Mari's work reflects the interdisciplinary nature of education, covering such topics as the tradition, pragmatism, social change, and social status of Arab village life and token Arabs in Israeli government; feminization of the teaching profession; job discrimination; physical security of Israeli universities; and television, informal education, and the rise of Arab Palestinian nationalism as it influences education.

Timely, empirical, and the first work of such scope, *Arab Education in Israel* is not only a thorough study of Israeli majority-minority relations. Its questions and conclusions are of universal significance for minority and third-world education. Eighteen tables, notes, and index are included.

Sami Khalil Mar'i received the B.A. and M.A. from Hebrew University and Ph.D. from the University of Wisconsin. A Palestinian Arab and Israeli citizen, Mar'i worked as an instructor in Arab schools and teacher-training colleges. He has served as research associate at the Hebrew University Institute for Innovation in Education and as director of the Institute for Research and Development of Arab education at the University of Haifa. The first Israeli Arab to receive the Ph.D. in education, Mar'i is senior lecturer at the University of Haifa and visiting associate professor at Michigan State University. Mar'i is the author of journal articles and monographs in Arabic, English, Hebrew and Portuguese.

Contemporary Issues in the Middle East

SYRACUSE UNIVERSITY PRESS

ARAB ED

Contempora

αRαB εδuCαTION
IN ISRαEL

Sami Khalil Mar'i

 SYRACUSE UNIVERSITY PRESS   1978

Chapter 2 appeared in modified form in Hebrew in *Studies In Education* 1 (1)
(April 1973):85–101.

Library of Congress Cataloging in Publication Data

Mar'i, Sami, Khalil, 1940–
  Arab education in Israel.

  Includes bibliographical references and index.
  1. Palestinian Arabs—Education—Israel.
2. Palestinian Arabs—Israel—Social conditions.
3. Israel—Social conditions. I. Title.
LA1443.7.M37   370'.95694   78–7389
ISBN 0–8156–0145–X

Manufactured in the United States of America

To Khalil and Rasha

Sami Khalil Mar'i received the B.A. and M.A. from Hebrew University and Ph.D. from the University of Wisconsin. A Palestinian Arab and Israeli citizen, Mar'i worked as an instructor in Arab schools and teacher-training colleges. He has served as research associate at the Hebrew University Institute for Innovation in Education and as director of the Institute for Research and Development of Arab Education at the University of Haifa. The first Israeli Arab to receive the Ph.D. in education, Mar'i is senior lecturer at the University of Haifa and visiting associate professor at Michigan State University.

Contents

Preface   **ix**

Introduction   **xi**

1. Background and Early Education   **1**
2. School and Society   **28**
3. Goals, Policies, and Administrative Status   **50**
4. Curricula   **70**
5. The Segregation-Integration Issue   **90**
6. Higher Education   **106**
7. Student Variables   **131**
8. Changing Socioeconomic and Political Conditions   **145**
9. Education at the Crossroads of Cultures   **173**

Appendix A: An Arab and a Jewish Student
  Argue on "Land Day"   **183**

Appendix B: The Study of Minority Education   **189**

Notes   **193**

Index   **205**

TABLES

1. Schools, Students, and Teachers in Government and Private (Arab-Moslem) Schools in Palestine (1914)   12

2. Number of School Teachers and Students in Government and Private Systems (1946)   14

3. Number and Percentages of Males and Females in Elementary Education (1920–45)   15

4. Gaps Between the Sexes in Elementary School Enrollment   20

5. Distribution of Jewish and Arab High School Students (1974)   22

6. Hours Allocated to Teaching History in Arab Junior and Senior High Schools   74

7. Percentage of the Total Hours Spent on General, Jewish, and Arab History in Jewish and Arab High Schools   76

8. Hours Devoted to Arabic Language and Literature in Arab High Schools   80

9. Hours Devoted to Hebrew Language and Literature in Arab High Schools   81

10. Hours Devoted to Language and Literature in Jewish and Arab High Schools   84

11. Number of Hours Specified for Arabic and Hebrew Language and Literature (1965 and 1973) in Arab Schools   84

12. Attitudes Toward Continuation in Secondary School   152

13. Determining Elements in the Decision to Study   153

14. Parents' Attitudes Toward the Future Occupations of Sons and Daughters   154

15. Hamoula Membership Compared to a Trade as Potential Contributors to the Individual's Social Status   158

16. The Position of Parents, Teachers, and Pupils in Regard to Vocational Education   159

17. Attitudes Toward Vocational Education   160

18. Distribution of Responses of Parents and Pupils as to Attitudes Toward Vocational vs. Academic Programs   161

Preface

I N ITS RECENT HISTORY the Middle East has been the scene of many wars, some outcomes of which were immediate and readily noticeable, while others must still be evaluated. One of these outcomes, of course, was the creation of Israel as a Jewish state in 1948, and the dismantling of Palestine as a political entity (under the British mandate). As Jews started leaving their diaspora and gathering in their newly created state, Palestinians were subjected to a continuous process of dispersion and geographic fragmentation. One segment of the Palestinian population, however, remained on its land to become an Arab minority in Israel. I. F. Stone, a well-known American Jewish thinker, observes that while every country in the world has its own Jewish minority, Israel is no exception. But, ironically, Israel's "Jews" are its Arabs. The book at hand is a comprehensive study of but one aspect of the lives of these Arabs in Israel—education.

This work could be viewed as a case study, but it also raises questions and exposes problems and issues of universal significance. As such, the book is a study of education and politics, a study in comparative education, a study of education in a developing society, a study of minority education, a cross-cultural study, and, of course, a study in Middle Eastern affairs. In fact, it fits into a sphere commonly shared by all these fields and is intended not only for professionals and students of the social sciences, but also for those who are involved in policy making, education, social action, cultural affairs, and politics.

This book was written while the author was at Michigan State University, on sabbatical and as a visiting professor. I am deeply indebted to the university in general and to Dr. Keith Goldhammer, dean of the College of Education, and Dr. Robert Green, dean of the College of Urban Development, in particular. Their cordial invitation and encouragement made the writing of this book possible. In addition, my stay at MSU was a rare opportunity by which I was able to detach myself from some daily burdens and concerns. Most important of all, my time there liberated me, though temporarily, from the immediate psychological pressures stemming from the uncomfortable political context in the Middle East. This liberation enabled me to maintain a more objective approach to the issues raised and discussed.

My thanks extend to my students and colleagues, both Arab and Jewish, in Israel, whose insights and comments were helpful in drawing my attention to some important variables and aspects of Arab education. Special gratitude is due to colleagues and friends at MSU for their critical comments on the manuscript. Nevertheless, they do not share responsibility for its weaknesses.

Anne Cauley has been a great aid to me in editing; her work contributed to a smoother and more intelligible text. And the efforts of Lynda Sanders in typing the final draft are appreciated.

Finally, my wife, Mariam, read the manuscript at different stages of its preparation. Her critical and, in some cases, uncompromising commentary made me rethink many points and arrive at a deeper understanding of the issues involved. Her patience and contributions are gratefully recognized.

East Lansing, Michigan   Sami Khalil Mar'i
Spring 1978

Introduction

ABOUT HALF A MILLION Palestinian Arabs live in Israel. When the state of Israel was established in 1948, these individuals found themselves Israeli citizens living within the boundaries of a state whose creation they, along with other Arab nations, had opposed. They were cut off from their fellow Palestinians, who became refugees, stayed in their land annexed to the kingdom of Jordan (the West Bank), or became affiliated with Egypt (the Gaza Strip). The life of the Arab minority in Israel can best be characterized by the contradictory aspects of their existence: they are citizens of a state which has been involved in what seems a never-ending war with Arab nations; they occupy a typical non-Western spot in a super-Western context; and, finally, until three decades ago, they were an overwhelming majority which abruptly became an overwhelmed minority.

Israel's Arab minority has recently been undergoing an intensive process of re-Palestinization. International as well as Middle Eastern political dynamics have awakened Palestinianhood among Arabs inside and outside of Israel. Though they are citizens of Israel, the Arabs in Israel have always felt they belonged to a larger Arab population. The Arab educational system in Israel has to operate within this fragmented sociocultural and psychological situation. The system is state controlled, by its clients (Arab children) do not fit the legal and ideological framework of the Jewish state.

Beyond that, the Arab community in Israel belongs to the general category of developing societies. In this respect, its members share common cultural, structural, economic, and political characteristics with the rest of the Arab world and many other societies in Asia and Latin

America. The field of education is no exception. Certain educational phenomena and dynamics reflecting educational achievements and the changing expectations and functions of education, result from the impacts of modernizing agents on the role of social institutions. Modernization itself creates cultural and social contradictions in any social setting, but in this case these contradictions are magnified because the Palestinian Arab minority in Israel is enemy affiliated, and the modernizing forces originate from the Jewish majority.

The Arabs in Israel are a minority, but it does not necessarily follow that they have developed a minority self-concept. Until 1948, they were the overwhelming majority. Moreover, their sense of belonging to the larger Arab population in the Middle East has increased with time. On the other hand, the Jewish majority in Israel seems to possess a minority's mentality. For a great many years before they immigrated to Palestine and then to Israel, the Jews occupied minority status in their countries. Thus, both Arab and Jewish Israelis' self-images contradict their present demographic status, and each group's self-concept is mirror-opposite to the other's. Arab-Jewish social and cultural contradictions are clear in light of the Arab-Israeli conflict. They become acute in the realm of education.

This is education at the crossroad of cultures. Arab education in Israel is caught in the middle of the Israeli-Arab conflict. The Arab teacher is expected to play two conflicting roles. If he emphasizes Israeliness, then he is playing the role which the authorities—his employers—expect him to play. If he emphasizes Arabness, he is playing the role which the community—his community—wants him to play. Whichever role he chooses, he finds himself in a difficult situation. The Arab educational system in Israel is not only pressured by the expectations of the authorities and the community. It is also caught in the internal cultural conflict of traditionalism vs. modernism—forces with great impact upon Arab education in Israel. Although traditionalism tends to reduce the options of the Arab and puts him at a disadvantage when he tries to compete in a predominantly Western-Jewish context, it is significant in helping the Israeli Arab to preserve his ethnic identity.

Arab society in Israel is undergoing a very intensive process of modernization, and as a result, it is not only facing the pains and stresses of becoming more modernized, it is also experiencing the agony and the challenge of being a national minority belonging to a state which has been, and still is, at war with their people. These facts pose many interesting yet difficult questions concerning not only the Arab minority itself, but the larger, predominantly Jewish, Israeli society as well.

One wonders about the web of political relationships between Arabs and Jews in Israel. How do Arabs behave politically? What kind, if any, of political power do they have in the internal Israeli political structure? How is that power reflected in the way they fare with the majority? How do Arabs relate to the state of Israel and its institutions? How does the Jewish state relate to its non-Jewish citizens, especially when they are Arabs? Should the Arabs in Israel participate actively in a peace-making process? And, if they should, in what capacity? As Israelis, as Palestinians, or as both?

What kinds of structural changes have taken place in the Arab and/or Jewish society as a consequence of this unique type of pluralism? How are the Arabs distributed in the larger Israeli social stratification structure? Does the fact that Israel has a fairly large Arab minority affect the way in which social institutions are developing in Israeli? And, keeping in mind the tremendous birth rate among Arabs in Israel, what are the demographic and political implications for the future of the Jewish state?

To what extent is the Arab labor force integrated in Israeli economy? What is the quality and distribution of that labor force? What are the social and political dynamics which determine, among other things, the economic status of Arabs in Israel?

In real-life situations the issues raised by these questions and others cannot be isolated and dealt with separately. However, as important as they are, such issues are not the focus of this study. This book is devoted, rather, to an examination of educational quality against conflicting historical, political, and social backgrounds—backgrounds which are forces that shape the educational scene among Arabs in Israel. It is the conflicting nature of these powerful forces which puts Arab education in Israel at the crossroad of cultures.

The background of Arab education in Israel is highlighted in Chapter 1, which provides political, sociocultural, and historical overviews of Arab society and education. Throughout the analysis of the different aspects of the educational scene this background is examined in terms of its causal relationship with educational phenomena and dynamics. The last section of Chapter 1 presents a statistical survey exposing the existing quantitative gaps between the Arab and Jewish educational system in Israel.

Chapter 2 explores the internal sociocultural dynamics in the Arab community, focusing on the development and modernization of Arab society in Israel. Processes of modernization and change are discussed in terms of their effect on educational variables, and the relationship between school and society are analyzed. Although Chapter 2 centers on internal social-structural and cultural dynamics pertaining to education, external forces and minority-majority interaction, on the one hand, and interactional dynamics between Arabs in Israel and the larger Arab nation as they influence Arab education in Israel, on the other, are discussed in chapters 3 through 8.

One of the most significant issues in the context of minority education is the underlying philosophical guidelines of Arab education in Israel. What, if any, are the goals of education? Who sets these goals and whom do they serve? What differences, if any, exist between the goals of majority education and those of the minority? Can these goals be identical? Should they be separate? If they should, then how is the fact that the minority and the majority hold conflicting cultural and national aspirations to be expressed in terms of educational goals? Furthermore, in such a state of affairs, who controls what in Arab education in Israel? What kind of administration is there to shape educational policies and to make decisions? And to what extent is there consistency between the way Arab education is administered and the sociopolitical status of the Arab minority on the one hand and the state-specified goals on the other? Finally, in such a politically loaded situation, to what extent is Arab education politicized through its administration? Chapter 3 focuses on these issues as they relate to the goals, policies, and administration of Arab education in Israel, and it concludes with the suggestion that in such contexts the educational scene is often an extension of the political one. However, alternatives to the current status are suggested in terms of their educational and political impacts.

Chapter 4 deals with the crucial issue of curricula. In Israel, curricula are specified by the state as carefully defined topics, course content, and the number of hours to be allotted to them in school. For example, as far as contents and goals are concerned, is Arab education in Israel really Arab? Is it Israeli? What about other, uncontrolled experiences which take place out of the school? The Arab educational system in Israel is challenged by this very powerful competitor—the nonformal education which takes place outside the school—which reinforces the national identity of the Arab in Israel. In this sense the experiences of the young Arab generations in their own community, and in the Jewish community, along with their continuous exposure to the mass media in the Arab Middle East are detrimental to the state-controlled school's efforts to achieve its goals. The issue of reciprocity of curricula in a pluralistic context (i.e., what is "Jewish" in Arab curricula, and what is "Arab" in Jewish curricula?) is also analyzed.

In Chapter 5 the issue of social and educational integration in a pluralistic sociopolitical context is addressed. After the topic of integration of the two major Jewish subcultural groups is highlighted, the efforts at Jewish-Arab integration in housing, municipalities, and education are surveyed and evaluated in terms of their motivations, implementation, and the outcomes they have produced. The dynamics at play in this realm of social and educational integration are of universal significance with regard to the majority's attempts at manipulation and control and the minority's efforts to achieve a better status. The basic issue in this chapter is: Does the strategy of "separate but equal" work, and to what extent should integration be pursued?

While separation of Arabs and Jews in Israel is practiced from kindergarten through teacher-training seminaries, Arab and Jewish students do mix as members of the same educational institutions at the university level. Chapter 6 is devoted to a consideration of higher education among Arabs in Israel and focuses on questions like: What gaps exist between Arabs and Jews in Israel? How does higher education among Arabs in Israel compare with that among their fellow Palestinians on the West Bank? Does the Palestinian experience of dispersion and discontinuity have different meanings for different segments of Palestinian society? Is higher education considered a channel for upward socioeconomic mobility? What are the noneconomic (sociopolitical) values of higher education? To what extent are Arab students in Israeli universities political activists? What are the changing nature and goals of that activism?

Chapter 7 addresses a few student variables. It considers what happens to students when they are at the crossroad of cultures. How do they achieve scholastically in comparison with their majority counterparts? Are evaluation measures valid? What impact does a minority status have on the level of students' achievement? How do the vocational aspirations and perceptions of the future of Arab students in Israel compare with those of their Jewish counterparts? Is the level of aspiration different? How does each group perceive the possibility of realizing its aspirations?

Thinking abilities and coping behavior are two other points of emphasis in this chapter. Arab samples from Israel are compared with Arab samples from the West Bank to detect differences between the two groups which could explain the phenomenon that while Arabs in Israel occupy a minority status and interact with the Jewish-Western majority, Arabs on the West Bank have maintained cultural continuity. The questions posed here are: What impact does intercultural interaction have on the young generation's abilities to think and cope? Does thinking ability increase coping ability? Or, is there a negative correlation? And, if there is, what are the intervening variables?

Chapter 8 is an investigation of how changing socioeconomic conditions are transformed culturally into educational needs. The major issue is the extent to which a minority's educational system is responsive to those needs. If it is responsive, then the question is, to whose needs? What are the educational implications when the majority and the minority are economically interdependent? What are the impacts of pluralism (Arab and Jewish) on the Jewish society's structure in Israel? To what extent is the minority being manipulated to serve as an outlet for the inconsistencies existing in the unique composition of the majority's society? The issues of equality of educational and economic opportunities are indispensable to the discussion presented in this chapter.

Chapter 9 reconsiders the universal issue of minority education at the crossroads of cultures. Conclusions and recommendations are extrapolated as they relate not only to the Arab minority in Israel but to education, politics, and culture in general.

1

Background and Early Education

Education CANNOT BE UNDERSTOOD in isolation from the background of the people it serves. Brief historical, political, sociocultural, and demographic background information will help provide a general perspective on Arab education in Israel. The society in which this education system functions belongs to two conflicting entities at the same time—to Israel and to the Arabs.

POLITICAL BACKGROUND

Palestine was under Turkish rule for four centuries (1517–1917). Immediately after World War I and as a consequence of it, Palestine, along with other Arab countries, was subjected to the British mandate. The mandate over Palestine lasted for three decades, directly after which, in 1948, Israel was established as a Jewish state on the major portion of Palestine. The remainder belonged to Egypt (Gaza Strip) and to Jordan (the West Bank).

Arabs were the majority in Palestine until 1948, when they suddenly became the dominated minority in Israel. Until that time Arabs and Jews in Palestine were involved in a continuous war which started on a semi-organized basis in the 1920s and has escalated since then. The most noticeable fighting periods were the late thirties and the late forties, before the establishment of Israel.

Arab-Jewish relationships in Palestine can best be characterized as a continuous bloody conflict. In times of relative quiet both prepared for the next round and lived separately in demographically "mixed"

1

cities.[1] An atmosphere of suspicion and overwhelming mistrust dominated the relationship for many decades.

On May 14, 1948, the British evacuated Palestine, and on the same
day Israel was declared a Jewish state. One hundred fifty-six thousand
Arabs remained within the boundaries of the newly created state. Although war had ended or, at least, seemed to have ended, mutual mistrust continued. One of the consequences of Jewish mistrust was the
subjection of the Arab minority to military administration, which lasted
until 1966. Military administration meant, among other things, curfews,
and special permits for most Arabs for them to be able to leave their
villages and towns to look for jobs, education, and trade.

The official rationale for subjugating Arabs to military administration
was the maintenance of security. Because of their national background
and because the Arabs were concentrated in border communities, the
government applied military administration as a safeguard against any
possibility of Arab subversion.[2] Many Jewish and Arab political leaders,
scholars, and political organizations, however, referred to it as un-
necessary, unjustifiable, and discriminatory.[3] It is also referred to as a
means of "hunting" for votes by the ruling party[4] as well as a reflection
of the assumption that a person (or a group) is guilty before committing
any crime.[5]

The Arabs who remained within Israel's boundaries could not
psychologically accept the new political and sociocultural reality. They
were part of a defeated group and suddenly became a national minority
facing a powerful majority who had just won the war against them.

The Arab minority has been continuously increasing absolutely as
well as in relation to the majority. In 1948, and immediately after the
establishment of Israel, there were 156,000 Arabs in Israel (less than
7 percent of the total Israeli population). In spite of the many waves of
Jewish immigrants to Israel the ratio of Arabs to Jews kept increasing.
In 1958, ten years after the establishment of the state, Arabs comprised
11 percent of the Israeli population, in 1976, almost 15 percent
(500,000).

This increase of 4 percent per annum among Arabs in Israel is due,
according to Jacob M. Landau,[6] to many factors, most important of
which are: (1) a very high birth rate of three times that within the
Israeli Jewish sector; (2) a significant decrease in infanticide due to the
improvement of health services; (3) family reunion policies through
which almost 40,000 Palestinian Arabs entered Israel to rejoin their
families from whom they were separated during the war and prior to the

establishment of the state; and (4) the very low emigration of Arabs from Israel.

The absolute and relative increases of the Arab population in Israel have far-reaching demographic and political implications. The relatively low birth rate among the Jewish population, the decrease in immigration of Jews to Israel, and the consistently increasing Arab population in Israel, coupled with increases resulting from the annexation of East Jerusalem and possibly other populated areas, are expected to change the demographic balance in Israel.

These trends have made Jewish Israeli leaders concerned regarding the future Jewish majority in the state. The Arab population in Israel, because it is concentrated in certain geographical locations and is consistently increasing in number, is becoming more demanding. Landau notes a "sense of uniqueness" among the Arab minority in Israel due to these two factors. "It is not surprising that the . . . increase among the Arab minority in Israel strengthens their sense of uniqueness and adds weight to their demands as a unit. The nature of these demands is also influenced by the relatively young age of the Arab minority members. . . . More than half the Arabs in Israel were born after the establishment of the state. Because of that, a recognizable part of their political behavior is conditioned by the dynamics of [their] life in Israel."[7] A major part of those dynamics to which the younger generation are exposed takes place within the Arab educational system in Israel.

Active political participation of Arabs in Israel is very minimal. Most of the political parties in Israel are extensions of pre-state Zionist movements, and for this reason it is most difficult for an Arab in Israel to identify with them and their ideologies. The parties themselves, although they always seek the Arab vote, do not encourage Arabs to become full members of the party. Also, the Arabs in Israel are not eager and enthusiastic to become party members, but even those few who are willing to try are usually denied the right of membership.[8]

The only political parties in Israel which accept Arabs as full members are Mapam, a socialistic-Zionistic party, and the Israeli Communist party. The former is losing popularity among Arabs in Israel because of its Zionistic ideology and also because it has joined the labor coalition which governs the country. On the other hand, the Israeli Communist party is gaining popularity because of its non- (or anti-) Zionistic ideology which also has more appeal to the Arab voter in Israel.

There have been repeated efforts to form an Arab political party in Israel. Most successful of these efforts were those of the El-Ard (the land) movement which started as a cultural movement and achieved legal status as a publisher of Arabic books and papers in Israel. Its newspaper was most popular among Arabs. After the movement had gained popularity and support, it was outlawed in 1964 by Israeli authorities for political and security reasons. Thus, before it became a political party, the El-Ard movement was legally abolished. Other groups which tried to organize a movement or an association out of which a party may emerge were discouraged by the Israeli government and/or the existing political parties.

Instead, the government and political parties encourage traditional leadership in the Arab society. Leaders are the elderly in a village or a town. Imposed upon the minority as socio-political leaders, the leaders enjoy the trust and encouragement of the establishment (government and other political institutions) but are losing the popularity and trust of their fellow Arab citizens. S. F. Geraisy suggests that "the government often supports patriarchal leadership and hamula [clan] functionalism, and it promotes young men who are prepared to support 'traditional' relationships both in the village and in its ties with the outside. The historical and social conditions that produced these forms of leadership might have changed, but the possibilities of using them for new needs are exploited and encouraged." The encouragement of the hamula leadership and structure is usually attributed to "certain intended or unintended policies of the Jewish authorities as a part of a general policy of divide-and-rule."[9]

Sabri Jeries gives two reasons for the lack of an Arab political organization or movement in Israel. First, during the first years after the establishment of the state of Israel, few Arabs thought in this direction. Because the minority lost its political leadership when they left the country in 1948, it took many years for a new leadership to emerge. Second, when this nontraditional leadership emerged a decade after the establishment of the state, it was paralyzed by the strict and suppressive policies of the government. In this state of affairs, those who wish to become involved in political activity and, at the same time, express their criticism and frustrations can do so only through the Communist party.

Although they constitute 15 percent of the total Israeli population, the Arabs in Israel do not have political power, nor is their vote united. It is scattered in the existing Israeli political parties, whose policies are usually irrelevant to Arab needs. They cannot be considered a pressure group as yet.

Political power gained by pressuring the ruling authorities has proved very instrumental in achieving benefits and improving group status. It is especially true in the Israeli political structure. The relatively small Religious (Jewish) Party, due to its political pressure and maneuvering, has achieved a separate and relatively autonomous educational system which is fully financed by the government. Another example of political pressure which has resulted in an independent educational system is the case of the Kibbutz movement.[10] These educational services are also financed by the government.

The lack of political power in the Arab minority in Israel is not the sole reason for the lack of autonomy of Arabs over their educational system. Although it is a major reason, it reinforces other existing political, legal, and administrative factors, all of which can be considered responsible for the majority's control over the minority's education. The lack of autonomy in education is being used to prevent or at least delay the emergence of political organizations and movements among Arabs in Israel. These issues are discussed in a later chapter.

SOCIOECONOMIC BACKGROUNDS

Arab society in Israel can best be characterized as a developing society occupying the status of a national minority to which the majority represents not only advantage and power but also modernism. It is to this process of developing from traditional to modern and the special status of minority that most developments or the lack thereof can be attributed. Most of the changes which take place in the life of Arabs in Israel can be related to modernization processes operating among them and/or to their socioeconomic and political status as a minority. The education of Arabs in Israel is especially influenced by these two factors.

More than 85 percent of Arabs in Israel are concentrated in over 100 rural villages in three areas of the country: the Galilee in the north, the Little Triangle in the (eastern) center, and the Negev (bedouins who are now settled in villages). There are only two Arab cities in Israel, one is a large village and the other Nazareth. The Arab population in Israel forms a rural society which, like all other rural communities in the world, is homogeneous, traditional, and relatively static.[11]

The social, cultural, economic, and political continuity of Arabs in Israel was severely interrupted in 1948, when the state of Israel was established. This disruption was not without some detrimental and debilitating effects as far as political organization, coping strategies and behaviors, and higher education are concerned. However, it also spurred democratization of the family atmosphere and improvement of intellectual functioning and female education. These effects and others are the major concern of this book. The background of these developments in Arab society in Israel is of special importance as a general introduction and framework to which these developments can be attributed.

Because of the concentration of Arabs in villages and rural areas there is a *de facto* segregation between the minority and the majority in Israel. This geographical separation is also responsible for educational segregation. Education of Arabs in Israel has been conducted and administered both structurally and culturally under the general principle of "separate but equal." New forces are emerging, however, which urge and demand limited integration.

Minorities are often barred from economic, social, and political opportunities, and their subordinate status often manifests itself in unequal access to educational opportunities.[12] One may argue the universality of these observations, however, the segregation of the Arab educational system, as is shown in different contexts in this study, hinders its development. This does not mean that only the Jewish majority in Israel is pursuing a separatist policy. It is equally true that the minority itself is not demanding full integration, mainly because of the threats against the cultural and national uniqueness of the minority which are inherent in a situation where full integration exists.

Integration has been especially frustrating in the economic life of Arabs in Israel. For a while after the creation of Israel Arab workers in Jewish urban centers enjoyed the economic opportunities available to them. In those early years Arabs perceived the job market as full of opportunities, especially when compared with what was available for them in their towns and villages. Compared with any period in their past, the economic status of Arabs in Israel has improved; however, not to the point of that of the Jewish majority.[13]

The rural Arab society in Israel depended on underdeveloped farming to survive, but farming is no longer the major source of living for most Israeli Arabs. Three developments have led to the shift from farming to a wage-earning labor force. First, most of the cultivatable land owned by Arabs was confiscated or expropriated by the Israeli authorities for "security" reasons and in order to provide the Jewish newcomers with land.[14] Two goals guide the policy of confiscation—"Judaizing the Galilee" and "balancing the population." In the Galilee, where most of the Arab population is concentrated, a Jewish city (Carmiel) was established; and near the Arab city of Nazareth another Jewish city (Upper

Nazareth) was also established.[15] When Arab villagers demanded their land back they were denied it and offered a compensation many regarded as too low and refused to accept it.[16] The loss of land has increased the need for employment outside the village.[17]

A second reason for a shift to an Arab wage-earning labor force is that even in those villages which have not lost much of their land, farmers find it more worthwhile to go to the city and become wage-earners. This is usually due to the deterioration of their land because of the kind and quality of crops they planted for many years. These crops may have been necessary for the Israeli market, but often they could not compete with comparable crops grown by more technically advanced Jewish farmers. Discriminatory policies in marketing and pricing of their products have put the Arab farmers at a disadvantage, especially the tobacco growers. For example, in 1962, the Arab tobacco grower earned only 68.7 percent of what his Jewish counterpart did for a ton of tobacco.[18]

Third, internal dynamics have reinforced this trend of wage-earning in the Jewish urban centers. The land-owning system in the Arab village was traditionally a feudalistic one. Few owned the land, and the rest (fellaheen) farmed it for a relatively small share. When job opportunities became available in the city for those who did not own land, they were the first to utilize this opportunity, and at the same time they were able to shed their subordinate socioeconomic status. This social structure transformation has far-reaching implications as far as education is concerned. Education becomes a channel for upward mobility for those of a traditionally subordinate status (See Chapter 2).

The change of the majority of the Arab labor force from a farming to a wage-earning force was a necessary and economically worthwhile shift when compared with the limited availability of jobs in their own environment. For many work outside of the village was a way to earn more, but more importantly, it liberated them from the rule of the land owners. While enjoying job opportunities and improving their economic situation, Arab workers have become increasingly aware of and sensitive to their low status as workers in the Israeli job structure. This, coupled with increased political awareness, has frustrated Arab workers in the Jewish urban centers.

Geraisy, in his extensive study of Arab workers in Jewish cities, has found that 72–82 percent of those workers have had no training whatsoever. The few who have had some training had it on the job.[19] This puts the Arab worker at a disadvantage and reduces, if not eliminates, his chances in competition for better jobs. Indeed, the Arab worker is

"pushed" into harder, yet lower paying jobs which his fellow Jewish
worker avoids. Aharon Cohen concludes that "in effect most of the jobs
remained closed for the Arab worker."[20]

In spite of the many difficulties faced by the Arab labor force in
the Israeli economy the economic situation in the Arab society in Israel
has improved. Outside labor has brought about tremendous structural
and cultural changes and transformations: extended family structure has
decreased to an almost unidentifiable minimum; achievement-based
status has replaced ascriptive social status; trade and labor unions are
being substituted for traditional social structures; the traditionally
subordinate social classes are rising; and modernization processes have
intensified. Such changes are usually manifested in a more democratic
family atmosphere, an uplifting of the status of females, and more
political awareness and activism.

While the Arab labor force is contributing to these changes through
its daily and continuous contacts in the modern Jewish industrialized
urban centers, it cannot be considered an exclusive change agent. Other
factors have contributed, too. Education, mass media (Israeli and Arab
countries' radio and television stations), modernization, and "the spirit
of the times" have also played a role.

HISTORICAL BACKGROUND

The historical background of Arab Education in Palestine is an important frame of reference while examining educational phenomena for
some of the basic educational problems of the Arab society in Israel
can be traced to the nineteenth century, and they have existed since then
on different levels of magnitude and significance. Three periods are
covered: first, prior to 1917, when the Turkish rule over Palestine
(then part of Great Syria) ended; second, from 1917–1947–48, during
the British mandate over Palestine; and third, the few years immediately
after the establishment of the state of Israel, the beginning of Arab
education in Israel.

PRIOR TO 1917

Schools such as those in the Western world were established in Palestine
during the last quarter of the nineteenth century.[21] The elementary school
was then called *rushdi* (maturity-inducing) and was established by the

representative of the Turkish Empire, the *wali* (governor) in Palestine, who was located in Acre at that time. It was a four-year elementary school maintained by the government and community and administered by a Turkish principal. The language of instruction was Turkish, while Arabic, the pupils' native tongue, was taught as a second language. The main function of the school was to provide a basic and religious (Islamic) education. The rulers encouraged the teaching of Islam because it was common to the Turks and the Arabs. The central government paid teachers' salaries, but communities had to provide physical facilities. Although females were not officially prohibited from attending schools, because of traditional backgrounds school populations were male only.

This school did not appeal to the Arabs in Great Syria, particularly the Palestinian Arabs, which resulted in a lack of support and limited attendance. The language of instruction was irrelevant to the masses, simply because they did not need it. Moreover, the shift at an early age from the native Arabic tongue to a foreign one was almost impossible. The fact that the principals were Turks only alienated the educational institution from the Arabs, and the principal, a foreigner, could not function as a recruiter of pupils for the newly created school.

From a religious point of view, the school should have appealed to the population, but other factors overshadowed this potentially attractive characteristic. The school tried to oppose the Arab national awakening in Great Syria and thus antagonized the Arab population. Moreover, the local mosque usually provided an alternative for religious education in the kuttab (a mosque-affiliated school). Another factor which contributed to the lack of popularity of the rushdi school was that the education led nowhere. In Palestine there was no possibility to continue education at a higher level and improve one's socioeconomic status. Those who sought higher education had to go to Damascus to high school, but because of the great distance, very few pursued a high school education.

High school was called *shahani* and consisted only of a two-year program. It was free, and the subjects emphasized in the curriculum were administration (secretarial and clerical skills) and the Turkish language. The few graduates of this high school were employed by the authorities, usually in the wali's headquarters or in local government offices, only a handful of Palestinians graduated from that highly prestigious high school.

The highest educational institution available during the Turkish Empire's rule over Great Syria (including Palestine) was the *Harbi* (military) Institute, located in Istanbul. The distance and limitations on admission made the school beyond the reach of the few Palestinians who wished to pursue a higher education. Admission was most difficult for Arabs because of the military nature of the institution, especially at that time when Arabs started demanding independence from Turkish rule.

Turkish government schools did not have a direct and significant effect as far as formal education for Arabs was concerned. They were rare, culturally imposing, nationally antagonizing, lacked continuity, and their only possibly attractive aspect, religious education, was already available in the mosque. Their basic contribution was probably that they increased awareness regarding the importance of formal national education. The two private school systems, Christian and Moslem, grew because of competition with each other and with the Turkish system. Their tremendous success was due to the fact that each made itself relevant to the communities it served in a different way.

Missionary Christian schools began during the Turkish rule, not as missions to convert people to the Christian faith, but to provide educational, health, and other services to the already existing Christian Arab minorities in Great Syria. They established convents, schools, hospitals, and cultural centers in most major cities in Lebanon, Syria, and Palestine. In Palestine, the Holy Land, Christians enjoyed special educational services. Although the justification for the establishment of these institutions was that the different European countries were interested in serving their respective Christian brothers under Turkish rule, there were also political reasons. Through these institutions European countries interfered in the domestic political affairs of the Empire.[22]

In spite of their political intentions, these were the first Western formal educational institutions to be established in Great Syria. They were popular, especially among Christian Arabs, because of their religious standing and because they provided an option to the Turkish school system. The principals and most of their teachers were from the country which supported them and were not associated with the local ruler. In fact, their political orientation was opposed to the ruler's. Moreover, because government schools sponsored by an Islamic (yet non-Arab) empire emphasized the Islamic religion of the majority, Christian missionary schools became increasingly attractive even though tuition was charged.

Turkish was not taught in these schools. Arabic was the primary language, although the language of the sponsor European country was prestigious and heavily emphasized. Despite heavy enrollment of Christian Arab boys and girls, Moslems also often utilized the modern educational opportunity offered by the schools. The Christian schools existed in Palestine as autonomous educational institutions under the British mandate, and some of them still exist in Israel with a lesser degree of autonomy (See Chapter Three).

The contributions of the missionary schools to formal education in Great Syria were significant. Not only did they introduce the structure and content of the modern, Western-type school, but they set an example for the majority in Great Syria (Moslem Arabs) to follow. The Arab group was already frustrated by the curriculum of the Turkish school and was ready to establish schools to serve their own needs and aspirations. Through the missionary schools the European know-how in private education and community initiative and organization were introduced.

The problem of formal Christian Arab education in Great Syria may have been solved by missionary schools. Moslems, on the other hand, could not fully identify with either Turkish schools (Moslem but not Arab) nor missionary schools (neither Moslem nor Arab) and had to create their own private educational system.

In 1867 *Hadiqat El-Akhbar* (The News Garden), an Arabic newspaper, published an editorial which said: "It is more suitable to the respect of Moslems to establish their own schools like other religious groups [Christians] in spite of the availability of the rushdi [Moslem] school which are established by the Wali of Great Syria." During the early 1870s the "Association of Good Will" (Jam'iyyat El Makased El-Kheiriyyah) was established in Great Syria as a Moslem organization. Its stated goals were: "To provide help and support for the poor, to provide schools for boys and for girls, and all this without involvement in politics." Private Arab-Moslem schools were also established in Palestine (Acre and Jerusalem), and although it was formally stated that these schools would not deal with politics, they began as a reaction to both Turkish (non-Arab) and Christian schools with an underlying political-nationalistic motivation.

Along with the cultural awakening of the last quarter of the nineteenth century, allowed by the liberal walis (i.e., Midhat Pasha, 1878–80), came a bloom in education. Arab-Moslem schools became widespread and extremely popular. They achieved a respectable reputation because the language of the institution was Arabic, modern secular subjects were added, and emphasis was placed on Arab nationalism, all without lowering the status of religious education. The schools were the result of communal initiative and participation, however, they started and remained elitist because they were maintained through the fees they charged, which only a few could afford. Some pupils from poor family backgrounds were admitted and the fees waived, but not a great many.

These schools arose as a communal and national response to the foreign school, and while doing so, emphasized a nationalism that antagonized Turkish authorities. Yet activities in education and culture, at least in the beginning, were permitted because they were considered an outlet for community activity. The nationalistic forces were encouraged to become involved in educational and cultural activities to divert their attention from active political opposition to Turkish rule. When the central authorities became aware of these activities the wali was invited for consultation, after which all Arab-Moslem schools were nationalized under strict supervision of the government. The government, however, did not intend to turn them into government schools, only to make sure that no antigovernment components were included in the curriculum. The number of Arab-Moslem schools continued to grow. In Palestine they increased from 2 schools in the 1880s (in Acre and Jerusalem) to almost 400 schools in 1914, when World War I broke out, a consequence of which was the collapse of the Turkish Empire.

With the beginning of the war, all Christian schools in Great Syria were ordered closed by the wali because of their close ties with anti-Turkish countries. Table 1 illustrates the Palestinian educational scene in 1914.

TABLE 1

Schools, Students, and Teachers in Government and
Private (Arab-Moslem) Schools in Palestine (1914)

Type of School	Number of Schools	Number of Students			Average Number of Students per school	Number of Teachers	Students per Teacher
		T	M	F			
Governmental (Turkish)	95	8400	7000	1400	38	234	36
Private (Arab-Moslem)	379	8731	8600	131	23	417	21

T = total; M = male; F = female
Source: Abdullatif Tibawi, *Arab Education in Mandatory Palestine* (London: Luzac, 1956).

From Table 1 it is obvious that the number of private schools increased beyond that of government schools. The relatively smaller average number of students per school in the private system is due to the fact that these schools charged a tuition while government schools were free of charge. This also explains the small average number of students per teacher. In other words, because the schools were private and elite a lower number of students in the classroom was maintained in order to provide better educational opportunity.

The number of female students is, in both cases, less than male students, with a noticeable difference between the two systems. The fact that a very limited number of females attended private schools is probably due to the preference of traditional families to invest in their male children. Females usually attended schools which were free of charge. This tradition of low status of females regarding education has continued for many years and is presently expressed in unequal opportunities for women at the higher levels of the educational hierarchy.

In summary, formal schooling was introduced in Palestine during the latter part of the nineteenth century and in most cases was limited to the elementary level. Three educational systems existed simultaneously: the Turkish governmental schools, in which Turkish was the language of instruction and which tried to oppose the newly emerging Arab nationalism; the missionary Christian school system, which emphasized the language and culture of the sponsoring European country; and the Arab-Moslem private school system, which introduced Arab nationalism in response to the Turkish schools and emphasized Islam as a reaction to the Christian school system. Not only did awareness of modern formal education increase during this period, but education became associated with nationalism. Moreover, local communities were successful in their efforts to control education and make it more relevant to their needs and aspirations. Religion retained a significant status in education, but the conflicts between government and community regarding religious, cultural, and national qualities of education among Palestinian Arabs remained unresolved during the British mandate.

THE BRITISH MANDATE PERIOD (1917-1948)

In 1917, as a consequence of World War I, Great Syria was partitioned into Lebanon, (small) Syria, Jordan, and Palestine.[23] In Palestine the British ruled in terms of "mandatory administration," a condition lasting until 1948, when the state of Israel was established. During the

British mandate Arab schools in Palestine continued under their original ownership. Arab-Moslem schools, seminationalized by the Turkish authorities, became mostly governmental, and a few remained private. Christian missionary schools, closed at the Turkish authorities' order at the outbreak of the war, reopened after three years.

Although elementary school consisted of seven years, most schools had only a four-year program. In the villages it was considered satisfactory if one achieved an elementary education. High schools were established in major cities to prepare manpower to fill the newly created positions of clerks and civil servants to mediate between government and the communities. English was therefore vigorously taught as a second language.

During the thirty years of the British rule over Palestine, free but noncompulsory education developed. The number of government schools increased from less than 100 in 1917, to 550 in 1947. While in 1917 only 8 percent of the school age children attended school, in 1947 one-third of the school age population had attended schools, if not for the full course of elementary education (seven years), at least for part of it.

The number of private Moslem schools decreased due to the fact that many of them belonged to the government system. The mandatory administration, while increasing and expanding the educational network, did not interfere in the private systems. The number of Christian private schools grew to exceed Moslem schools, as Table 2 clearly shows. In fact, many Moslem children attended them because they were modern and better equipped to teach foreign languages, including English, the language of the British employers.

TABLE 2

Number of School Teachers and Students
in Government and Private Systems (1946)

Type of School	Number of Schools	Number of Teachers	Number of Students
Government	478	1872	81,662
Private (Moslem)	135	432	14,169
Private (Christian)	182	1468	22,504
TOTAL	795	3772	118,335

SOURCE: Abdullatif Tibawi, *Arab Education in Mandatory Palestine* (London: Luzac, 1956).

Table 3 clearly shows the development of elementary education in Palestine, particularly the development between the two sexes. While the percentage of females had consistently increased (except in 1945–46), the gap was still great because the number of males had also increased every year, counter balancing the gain in the percentage of female education.

TABLE 3

Number and Percentages of Males and Females in Elementary Education (1920–45)

Year	Total Number of Students	Males	Females
1920–1921	16,442	13,656	2,786
	(100%)	(83%)	(17%)
1925–1926	19,737	16,146	3,591
	(100%)	(82%)	(18%)
1930–1931	24,288	19,346	4,942
	(100%)	(80%)	(20%)
1935–1936	42,747	33,035	9,712
	(100%)	(78%)	(22%)
1940–1941	45,645	42,661	11,984
	(100%)	(77%)	(23%)
1945–1946	81,042	64,536	16,506
	(100%)	(79%)	(21%)

SOURCE: Abdullatif Tibawi, *Arab Education in Mandatory Palestine* (London: Luzac, 1956).

Overall, Arab education in Palestine developed significantly under the mandatory administration. Schools were established in many villages, making educational opportunities more accessible. Secondary school education increased and became strongly associated with the achievement of a white collar job, usually as a cleark or a civil servant who not only enjoyed economic mobility and security but also a higher status due to his association with the rulers.

However, this educated elite of secondary school graduates was soon nationally aware and politically active. Teachers in Arab schools in Palestine were not an exception. In many cases they came to express their disappointment and frustration at the lack of autonomy for Palestinian Arabs over their educational system which was directed and

supervised by British officials. Those feelings of frustration began during
Turkish rule over Palestine as part of Great Syria, when the education
system was also governed by foreigners. The feelings were magnified
for the following reasons:

1. Through revolutionary movements Arab countries joined the
   Allies in their war against Turkish rule in the Middle East.
   Their expectation was not to become protected and governed
   by the Allies but to become independent. The educated were
   most aware of these national feelings and political dynamics
   because of the national significance of their occupation as
   "nation builders." Therefore, when they were subjected to
   another kind of foreign rule they were extremely frustrated.
2. Arab educators in Palestine had a precedent to follow. The
   Jewish Zionist education system, although serving a minority of
   less than 10 percent, was an autonomous one. All citizens were
   under the same rule, yet they were treated differently. This
   created and magnified antagonistic feelings toward the British
   administration in Palestine. Moreover, Arab educators were
   aware of the Balfour Declaration. On November 2, 1917, while
   addressing the Zionist Federation of England, Arthur J.
   Balfour, then the British foreign minister, declared that: "Her
   Majesty's government views with favor the establishment in
   Palestine of a national home for the Jewish people, and will use
   their best endeavors to facilitate the achievement of this
   objective."
3. Political and national awareness became increasingly widespread, especially during the British mandate period when
   various wars continuously took place between Arabs and Jews
   in Palestine.

The role of the British, as a consequence of the Balfour Declaration and through their mandate over Palestine, was to be "responsible
for creating in the country such conditions as would secure the establishment of the Jewish National Home, for facilitating Jewish immigration [to Palestine] and for encouraging settlement of the Jews on the
land." Professor Aharon Kleinberger of the Hebrew University suggested
that "a Jewish agency was to advise the administration in all matters
affecting the establishment of a Jewish National Home and to cooperate
in the development of the country."[24]

The Arab teacher in Palestine had to function in this tense atmosphere. Not only was there a lack of autonomy over education, but there was also a real threat to the Palestinian Arab national identity and unity. Indeed, when Balfour visited Palestine in 1925, Arab teachers and students declared a strike as an expression of their antagonism toward his declaration. This was not the only expression of frustration and disappointment to take place within the Arab educational scene in Palestine. Similar nationalist involvements and political activities also took place in 1936 and 1946, when Arab teachers, students, and scouts demonstrated in opposition to the mandatory policies in Palestine.

Dr. Khalil Totah, an Arab educator during the mandatory period, stated that Arabs in Palestine had no control whatsoever over their educational system. The education of Arab youths was far from nationalistic, as was apparent in the goals, policies, personnel, curriculum, and general nature of education.[25] Because of these criticisms and repeated demands for educational autonomy, the mandatory administration established an Arab Advisory Council to participate in policymaking in Arab education in Palestine. The councils did not have any power, however, and they often collapsed shortly after their establishment.

The assistant to the director general of the mandatory Department of Education opposed the demand for autonomy. His rationale was that a nation able to direct its education autonomously also needs political autonomy, and he saw the Arabs of Palestine as people who needed mandate. Educational services, therefore, were the first to be controlled by the British mandatory authorities and the last to be relinquished.

Overall, a great many quantitative developments in education took place during the British mandate over Palestine.[26] Even though elementary education was not compulsory, it nonetheless spread into villages which had never had schools. On the qualitative level, new methods of instruction were introduced, textbooks were published, and teachers were trained in two training centers, one in Ram Allah for females and the other in Jerusalem. Schooling of Christian Arabs in Palestine increased in terms of overall enrollment and especially in female enrollment.[27] Although more prevalent than during Turkish rule, education remained the privilege of the few. As late as 1946, only 30 percent of the school age population was enrolled, as compared with 8 percent in 1914 during the Turkish rule.

Along with these developments there was a growing sense of frustration and antagonism due to the efforts of the British mandate to denationalize Arab education in Palestine and prepare ground conducive to the establishment of the state of Israel. Textbooks in Arab schools, however, did include comments against Zionism and nationalist poetry and songs as a limited outlet for the strong feelings of bitterness and frustration.

Arab education in Palestine became more nationalistic that it had been during Turkish rule. This was not due so much to formally approved curriculum as it was to hidden and implied lessons and to the political activism of students and their teachers, which accompanied a period of continuous threat against the national identity and national unity of the Palestinian people and the establishment of Israel as an independent Jewish state in 1948. Some of the old issues remained open, some became sharper, and new problems and issues emerged.

POST-1948

The Arabs who remained within the boundaries of the newly created state of Israel can best be characterized as emotionally wounded, socially rural, politically lost, economically poverty-stricken, and national hurt. They suddenly became a minority ruled by a powerful, sophisticated majority against whom they fought to retain their country and land. It was an agonizing experience, for every family which remained had immediate relatives on the other side of the border, and the borders were "hot" and tense.

Arabs in Israel were left without political leadership and an educated elite. The vast majority of the educated left behind schools without teachers, and the lack of teachers was devastating to Arab education in Israel. When schools were ordered to reopen immediately after the declaration of independence of Israel and the compulsory education law was passed in 1949, Arab schools were flooded by pupils, and the few teachers who remained could not handle the situation. Educational authorities in Israel therefore appointed many unqualified teachers. In fact, during the early 1950s as many as 70 percent of Arab teachers were unqualified. Some of those teachers became formally certified through intensive summer courses and examinations. Despite tenure, some still have a negative impact on Arab education in Israel.

Physical facilities (e.g., buildings and equipment) were unsuitable and too limited to accomodate the many students who attended schools. The school was often spread all over the village in rented rooms to meet burgeoning needs. A shift system allowed two groups of students to attend each school each day, and many of the teachers spent most of the class period walking from one rented classroom to another. The mandatory period curriculum was cancelled without providing a substitute. Textbooks were outlawed by Israeli educational authorities because they included some anti-Zionist information, and in most subjects substitute texts were lacking. Schools at that time had very little educative effect.

Arab education became closely associated with the military administration, which appointed new teachers and paid salaries. This imposed association of Arab teachers with the military administration continues to have impact (even though this administration was abolished more than a decade ago) in terms of a deterioration in the formerly respected social status of teachers.

A separate Arab Education Department was established within the Israeli Ministry of Education and Culture. Most of the supervisors were of Jewish background, which added to the estrangement of the system from the society it serves. The fact that the Arab Education Department is headed by a Jewish majority member has created a model for other Arab departments in the government, all of which are run by Jewish individuals.

During the mandatory period, and more so during the Turkish rule, Arab education in Palestine was controlled by rulers who represented a different culture and nationality. In the case of Arab education in Israel, however, the situation is even more polarized because the Arab minority has never in its recent history achieved autonomy over its own educational system despite many efforts and resents the Jewish majority governing its education.

A QUANTITATIVE OVERVIEW[28]

A comparison of statistics of the Israeli Arab and Jewish populations traces the development of Arab education in Israel. This section presents numbers and ratios of population in general; potential elementary school population (5–14-year-old children); actual school population; gaps between the sexes; high school population; teacher training institutions; university students; and statistics related to teachers and teacher-to-student ratios.

In 1973 the total population in Israel was 3,307,600, of which fifteen percent (497,200) were Arabs. The potential elementary school population (5–14 years) was 670,700, of which 22.2 percent (148,900) were Arab children, however, only 18 percent of the actual elementary school population in Israel were Arabs. This means that the compulsory education law is less enforced in the Arab population. In the Jewish population elementary school enrollment exceeds 99 percent, while among the Arab population it averages 82 percent (85 percent of Arab male school age children are enrolled and 78 percent of the female).

These figures reflect a gap between Arab and Jewish education in Israel, despite a continuous increase in school attendance of the Arab elementary school age population. In 1946, when elementary education was not compulsory, only 30 percent of Arab school age children were enrolled. In 1955, four years after the compulsory education act was implemented in Israel, the enrollment increased to 59 percent; in 1965, it became 75 percent; and in 1973, 82 percent.

Table 4 reflects the development of education of females in elementary schools. There has been an increase from 32 percent females in 1955, to 46 percent in 1973, and by 1980 it is expected to increase to nearly

TABLE 4

Gaps Between the Sexes in Elementary School Enrollment

Year	Total Number of Pupils	Males	Females
1953	33,674	22,966	10,708
	(100%)	(68%)	(32%)
1958	39,356	26,605	12,751
	(100%)	(68%)	(32%)
1963	56,793	33,905	22,888
	(100%)	(60%)	(40%)
1968	90,881	52,802	38,079
	(100%)	(58%)	(42%)
1973	121,634	65,561	56,073
	(100%)	(54%)	(46%)

SOURCE: Sami Khalil Mar'i and Nabih Daher, *Facts and Trends in the Development of Arab Education in Israel* (Haifa: The University of Haifa, Institute for Research and Development of Arab Education, 1976).

50 percent. A noticeable jump took place between 1958 (32 percent) and 1963 (40 percent), because of increasing awareness of the relevance of female education to the improvement of the economic situation and the fact that females were no longer needed for agricultural work due to land confiscation and higher income from outside work.

The trend in female education was initially recognizable in

Palestine during the British mandate. At the turn of the century during Turkish rule the percentage of females in elementary schools was less than 8 percent; in 1941 female enrollment had increased to over 23 percent (see Table 3). In 1946, however, this dropped to 21 percent because many schools closed during the war between the Arabs and Jews in Palestine.

These ratios of enrollment, particularly female enrollment, while higher than in the rest of the Arab world, are equal to, or slightly lower than, the percentages among Palestinians on the West Bank, who until 1967 were not under Israeli rule. In the Arab world the average elementary school enrollment is 65 percent of school age children.[29] Among Palestinians on the West Bank it exceeds 87 percent.[30] Palestinians (including Arabs in Israel), unlike some other Arab people, became familiar with formal education as early as the second half of the nineteenth century, and when opportunities were available in Israel and Jordan enrollment rates were higher. A gap in enrollment rates still exists, however, between Arabs and Jews in Israel, due probably to the difference in modernization (Westernization) each type of school has achieved as well as differences in economic status and the availability of educational opportunities.

Although Arab student population constituted almost 20 percent of the total Israeli 14–18-year-old population, their percentage of enrollment in high school is less than 10 percent. This means that only 50 percent of potential Arab students are actually enrolled in high school. The most important reason for this is the curriculum offered in Arab high schools. There are not enough vocational programs to absorb those students who do not wish to pursue their high school education in an exclusively academic program. There is also a tremendous lack of schools, especially in the small villages. A third reason is that youth often drop out as early as the end of elementary school and join the Arab labor force in the Jewish urban centers. Employers are legally barred from employing youth of high school age without certain regulations, such as enrollment in night school, but many Arab youths are employed nonetheless.

Table 5 shows the distribution of Jewish and Arab high school students academic, vocational, and agricultural programs. In the Jewish sector more students are enrolled in the vocational track than in the academic (51.4 percent and 43.4 percent respectively). When a Jewish student does not wish to enroll in a purely academic track he also has a rich variety of vocational-technical programs in which he can enroll to suit his capabilities. The programs are not meant only for

TABLE 5

Distribution of Jewish and Arab
High School Students (1974)

	Total	Academic	Vocational	Agricultural
Jewish	124,596	54,064	64,068	6,464
	(100%)	(43.4%)	(51.4%)	(5.2%)
Arab	13,456	11,397	1,456	603
	(100%)	(84.8%)	(10.8%)	(4.4%)

SOURCE: Sami Khalil Mar'i and Nabih Daher, *Facts and Trends in the Development of Arab Education in Israel* (Haifa: The University of Haifa, Institute for Research and Development of Arab Education, 1976).

low-achieving students, and the selection ranges from highly sophisticated academic to skill-oriented programs.

In Arab schools, on the other hand, only 10.8 percent of high school students are enrolled in such programs, which are often of poor quality. The majority of students (84.8 percent) enroll in academic tracks not out of choice as much as out of necessity (see Chapter 8). The majority of elementary school graduates either join the labor force or continue in academic tracks because vocational-technical programs do not exist. This affects the quality of Arab manpower (mostly unskilled) in the Israeli job market, for the majority of the dropouts, as well as many of the high school graduates, enter the job market as unskilled workers and must compete for lower paying, less secure, and less status-assuring jobs.

The third level of the educational hierarchy in Israel is the government teacher training institute, whose role is to prepare qualified kindergarten and elementary school teachers (secondary school teachers are prepared at the university level). Until 1948 there were two Arab teachers' institutes in Palestine; one in Ram-Allah for females and the other in Jerusalem. When the state of Israel was established, however, Palestinian Arabs who remained within the borders of Israel could not attend these institutions because they belonged to Jordan, along with the West Bank.

Only ten years later, in 1958, an Arab teachers' seminary was established by the government Ministry of Education and Culture in Jaffa. The same year there were 2,768 Jewish students enrolled in teacher seminaries and only 40 Arabs in the seminary in Jaffa, representing only 1.4 percent of the overall Israel student-teacher population.

Arab school age children were 12.7 percent of the total elementary school age population in Israel. Another Arab teacher seminary was established in 1968, and by 1974 the enrollment for both was 587 Arab student-teachers, comprising only 7 percent of the total student-teacher population in Israel. Arab school age children in 1974 totaled more than 22 percent of the total Israeli elementary school age population.

This lack of teachers prepared at certified institutions has led to other problems. In Arab schools there has always been a shortage of qualified teachers. As a consequence, unqualified high school graduates were employed, lowering the quality of teaching in Arab schools. Today, more than 40 percent of the teachers in Arab schools in Israel are unqualified, however, in Jewish schools the number is negligible— a difference due to the fact that Jewish teacher training institutions existed to fill the demand for qualified teachers.

Arab students at Israeli universities constituted less than 2 percent of the total student population in Israel in 1974. During the year 1976–77 the number of Arab university students in Israel almost doubled to 3.5 percent of the student population. There were many reasons for this lack of students. Until 1966 Arabs in Israel were subjected to military administration and needed a special permit to move about or travel, including to and from the university. It was difficult for a family to financially support a student and for students to rent a room or an apartment in a Jewish city. The few who could overcome these barriers found it difficult to compete in a culturally different entrance examination. Moreover, Director of the Arab Education Department in the Ministry of Education and Culture Emanuel Kupileivitch suggests that Arab students are not allowed to enroll in certain departments such as electrical engineering or physics at Israeli universities because of security reasons.[31]

When such difficulties are not encountered by Arab students, their numbers increase significantly. At the University of Haifa, located in the northern part of the country where more than 65 percent of the Arab population is concentrated, distance, housing, and expenses are not problems, and most students commute daily. The university consists of three colleges (education, humanities, and social sciences), none of which offers programs where security is a problem. The university has adopted a policy of increasing its relevance to oriental (Sephardic) Jews and to Arabs. One of these measures was to accept Arab faculty members. Indeed, six out of the nine Arab university level professors in Israel are at Haifa, while the six other universities in Israel have a total of only three Arab faculty members. As a consequence, 45 percent of the Arab student population in Israel attends the University of Haifa.

Kupileivitch considers "security" the main problem encountered by Arab students in Israel, but he also recognizes four others: The low quality of the Arab high school, particularly the science programs, puts the Arab student at a disadvantage in applying for admission; the fact that instruction takes place in Hebrew complicates adjustment; the Arab student does not have an opportunity in his school to be socially and politically prepared for a university atmosphere, especially when the student population is predominantly Jewish; and there are difficulties in the transfer from one cultural environment to another.

Discrepancies in other areas also exist. For example, the average number of pupils per teacher in the Jewish sector was 22.7 in 1974. In the Arab sector it was 32.8. To close this gap 1,500 Arab teachers are needed for the Arab elementary school pupil to have pupil-to-teacher ratio equal to that of his Jewish counterpart. The employment of such a number of teachers would cost the government at least fifty-four million Israeli pounds per year for salaries alone.

This discrepancy is related to that of crowded classrooms. In 1970, while 24 percent of classrooms in the Arab sector had more than 40 pupils each, in the Jewish sector only 7 percent had more than 40 pupils. Forty-six percent of the classrooms in Arab schools held more than 35 pupils in the Jewish schools only 24 percent. Between 1970 and 1974 there was improvement, but a discrepancy remained. In 1974, 40 percent of classrooms in the Arab sector included more than 35 pupils each. In the Jewish sector, on the other hand, the percentage dropped from 24 percent in 1970, to 20 percent in 1974. In 1973 Kupileivitch, suggested that 1,720 classrooms needed to be built for Arab children.[32] Likewise, in 1974 there were only four special education schools in the Arab sector as compared with 167 such schools in the Jewish sector.[33]

In Israel there is a long tradition of dealing with potential high school dropouts by establishing "schools for the working youth." These schools provide vocational and academic training through night classes and are especially important for Arab youths, among whom the dropout rate is high. In 1974, however, only four such schools existed in the Arab sector as compared to ninety in the Jewish sector.[34]

In Israel there are also regional pedagogical centers meant to serve the schools as teaching aids and in educational technology. Thirty such centers exist, none of them for the Arab schools.[35] Arab teachers are encouraged to use these facilities, but when they try, they find that due to differences in language, culture, and curriculum the facilities lack relevance for their pupils because they were developed for Jewish schools.

One way to evaluate the development of Arab education in Israel is to view it as a "closed" system, not comparable with situations in the Jewish sector in Israel. In this case the trends of improvement in Arab education which started long ago, continued after 1948. In elementary education, for example, in 1914 females comprised 8 percent of the total elementary school population, but in 1944, during the British mandate over Palestine, the figure was 23 percent, and in 1973 it had increased to 46 percent. Moreover, in 1946, two years before Israel was created, 30 percent of the total elementary school age children attended school and in 1974 this increased to 82 percent. Similar developments have also taken place among other sections of the Palestinian society.

Another way to evaluate the development of Arab education in Israel is to compare it with education in the Jewish sector in Israel. For the last three decades both Arabs and Jews have been governed by the same laws and administration, however, a clear pattern of discrepancies exists between education of the Arab and the Jewish populations in Israel. *The higher the educational level the greater the discrepancy.* In 1974 Arab elementary school age children represented 22 percent of the total population of this age. In actual enrollment, however, Arabs constituted only 18 percent of the total school population. In high school Arabs totaled only 10 percent; in teacher training institutions 7 percent; and at the university level the discrepancy becomes the greatest, with only 2 percent of the total university student population in Israel Arab students.

SUMMARY

The Arab minority in Israel is trapped between conflicting forces. They are Arab nationals and Israeli citizens at the same time, a dual loyalty demand which places them in a difficult situation. They have no direct contacts with the Arab world, nor do they have any political power in the internal Israeli political structure—a lack of power due both to choice and to force. For almost two decades in their thirty-year history as a minority under Israeli rule, Arabs were subjected to a military administration which, among other things, suppressed the emergence of political leadership. In combination these political dynamics are probably the most powerful forces which shape Arab education in Israel, its goals, policies, administration, curricula, and even teachers' behavior in the classrooms.

Arab society in Israel is a rural-traditional one, though it is undergoing intensive processes of urbanization and modernization. Because of historical factors and patterns of settlement, integration in housing and education between Arabs and Jews in Israel is extremely rare. Even in mixed cities, fully separate educational systems are maintained, however, sociocultural contacts between the two groups are not lacking. Flocks of Arab laborers commute daily from their towns to the Jewish metropolitan centers to earn their living.

The economic status of the Arab minority in Israel is quite susceptible to the fluctuations in the Israeli economy. While most Arab-owned cultivatable land was confiscated by Israeli authorities, other economic resources and job opportunities were not created and developed, resulting in economic dependency of the minority. Although the economic situation of Arabs in Israel has improved considerably, differences still exist between the Arab minority and the Jewish majority with regards to the distribution of opportunities, wages, and status within the job structure. These economic and social conditions have resulted in many transformations in the structure of Arab society in Israel and have changed community attitudes towards education tremendously.

Although traditional religious formal schooling has never ceased to exist among Arabs in Palestine, modern Western-type schools were introduced during the second half of the nineteenth century. At that time, under Turkish rule, state-provided public education was introduced in Palestine, a system which has grown during the last few decades to a point where more than 85 percent of the elementary school age children are now actually enrolled. Nevertheless, great gaps still exist between Arab and Jewish educational systems, and the higher the educational cycle, the greater the discrepancy.

Two basic Arab concerns have influenced the interaction between the political context and the educational system in the history of Palestinian education. First, Palestinians have never ceased to demand national and cultural relevance in the education of their children. This demand led to developments in private education under Turkish rule and the establishment of a school system which was not only religiously but also nationally relevant. Later, under the British mandate, there was a continuous call for additional national elements in school curricula and a strong demand for fuller autonomy in education—issues still unresolved in the case of Arab education in Israel.

Second, Palestinian Arab teachers and their students have always been active in the political scene, a phenomenon most apparent during the British mandate over Palestine. Through their writings, organizations, strikes, and demonstrations, teachers fought not for professional benefits but for national causes. This tradition is still followed, for example, on the West Bank, where the school serves as a common place for resisting Israeli occupation. Teachers were, and to a certain extent still are, the community leaders in most segments of Palestinian society. Among Arabs in Israel, however, this does not seem to be the case. Although they are politically aware and sensitive, especially to matters related to education and politics, teachers have lost much of their traditional role as community leaders and are not involved in political activism, at least not as a group. This noninvolvement is probably due to internal Israeli political dynamics and pressures. The following chapter is devoted to a discussion of these intricate relationships between school, particularly the teachers, and society among Arabs in Israel.

School and Society

THE RESULTS OF AN INVESTIGATION based on conversations and discussions with individuals and groups and on prolonged observation of actual situations both in and out of school reveal much about school and society in Arab villages in Israel. This research had two principal aims. The first is to discuss the subject of the position of the school (mainly the elementary school) in the Arab village in Israel, as seen in the various attitudes of parents and other social groups towards the school, its teachers, pupils, curricula, methods, and aims. The success or failure of education is in no small measure dependent on the way parents and teachers regard education. Their attitudes—whether negative or positive—are usually transferred to the pupils and, to a great extent, tend to determine student success.

The second aim of the investigation was to define the nature of the relationship between the educational institution and rural Arab society in order to reveal the variables which seem most basic and significant. Such a discussion of problems, attitudes, and other variables serves as background and as a point of departure both for those engaged in educational practice and for those engaged in educational theory and research.

Arab society in Israel is rural and traditional. Like other societies of this kind, Israeli Arab society has a clear and well-defined system of values and customs that guides, directs, and regulates the behavior and the interpersonal and intergroup relationships within the society. It is possible to distinguish predetermined modes of behavior and frequently even to predict how a particular individual will behave in a particular situation, for tradition determines how he should behave in many

varying situations. This being the case, the individual in the society is
"outer-directed."[1] This is an example of externalization, in which the
controls over the individual's behavior are external rather than internal.
It is a logical outcome of traditionalism, rather than of conditions and
educational neglect or of conditions of affluence, characteristic of
modern society.[2]

Following the drastic change in the political map in 1948, a change
which brought in its wake other momentous changes, decisive shifts
occurred, and are still occurring, in the social structure, the value
system, and interpersonal relationships in Arab society. These changes
have required abandoning regular and established life patterns and behavior patterns. For example:

1. There have been transformations in employment.[3] Agriculture
   is no longer the primary source of earning a living and has
   begun to take a marginal place in Arab society in Israel. Outside work replaced agriculture as the primary source of income,
   creating a proletarian class with a rural mentality. In other
   words, the main work force in the Arab village turned from
   agricultural work to direct participation in the industrial economy in the Jewish cities and settlements.[4]
2. This change in the sources of livelihood is constantly increasing and brings about daily and intensive contact with urban
   Jewish society. In the eyes of the Arab citizen, Jewish society
   symbolizes modern society, with different and varied styles and
   living patterns—a society which is much more dynamic than
   the rural Arab society, and which, like every other modern,
   Western society, has room for individual initiative and personal
   responsibility.
3. Leaving the village for outside work lessened Arab dependence on existing cultural patterns and social structures. Paid
   work and the possibility of work outside the village accelerate
   the breakdown of the extended family as the economic-social
   unit in rural Arab society in Israel.[5]

These structural and cultural factors contributed to the emergence
of a process of individualization in rural Arab society. The individual
has become more and more autonomous and less dependent both on the
social frameworks to which he belongs and on the cultural patterns
customary in the village. Individualization depends not only on the
daily confrontation with different values and behavior patterns and the

relative weakening of the dependence on social structures, but also on an improvement in the economic condition of the village, particularly for the workers.[6] An improvement of this nature strengthens the feeling of autonomy of the individual, especially when he is a part of the working class, for most of the parents of such people worked the land of others in return for only the most basic subsistence.

It appears that the increasing emergence of individualization is one of the most decisive changes, both structurally and culturally taking place in the Arab village in Israel. Modernization and its processes and outcomes in Arab society in Israel have not been sufficiently investigated, and it is strange that even the little research that was undertaken has not been continued and did not focus on the phenomenon of individualization. This is not the place, nor is it our purpose, to discuss this phenomenon and the tensions aroused in the individual and within the social group which accompany this and other manifestations of modernization.[7] We shall look, rather at the effects of modernization and its processes on the relationships between parents and the village school.

PARENTS AND TEACHERS

There has been a transition in Arab society from heteronomy, a rather strong dependence on a collective social system, to a situation requiring autonomy and independent and responsible activity. This transition has not been smooth and most certainly not lacking in tensions and problems. It has been difficult and drastic, accompanied by feelings of bitterness and perhaps even by a sense of loss of identity.[8] It took place with no self-awareness and with no concept of the reasons and logic inherent in the conditions demanding such a transition. The demands of the new political-economic situation in which the individual Arab in Israel found himself caused, at least at the outset, a relative loss of orientation. The conditions, the manner, and the content of the transition have resulted in a sense autonomy that was not authentic, not at all something which came about as a result of education and of compelling values. Rather, this illusion of autonomy[9] is a result of the rapid social and cultural changes following the sudden transition from an agricultural society to a society involved in an industrial economy; from internal work within the familial social-cultural context to outside work within an utterly different social-cultural context; and from an objective and subjective dependence on rigid, collective social frameworks to objective independence and personal responsibility. The individual's sense of autonomy necessarily results in many changes in his perception of himself and in the way he sees the world around him, including the school.

For the most part an Arab parent feels that it is he who makes the decisions in all matters concerning members of his family. He tolerates no direct interference even if offered with the best of intentions in order to help him. Before the social changes mentioned above, however, the traditional Arab parent not only acquiesced to direct interference in his life and the life of his family, but he often acted in accordance with such intervention, which had generally come from a clan or feudal leader. Such intervention is now seen as an affront to his autonomy, and it arouses his opposition.

The parents still see the school as an institution that should be as authoritative and traditional as possible. They maintain that the school must be authoritative as it was in the years before 1948, during the British mandate. The typical expression of such authority is seen in the administering of severe physical punishments, for "herein lies the worth of the school educator." Yet observations in schools showed that many parents viewed the authority of the school as an infringement on their own authority and came to school to complain angrily and even threatened violence when they found out that corporal punishment had been meted out to their children. It is interesting that in conversations the parents expressed themselves in a way that approved of corporal punishment, but in school they exhibited contradictory behavior.

This was also confirmed in talks with the teachers. A claim frequently voiced was that "parents say one thing and do the opposite" in connection with authority and its expressions. "They are merely words. . . . When we do what the parents say, they want and use corporal punishment, they not only don't accept it, but they complain and may even threaten to turn to the police or the courts." An angry parent, whose son had been beaten by one of the teachers, arrived at the school and shouted at the headmaster, "By what right did your teacher strike my son? What is this? Doesn't he have a father to educate him? Your job is only to teach. Leave his upbringing to me. I know how to raise well brought up children and I don't need your help." In the beginning of the school year the same parent had come to the school and asked the same teacher and headmaster "not to spoil" his son.

All this is better understood if it is remembered that, in fact, "to educate the child" was always considered the indisputable function of the traditional school. Such interference in the education of children did not, in former times, result in parental opposition. Furthermore, the teacher was seen by the parents as so authoritative that they used to threaten their children when they misbehaved by saying that they would report them to the teacher. Such threats have disappeared, and apparently the perception of the teacher as "the educating figure" is also fading.

In conclusion, it appears that opposing forces exist in the personality of the parent.[10] He is exposed to the processes of socialization and "patternization" within the traditional-cultural context in which he grew up, then later exposed to the intense and continuous influence of modern values, life styles, and behavior patterns. These two components in the personality of the parent are in sharp conflict and express themselves in contradictory and inconsistent behavior. Actually, a situation exists in which the value and cultural orientation of many parents has been lost, their self-confidence has been weakened, and even their authority, derived from tradition, is breaking down. This is all due to the rapid cultural changes to which the parents were exposed without the possibility and the capacity to view them critically. The familiar conventions of the traditional culture no longer have the same force, and new conventions have not yet developed. With this in mind, the oversensitivity on the part of the parents and the contradictions and lack of consistency in their behavior is understandable.

THE SCHOOL AND THE CLAN

Two contradictory processes are sweeping through the rural Arab society in Israel. One process is that the clan formation is breaking down, and other social frameworks are gradually being created (classes, associations, and partnerships) that in time will take the place of the clan in the social organization. The emphasis is being transferred from the collective to the individual, although a counterforce, expressed unexpectedly in the strengthening of the clan-tribal identity, has developed for two principal reasons.

The first reason is that generally one or two clans held power in the village and the other clans—because of their economic condition and the inferiority of their position—had no representation in the village leadership. The same clans that did not enjoy a favored position before the processes of modernization began to change the society are now struggling to achieve such a position, simply because they are no longer socially inferior. Feudalism no longer exists, the landholding regime which was characteristic of the Arab village has disintegrated, and the society in general no longer relies on agriculture as the sole source of income. The second important reason is an external strengthening of the clan structure and tribal identity. The Israeli establishment, the military government until 1965 when it was abolished, and particularly the ruling political parties strengthened clan structure and tribal identity to create a point of weakness to be used in their attempts to gain influence in the Arab village in Israel.[11] The continuing existence of these social structures helps Israeli political institutions control, to a large extent, the Arab community in Israel.

These two processes act on the clan structure in opposite directions, creating both intraclan and interclan tensions within the village. The question in this context is, how are these social tensions reflected and expressed within the school and in its relation with the society in which it operates?

Research conducted in various villages shows that in the present social reality all social levels and all the clans are generally represented by the teachers in the village school. Before the establishment of the state this situation was different. For the most part only the sons of well-to-do families were able to obtain a secondary school education, and it was natural, therefore, that the teachers, themselves sons of the village, belonged to the upper social stratum, the ruling clan, of the society.[12] This prevented the creation of tensions on a clan basis among the teachers, since they all belonged to the same clan. It even prevented tensions between the school and the society, for in any case the teachers' clan was the one that held control in the village, therefore the teachers were leaders not only by virtue of their jobs, but also by virtue of their clan membership. Furthermore, most of the pupils going to the school were sons of the ruling and land-owning clans, for they had the right to education.

Another factor which in the past tended to prevent the creation of tensions within the school and between the school and the society was that during the mandate period, a considerable number of the village teachers came from the urban population, since there were not enough secondary school graduates in the villages to fill the need. Such a teacher was a stranger not expected to identify with any particular clan within the village. His presence in the school did not cause social tension because of his lack of involvement and membership in a specific social framework. These teachers were generally regarded with respect and sympathy because they were neutral and not directly involved in the social structure and its potential tensions. The teacher's status as a stranger within the cultural context discussed here increased the regard in which he was held, inasmuch as a stranger is very highly regarded in accordance with the dictates, traditions, and rules of hospitality. When there was any fear that certain teachers might cause tension within the school or the society the mandatory Ministry of Education was careful not to employ them where they lived or in any place where their presence might have caused problems. They were placed in positions where they could remain as neutral as possible.[13]

Today, not only do the teachers tend to represent all of the clans of the village, but as a result of a planned effort and because of clear educational considerations on the part of the Ministry of Education, most of the appointed teachers work in the villages where they were born. Only in those cases where there are not enough teachers in a particular village does the ministry transfer teachers to that village from settlements with a surplus of teachers. A degree of involvement, then, in everything taking place in their village can naturally be expected on the part of teachers who are village members, with all of the positive and negative aspects of such involvement. In general, every individual identifies with the clan to which he belongs, and in time of crisis, when interclan tension is at its height, the teachers also intervene in one way or another.

Tensions exist in the school just as they exist in every other social institution. Teachers of one clan may unite against teachers of another hostile or competing clan, forming groups on the basis of a clan or a coalition of clans. Such groups are active and exert pressure within the school and outside it. With this in mind, it is possible to understand the tensions and misunderstanding which often arise in school among teachers and between them and the headmaster. Such tensions within the school tend to emerge in the wake of tension within the village, with the teachers identifying with their own clans.

The school is often considered by the villagers as the property of a particular clan within the village, especially if the headmaster or most of the teachers belong to that clan. Parents whose clan has no representation among the teachers in the school are often embittered, for they interpret the teachers' behavior toward their children in terms of clan background: "Of course he is more concerned with his own relatives"; "He beats and insults my son and teaches him badly because my son belongs to another opposition clan"; "I asked the headmaster to transfer my son from that teacher's class to the class of another teacher because the second one is my cousin." In one village after a disagreement between two clans the children of these clans began to quarrel. According to a neutral teacher, the teachers belonging to the larger clan incited the pupils of their clan against the other smaller clan. The supervisor who was once responsible for that school verified this account.

Occurrences as serious as this do not take place in every single village or in every single school. Phenomena of this kind generally depend on the composition of the teaching staff in the school, the balance of power within the village, and the educational-cultural level of the community. Furthermore, situations of acute tension are not constant and permanent even in those villages where the social structure and the composition of the teaching staff provide fertile ground for tension. Sometimes there may be tension without active enmity, resulting in the most positive kind of involvement in support of the school and its development. A sixty-five-year-old "mukhtar" (village head) considered the problem of the clans and the school. His words are an attempt to express in analogical form the variegated web of relationships between the society (the clans) and the school.

> The relation between the society and the school is like the relation between the weather and our crops in the field. The weather is sometimes hot and sometimes cold. . . . It depends on the season. The heat is sometimes good, because it ripens the fruit and helps it to grow . . . and sometimes it's harmful because it scorches and destroys the fruit and the tree. It's the same with the cold; sometimes it's good because it allows us and our crops to rest and sometimes it's harmful, because it freezes the crops and destroys them.

In saying "the heat is sometimes good," he means that at times interclan involvement and rivalry result in an enthusiasm to assist the school and support it (e.g., in construction and repairs). "The heat that scorches" symbolizes a negative involvement and destructive enthusiasm which disrupts cooperation and is even likely to bring about an active attempt to create havoc. The "good cold" symbolizes an absence of excitement, or a state of calm, freeing the inhabitants from participation in the expenses of development and construction, while the "cold that freezes" in that condition in which there is a lack of involvement of a kind which causes apathy towards the school.

As a natural extension of this point, it is necessary to examine the social-cultural dynamics which underlie the conditions of social tensions or their relative absence. The quality of interaction between the school and the community within which it functions should be emphasized. It is to be expected that a thorough investigation of these variables can

make a significant contribution towards an improvement in the functioning and status of the village school in general, and towards the
consolidation and efficacy of its functioning as an agent of social-
cultural change, in particular.

Education and teachers can serve as agents of social-cultural
change in the society in which they function.[14] This is especially true of
teachers in a developing society and under conditions of transition from
a traditional to a modern society.[15] The function of the teacher as an
agent of social and cultural change is expressed in his relationship with
the pupil, his attitude toward modernism, and his values and patterns
of behavior. Today the teaching group is one of the main representatives
of modernization in rural Arab society, fulfilling this function because
of two factors. First, the teacher functions as an adult who, with his
particular capacity (knowledge, skills, and values), comes in repeated
contact with the young generation of the society. This contact is particularly significant considering the level of general education in rural
society. For instance, the basic skills for acquiring knowledge (reading
and writing) are nonexistent among the majority of the society's adults.
In surveys carried out in various villages the illiteracy rate in very developed villages averaged 30 percent, and in underdeveloped, remote
villages illiteracy among the inhabitants over the age of thirty averaged
70 percent.[16]

The second factor strengthening the function of the teacher as an
agent of social-cultural change, not only within the school but also
outside it, is the fact that the teaching group constitutes the educated
elite in the village. The teacher comes in continuous contact with the
sources of modernization, and therefore, its processes affect him both
during the period of his studies in the institutions of teacher-training
and afterwards. Furthermore, teachers are frequently expected by the
community to understand, digest, and translate the phenomena and
expressions of modernization to their society within the village. These
phenomena may be expressed in changes in the social structure (local
councils, associations, organizations) or in values and new and strange
behavioral conformations (e.g., ways of eating and drinking, interpersonal relationships within the family, and relations between the sexes
within the village). There are many teachers who are uneasy precisely
because they are agents of social-cultural change. They belong, in one
way, to traditional social frameworks, have absorbed traditional values,
and have learned patterns of behavior characteristic of their traditional
society; yet as agents of social-cultural change, they operate in directions different from, and even contrary to, the tradition to which they

belong. This conflict in roles exists among the teaching group at different levels of consciousness and strength.

Although the teachers belong to the clans—the structural frameworks of their society—they may operate in many ways and with different degrees of awareness towards a social-cultural change, often resulting in a structural change in the society. This change is expressed primarily in the dissolution of the clan. As teachers they are expected (and attempts are made to act according to the expectations) to teach all the skills of reading, writing, studying, and thinking and to develop autonomous personalities, initiative, and nonconformity in their students. Yet they are also expected, particularly by their society, to impart the heritage, tradition, values, and traditional behavior patterns (heteronomy, obedience, and tribalism) to the students in order to preserve cultural continuity. Many teachers are caught up in this conflict with insufficient insight into the forces pulling them in opposite directions. Thus the conflicts between the content and variables in the traditional personality and the much broader, more modern self-image may result in all sorts of contradictory and inconsistent behavior.

Another conflict affecting the teachers is that of dual allegiance. They have a greater sense of national Arab identity than the average villager because they are educated and their identity is less involved with tribe and clan. On the other hand, they are expected to be actively loyal to the state of Israel by identifying with it and with all of its aspirations. They are required not only to identify, but also to develop and nurture such identification among their pupils under all circumstances and with the various means and capacities available to them.

The teachers, then, find themselves in a difficult situation: a nationalist force attracts them and assumes that they will emphasize the nationalistic aspects in teaching the young generation, and a second force emphasizes good and loyal citizenship towards the state in which they live as citizens. A young teacher expressed the conflict he was confronted with in the following words: "I am absolutely going mad. . . . When I educate my pupils towards loyalty to the state I am considered a traitor . . . and when I emphasize the national character of my pupils and try to nurture in them a sense of national pride, I am told I am a traitor." It is true that the roots of this conflict are inherent in the overall conflict between Israel and the Arab countries, but it is unfortunate that these teachers have been abandoned in the midst of this entanglement with no directed attempt to guide them and help them cope with the problem.[17]

In the eyes of the parents, the teachers are government agents. A number of factors are responsible for the emergence of this attitude.[18] The teachers are employees of an official state institution which is one of the arms of government. The parents perceive the teacher as a person serving the ruling authority because he was appointed by it. The roots of such an outlook lie in the fact that immediately after the establishment of the state, and for a number of years thereafter, the teachers in the Arab villages were directly dependent on the military administration for appointment and salary. In the course of time, therefore, the image of the teacher of the average person in the Arab village in Israel was that of an Arab "who lived off the Israeli regime and served it," as one parent observed.

Another factor which strengthened this concept is that teachers, as has been mentioned, are among the principal agents of modernization. The expressions of modernization are viewed by the average villager as characteristics of the Jewish society—a society which symbolizes modernity in the eyes of the Arabs in Israel. It follows that the teacher—in his attempt to reinforce the processes of modernization, which, in any case, are taking place in the Arab villages—is perceived by the villagers not as an agent of modernization but as an agent of the Jewish Israelis. "They (the teachers) want to turn us into Jews." A third and very significant factor is that many teachers are politically active in the various parties, particularly the majority Israeli party. Their activity is explained by the parents by saying, "They must serve the regime in order to keep their jobs."

As an agent of the government, the teacher receives harsher treatment because of the class struggle taking place in the Arab village. New dimensions of class tension have begun to emerge, indicative more of modern than of traditional society. The tension exists between members of the white collar class, of which the teachers make up the decisive majority, and members of the blue collar working class. Workers generally express it thus: "How does a teacher get his appointment if not through 'pull'? He isn't free. He has to shut up and serve his bosses. If I were offered a job as a teacher I wouldn't accept because I don't want to be considered an agent."

Not only teachers are caught up in these situations characterized by a lack of harmony and coordination. Other groups are faced with the same situations in different forms and at different levels of conflict and duality. The conflict of dual allegiance affects the entire Arab society because of the political reality of the Middle East. Among Arab teachers, however, it is more acute, more powerful, because they find themselves caught between the demands of the ruling authority and the expectations of their society. The contradictions which exist between traditionalism and modernity are characteristic not only of the teaching group, but of other social groups as well. The conflict becomes greater because of the special function of the teacher as an agent of social-cultural change, his relative awareness of the contradictions, and the aspirations of the society for cultural continuity.

Nor are teachers the only agents of modernization in the Israeli Arab village. The worker no less than the teacher carries the seeds of modernization back with him when he returns to the village from his work in the city. The qualitative changes in the economic structure of the society, the changes in the level of the average income, the paving of roads, the supply of water and electricity, the establishment of clubs, and—even though in small measure—mass communication, serve to stimulate acceptance and acceleration of the processes of modernization in the Arab village in Israel.

The influence of teachers is stressed because of their awareness—greater than in other groups—of social-cultural change, and because they come into constant and intentional contact with the society at large, especially the young generation. One of the purposes of this contact is to bring about change or to impart skills and develop personalities which will be compatible with the changes taking place. In discussing teachers, their difficulties, the contradictory forces affecting them, and their image in the eyes of the society special importance and consideration must be given to women teachers under conditions of cultural transition.

THE FEMINIZATION OF THE TEACHING PROFESSION

Carl Frankenstein[19] calls attention to the contradiction existing in Western culture as a result of the feminization of the teaching profession. Although the values prevailing in this culture are traditionally more masculine than feminine (achievement, competition, aggressiveness), we are witnessing the transformation of teaching into a feminine profession. The contradition is that it is the function of women teachers to foster masculine values among their pupils. Despite the feminization of the teaching profession, it appears that this phenomenon does not create a negative attitude towards the school. Modern society does not reject the woman as an educating figure and, generally speaking, the differences between the sexes are becoming more and more blurred,[20] leading to a partial resolution of the contradiction.

It is not possible at the present time to speak of the same degree of feminization within rural Arab society in Israel. In the Arab educational system women teachers make up only one-third of the teaching force.[21] In Arab rural society there does not as yet exist a strong contradiction between the prevailing values (more obviously masculine than in Western society) and the educating figure who is expected to develop and nurture these values among the younger generation. The presence or absence of such contradictions is not a direct consequence of the number of female teachers in the educational system, for any given percentage of female teachers becomes significant in the creation of cultural contradictions only by virtue of the interaction between it and its social-cultural context.

In Western society, where women make up the decisive majority of the teaching force, their relatively noninferior status negates this contradiction. But in rural Arab society women teachers are still far from being a decisive majority. Because of values and traditions which establish an inferior status of the woman, even the small percentage of women teachers creates a condition ripe for cultural contradictions. One of the typical expressions of these contradictions is the unwillingness of the parents to accept the fact that the education of their young children in school is in the hands of women rather than men teachers.

Most of the women teachers in the Arab educational system work in kindergartens or in the lower grades of the elementary school.[22] This practice accommodates the educational principle of preserving a continuity between the home and the school and of responding to the psychological needs of children of this age. Educational play has a very important place among the educational and teaching methods used at this age, however, rural society does not recognize the educational values of play.[23] The transformations and adaptations to these educational principles and concepts on the part of Arab parents express their attempts to resolve the contradiction with which they are faced.

The parents in the village are confronted with the appearance of women teachers in the elementary grades along with play as the main educational tool and interpret the phenomenon in accordance with their own social-cultural background in the following manner: Children at this age are unable to learn anything in any case, so they are permitted to play. Were children at this age able to learn, then they would not be permitted to play because that is not a serious way to learn anything. The way to learn is not through play but through a strict and authoritarian relationship. Since women teachers have no authority and are unable to educate, the young children are entrusted to women teachers who play with them. Were children at this age able to learn, then men would teach them; not through play, but "seriously." In this way the parents in the village attempt to resolve the contradiction they face entrusting education to women and the contradiction between learning and play.

The attempts of the parents to solve the problem of the cultural contradictions surrounding them are evidenced in their involvement in the education of their children. In the matter of women teachers and play this involvement is really a demonstration of their opposition to, rather than their acceptance of, what is taking place in the school. The traditional culture is trying—in its own way and in accordance with its own conceptions—to digest all kinds of phenomena which are in contradiction to the conventional cultural attitudes and concepts. These phenomena of modernism inevitably arise in conditions of transition. In this way contradictions are resolved. Otherwise, the parents' continued awareness of these contradictions are accompanied by tensions which are not easy to endure.

One conclusion of this discussion is that the society—by means of cultural rationalizations—prepares for cultural change and copes with it in its own way and through the conceptual-cultural framework and the cognitive spaces[24] inherent in it. The parents are becoming reconciled to the education of their children being entrusted to women teachers. Their opposition is getting weaker, primarily because of their experience in solving the existing contradictions. It seems that the contradictions of women teachers in traditional Arab society will be resolved in the same way that it is in Western culture, that is, through the blurring of the distinctions between the two sexes. Here the question arises as to what are the direct or indirect contributions of women teachers as a part of the educational establishment toward the acceleration of the processes of cultural change, one result of which may be the lessening of the differences between the sexes in Arab rural society in Israel?

One of the most significant contributions of the presence of female teachers in the schools—at least in the present stage of development of education in rural Arab society—is that many parents agree to their daughters attending school. The prospect of a daughter leaving home to attend school does not arouse opposition when other young women are working in the school. The resistance of many parents was broken when they realized that there were women teachers in the school who provided an educational model for their daughters to imitate and that the female pupils mainly come in contact with women teachers. The implementation of compulsory education for girls as well as boys would probably have been delayed had no women joined the teaching corps.

Another social function fulfilled by the presence of women teachers in school is perhaps more significant in the long run. Women teachers are demanding for themselves and from others, especially administrators, the right to educate children and not just baby-sit. They are gradually taking on responsibility as educators, not only because of their increasing numbers, but also because since 1959, most of them have received specific training in seminars for Arab kindergarten and elementary school teachers and see themselves as active educators and not marginal figures.

One mother expressed herself in the following manner after having visited the school a few times at the invitation of the teacher: "If she can educate my son and other people's sons, and even get money for doing it, than I can also educate my children at home and not just threaten them by saying that I'll tell their father when he comes home." Consequences of the interaction of the women teachers and the parents, especially the mothers,[25] go beyond the cooperation between parents and teachers in the education of the child. The role of the woman in the Arab village is gradually changing as her functions become more diversified. Her status is improving, and the parents' interaction with the women teachers intensifies and reinforces these processes.

From this discussion of female teachers and their status in conditions of cultural transition and of the various conflicts they face, many ideas present themselves which cannot be explored within the framework of this discussion. However, one deduction must be emphasized: in the course of the training and qualification of the teaching personnel who will be working within Arab society in Israel, wherever the training takes place, it is essential that those aspects connected with the function of the educator within and without the school and not only on the teaching skills are stressed. Direct and conscientious involvement, observation, and analysis of the sociocultural complexities must be the basis of such training.

Creating and intensifying the awareness of teachers of the different and often contradictory forces acting upon them, the various contradictory expectations of them, and the dynamics and problems inherent in social-cultural change and their role in that change, can make a significant contribution to the teachers, the pupils, and the society. Only if and when the teaching corps can cope with the problems of modernization, nationalism, and citizenship in a way which is educational and relevant to present-day reality, will Arab education in Israel (its content, methods, and aims) not estrange itself from the society in which it is functioning.

THE RELATION OF THE SOCIETY TO EQUALITY OF EDUCATIONAL OPPORTUNITY

The problem of equality of educational opportunity has recently merited considerable attention throughout the world. Particularly well-known are the works of James Coleman[26] and Christopher Jencks,[27] who investigated to what extent genuine equality of educational opportunity exists in regard to different social classes and different ethnic and/or cultural groups. Approaching the problem from a different angle, the positions taken by the parents in the village concerning the fact that the school is egalitarian, in that it has room for every pupil regardless of his clan membership are quite interesting. This is a relatively new phenomenon in Arab rural society in Israel, for although there always was a school, the availability of its services was not equal among all the villagers because of the clan phenomenon.

In the past formal education was primarily the privilege of sons in well-born, influential, and affluent families and a token of a high social position within the Arab village. Today, because of compulsory education and economic, cultural, and social changes education is the right and the obligation of the *entire* young generation in the village regardless of sex or social origin. Not only is there equality in law in regard to all classes, but equality of opportunity exists and is utilized by the children of all strata. It is not only permitted that the less well-to-do attend school, it is compulsory, and there is a widespread recognition of the necessity and importance of an education.

The significance of formal compulsory education is viewed differently by parents in accordance with their status, their education, and their opportunities. In the past, education was significant for parents of well-born origin as a token of their respected and high status. Whereas for parents of a lesser status, education was a luxury difficult to achieve because they felt no need for it, nor could they bear the financial burden. Today education is seen by the less well-to-do parents as having an importance beyond its pragmatic value. For them education constitutes an expression of equality with the well-born.

A formal education has ceased to be a status symbol in the Israeli Arab village. It has contributed to a partial elimination of the traditional class differences which had been clearly defined, strengthening the function of the school as the main factor in social-cultural change. Because of interclass/interclan stresses[28] within the society the relationship of parents to the egalitarian school differs in accordance with their class/clan membership.[29] That is, parents of a well-born background relate negatively and with misgivings to a school which is egalitarian, while parents of a less well-born background relate to it positively.

In examining the reaction of the different groups in rural society to the modern, egalitarian school in the Arab village in Israel in terms of the fundamental right to education and the practical possibility of attendance, it becomes evident that a reaction to the school as an egalitarian institution is determined by the interaction of two variables. The first is the age of the parents, for which two groups were defined: *older parents* (usually above 40) and *younger parents* (between 20 and 30). The second variable is the economic distinction between well-born and less well-born. In this way four groups are formed as a result of the interaction of age and the degree of family distinction: a well-born elder parent, a not well-born elder parent, a well-born young parent, and a not well-born young parent.

The *well-born elder parent* is inclined to reject the egalitarianism of the school, whose doors are also open to pupils from the not well-born families. His rationalization is that this lowers the standard of education. It seems, however, that other reasons are concealed in this rejection. Egalitarianism could cause the lessening of social differences of status. The well-born are engaged in a bitter struggle in the society to maintain their hold on local rule and social leadership. Furthermore, education has been a status symbol, differentiating and reinforcing the ascriptive status within the society. The fact that this identifying mark has become blurred in the wake of the transition from ascriptive status to achievement based status has created a feeling of bitterness and disappointment among the well-born elder parents.

The *not well-born elder parent* is inclined to approve of the egalitarianism of the modern school but often with hesitation and confusion. In the school he witnesses for the first time a situation that allows equal status and rights. This may cause the weakening of an inferior self-image that has developed over many years. Fear of achievement, initiative, and competition is conspicuous, expressed by the following state of mind: "Equality is a good thing, but since when have we schooled our children? It's not necessary to turn the world upside down. We have to know our limitations." Apparently the not well-born elder parent has misgivings concerning his ability to compete, to get ahead, and to win, because he has never experienced these feelings.

An interesting phenomenon is that the *well-born young parent*—like the not well-born elder one—approves of the equality of opportunity in school, but also with reservations. He belongs to the well-born group which, were it not for the equality of opportunity, would afford him a high status. Now he must make a greater effort and compete with others, causing him to waiver in accepting the principle of equality. But he also belongs to the generation brought up in Israel which has had some contact with the Jewish society—a generation that was in touch with the sources of learning, modernization, and equality. For the most part he sees himself as modern and progressive. Therefore, the well-born young parent must reconcile himself to equality and his negative feelings about it. He accepts egalitarianism because it is compatible with his liberal self-image but rejects it because he has to compete to achieve status.

The reaction of the not well-born elder parents is very similar to that of the well-born young parents regarding the principle of equal educational opportunity, yet each group arrived at this point for different reasons. The not well-born elder parent approves because he is likely to benefit from the opportunity but hesitates because he is not prepared for the competition. The well-born young parent approves of equality of opportunity but hesitates because he is likely to benefit less. Both groups exhibit a conflict between self-image and concrete opportunity. It is this conflict which causes an ambivalence on the part of both groups towards equality of opportunity.

The *not well-born young parent* approves of equality of opportunity in school. The young generation from not well-born families does not feel status inferiority because they grew up and were educated after the breakdown of the feudal regime and actually competed (in outside work in the city) with well-born colleagues. This was the first real opportunity for them to be on an equal footing with the sons of the well-born, and for the most part they stood up to this competition and achieved more in terms of vocation and income. They approve, therefore, of equality of opportunity with unparalleled enthusiasm and demonstrate a certain harmony between self-image and the actual possibility of competing and becoming educated.

These conclusions parallel some observations concerning social tensions. Maximum tension exists in the Arab village between the well-born elders and the not well-born young men, the former despising the latter because they symbolize the threat against their position. The well-born elders symbolize the past to the not well-born young men and are seen as an obstacle to equality. These tensions are expressed in often violent quarreling and competitiveness over village rule. The other two groups are becoming relatively marginal in this struggle and do not, as a rule, create tension. If anything, they participate as a result of a feeling of identification with their own group after the tension already exists. Thus, in conditions of tension in the village, the well-born young men are involved by virtue of identification with their fathers, and the not well-born elders are involved by virtue of identification with their sons.

CURRICULA, METHODS, AND AIMS

Reality has a pragmatic utilitarian significance for the man in the Arab village.[30] This principle is expressed in the villager's search for the tangible and immediate profit of everything he does and an inability to see the distant future and plan for it. If there is another dimension characteristic of the concrete, pragmatic approach, it is that of immediacy. Frankenstein,[31] in his analysis of the transition from the traditional state (the rural, in the Arabs' case) to modern culture, maintains that the villager is chained to the known. This attachment to the tangible indicates an inability to break out of the most narrow bounds of the ego and a weakness in the ability to abstract and project the future.

In the same model which Frankenstein uses to analyze this transition, there is an intermediate stage which he calls "contaminated traditionality" in which the purity of traditionality is weakened and the personality reveals traditional expressions along with modern ones.[32] At this stage the person can often plan for the future and rise above— even though only partially—the concrete and reach the abstract.

With this model in mind, the Arab village was approached in order to understand the relationship of the parents to the school and their perception of the curriculum, methods, and aims. The older generation, characterized by rural traditionality, stands bewildered in the face of the school in which there is "a lot of wasted time and even damage to the young generation." This was the typical opinion of the older generation in the Arab village in Israel. They had many questions: "What use is there in educating children for so many years? What do they do there and how does it help them in their everyday lives? Is all this worth anything or is it all just a waste of time? And let's say it helps the boys a little, what good is it to the girls?"

The older generation usually denies any value in the existence of the arts in school, because "you can't make a living from that"—a reflection of the fact that this generation worked at hard, physical labor in previous years, especially during the feudal regime, in order to subsist. The general agreement was unequivocal as far as the curriculum was concerned: The only important thing is what helps the child in his daily life and more or less in an immediate way. They prefer that Arabic studies are stressed so that the child will be able to read and write his own language; arithmetic, so that he can carry out essential, elementary problems; Hebrew, because it is the language of the ruling majority and useful in daily life; and religion, so that the child will not shun tradition and deteriorate into one of the "group of heretics" or "the immoral ones." The system thought by the older generation the most effective way to achieve all this is one of almost absolute authoritarianism, enforced by corporal punishment.

For this reason the modern school in the Arab village is seen by the older generation as an institution in which time is wasted and the young are corrupted because of their alienation from tradition due to the lack of emphasis on religious studies and the absence of physical punishment. It is considered an institution which uses up many years for very little. The prevalent opinion is: "If they taught them trades which would help them more in life, then all the years in elementary school would be justified."

The younger generation is the first in the Arab village which has been continuously exposed to the processes of modernization and its manifestations. Their level of education is higher than that of the elders, however, their regular and intensive contact with the Jewish society and communication media has resulted in their being characterized by "contaminated traditionality." They relate to the school, its curriculum, and its functions differently than the older generation. They are more aware and committed nationalistically, and they stress the basic skills of reading, writing, and arithmetic, not only because of their practical value, but because they are tools for social-cultural advancement. They perceive the school as an instrument of social-cultural change.

The difference in viewpoint reflects a difference in the life experiences of the two groups. The pragmatic position taken by the older generation of the village in regard to the basic skills is a reaction to degrading experiences they are having by not knowing how to read or write. They emphasize what *they* feel is needed, but fail to grasp the importance of education beyond the basic skills. The broader and more abstract viewpoint of the younger generation is a result of their experience in intercultural conditions in which they realize that education is the main factor in the differences between a developed and underdeveloped society.

The younger generation also stresses the study of Hebrew because they see its practical communicative value with the Jewish majority in the state. They favor drawing people closer and aiding understanding with the Jewish majority, contrary to the viewpoint from that of the older generation.

In general, the study of religion and tradition is the object of harsh criticism by both generations. It is known that the study of religion, Arabic literature, and the history of Islam are not particularly stressed in Arab schools (see Chapter 4), nor are they stressed to the same degree that the parallel subjects are stressed in Hebrew education (Jewish schools).[33] The older generation is inclined to have reservations about the school because they feel it causes alienation of the young from religion. The principal goal of the older generation is religion for its own sake. Most of the young people in the Arab village, however, are not religious. They reject religion and religious behavior because they see it as an external sign of traditionalism and backwardness. They prefer that schools emphasize the study of religion and tradition, not in order to mold the pupils into religious personalities, but to develop their sense of national identity through its connections with religion, history, and heritage. In this case, religion is not an end in itself as it is among the older generation, but it is a means to another end.

We may assume that because of the experience gained by the younger Arab generation in intercultural situations charged with conflict and stress, they are searching for identity and the nation-building processes. To a certain extent a solution may be found in the living connection with the heritage of the past. This heritage can only partially be transferred to the young generation by the elders through recollection. Therefore, one of the main functions of the school, as seen by the young generation, should be the development and consolidation of the pupils' cultural and national Arab identity.

An analysis of these various attitudes leads to significant conclusions and implications for the curriculum and functions of the education to be provided for Arab children in school. But only after further careful and concentrated examination can practical conclusions be used as a firm infrastructure for the greater efficiency, improvement, and strengthening of the educational institution in the Arab village in Israel.

Some of the issues are discussed at greater length in the following chapters, and some of these issues will remain open as long as the Israeli-Arab conflict remains unsettled. Others demand an immediate action for change on the part of both the community and the authorities. Certain dynamics of minority status and majority rule are beginning to take place independently of the Israeli-Arab conflict. Socioeconomic forces within Israeli society are beginning to have greater impact on the Arab minority in Israel and its educational system. The following chapters show that certain internal dynamics influence Arab education in Israel in the same way as do the commonly acclaimed external factors attributable to the conflict in the Middle East.

Goals, Policies, and Administrative Status

THE INFLUENCE OF IDEOLOGY on education[1] is especially noticeable in pluralistic situations wherein nationally different (or opposing) groups live side by side and where goals and policies are often defined by the dominant group.[2]

GOALS AND POLICIES

The law of state education of 1953 specifies the aims of education in Israel as follows: "To base education on the vaues of Jewish culture and the achievements of science, on love of the homeland and loyalty to the state and the Jewish people, on practice in agricultural work and handicraft, on pioneer training and on striving for a society built on freedom, equality, tolerance, mutual assistance, and love of mankind."[3] When the Israeli Knesset (parliament) so defined the state education law it also specified the goals of education in Israel. Goals for Arab education were not mentioned at all, indeed, in his extensive discussion of the problems of Arab education in Israel, Emanuel Kupileivitch, the director of the Arab Education Department, has determined that for the past three decades Arab schools in Israel "have been functioning without a defined goal."[4] This deficiency exists despite the fact that the minister is empowered by the same law to decide upon regulations concerned with "*adaptation* of rulings under the Law, in whole or in part, to the needs of *elementary* education of *non-Jewish* pupils, and the setting up of Advisory Councils for such education"[5] (emphasis added).

By law, the minister of education is responsible only for adapting goals defined for Jewish education to Arab education. The adaptive restriction may be undertaken with regard to *elementary* education only. Course content which helps develop national identity and ethnic awareness is more effective at the high school level than in the elementary schools. During the adolescent years in high school youth not only have the intellect required to grasp the abstract concepts of nationality and culture, but also at this age they seek to define their identity. Thus, the law has, in effect, deprived Arab students of the possibility of obtaining culturally and nationally relevant course content (see also Chapter 4).

Dr. Joseph E. Bentwitch, an eminent Israeli educator and a recipient of the Israeli-acclaimed Bialik Award, discusses this controversial issue of goals (or lack of goals) for Arab education in Israel:

> The definition of aims and content is perhaps the most difficult problem in Arab education. With regard to administrative problems, e.g. buildings, textbooks, supply of teachers, there are at least *plans*, . . . But with regard to aims, it would seem as if there was not even a plan. Indeed, so long as the Arab states continue to declare themselves at war with Israel, and as a result, the Arab population in Israel is subject to discrimination, it is difficult to make educational demands. It is difficult to preach loyalty to the State of Israel, or to set up as a goal a society built on freedom and equality when Arab youth regard themselves as deprived of freedom and equality.[6]

Furthermore, Bentwitch suggests that, as a consequence of the political situation and contradictory national aspirations, government has concentrated only on providing knowledge in addition to formal demands of order and discipline, but not much more.

Kupileivitch distinguishes four trends of thought among educational authorities in Israel with regard to the desired goals of Arab education. First, there are those who emphasize the point that Arabs are citizens of Israel and must be brought up as Israelis, expressing "the intention to blur the national identity of Arabs in Israel."[7] Second, there are those who stress the cultural uniqueness and national identity of the Arabs as educational goals. Kupileivitch, suggests however, "in this, they express a contradiction to the fact that these Arabs are citizens of Israel and obliged to be loyal." Third, there are those who advocate a balance between Arabness and Israeliness; they are of the opinion that it is possible to reconcile these two conflicting entities in such a way that the product will be an Israeli Arab who is loyal to both his nation and the state of Israel. The fourth trend is represented by those who claim that this problem of goals for Arab education needs more time to work itself out, and the best the authorities can do is *not* to form a clear policy. Kupileivitch concludes that this last trend of "do nothing" is the dominant one; the lack of policy has become policy itself.

While Bentwitch recognizes the difficulties in imposing the goal of loyalty to Israel, others view it as unquestionably legitimate. Although Kupileivitch suggests that it is unacceptable to educate the Arabs in loyalty to the Jewish people and in knowledge of the Jewish culture, he does maintain that "the achievement of science . . . love of the country and loyalty to the State" can be considered as legitimate aims of Arab education.[8] Bentwitch responds to these "acceptable" goals as follows: "And yet it is not to be supposed that Arabs in Israel can be content with such general and 'Jewish' aims as these. How well do we know from our own [Jewish] history that acquisition of full citizenship in a foreign nation, even when it is accompanied with fine national or cosmopolitan ideals, is not yet sufficient to instill self-respect. . . . Just as Jewish education is based on the values of Jewish culture, so, in Arab education, the values of Arab culture must take a central place."[9]

The first effort to address this problem of setting goals for Arab education was made by the Israeli educational authorities in 1972, when Deputy Minister of Education Aharon Yadlin headed a committee organized for the purpose of defining the goals of Arab education in Israel. The goals set by this committee, which were published in what is referred to as the Yadlin Document,[10] are:

1. Education in the values of peace.
2. Education for loyalty to the state by emphasizing the common interest of all its citizens and the encouragement of the uniqueness of Israeli Arabs.
3. Forming of a plan to make the economic and social absorption of Arabs in Israel easier.
4. Educating females for autonomy and for the improvement of their status.

In the discussion following the list of goals, the Yadlin Document also adds "to educate for the identification with the values accepted by the Israeli society—i.e., democracy and social ethics; and also with the culture of interpersonal relationships accepted by it—relationships between the individual and his friend, relationships in the family, and the relation of the individual to society."[11]

In 1973 a committee of seven Arabs and seven Jews headed by Dr. Matty Peled, was formed by the director general of the Ministry of Education and Culture "to define the national and cultural framework for the education of minorities" and "to determine a framework for the reduction of gaps."[12] The committee was also to advise on these issues and to recommend plans and policies for Arab education during the 1980s. The reaction of this committee to the Yadlin Document was the following:

> The limitations of these guidelines are found in not giving an answer to the question of contradiction in the life of the Arab citizen in Israel between his identification with the Arab nation and his interest in living in peace in the State of Israel—a contradiction which stems from the political reality overwhelming Israel. It is clear that the cry for loyalty by orders cannot be a basis for positive education in the school, and the emphasis on important social problems such as the question of female education, etc. cannot be a substitute to the discussion of the basic problems in the existence of the Arab in the State of Israel.[13]

It seems that the Yadlin Document does not only try to de-emphasize and blur the national identity of Arabs in Israel, but it also tries to cancel out their culture by imposing morals and values accepted by the predominantly Jewish Israeli society upon them through a government-controlled educational system. One must then wonder what is left in a culture after the "social ethics," the values which govern "personal relationships," "family interrelationships," and the "relation of the individual to his society" are cancelled out.

Arab youth are often committed to the improvement of female status. As this improvement appears in the context of the Yadlin Document, however, its intentions become questionable, for the goal of a woman's liberation is to become liberated in her own direction and within her own cultural context, and not to become what the Israeli society accepts or does not accept.

In 1975, after expressing dissatisfaction with the Yadlin Document, the Committee on Arab Education for the Eighties suggested that the minister accept the following as goals for Arab education:

> The goal of state education in the Arab sector in Israel is to base education on the foundations of Arab culture; on the achievement of science, on the aspiration for peace between Israel and its neighbors,

on love of the shared country by all citizens, and loyalty to the State of Israel—through emphasizing their common interests and through encouraging the uniqueness of Israeli Arabs, on the knowledge of the Jewish culture, on respect for creative work and on the aspiration for a society built on freedom, equality, mutual help and love of mankind.[14]

This statement is the first to explicitly require that education for Arab children be based on the essentials of Arab culture. The statement of goals on Jewish education quoted earlier does not mention "shared homeland," nor does it relate to the "aspiration for peace." It does not refer to the "common interests" between all (Arab and Jewish) citizens nor require knowledge of the Arab culture. The suggested goals for Arab education presented above, on the other hand, does not have an equivalent of "loyalty to the Jewish people." Through all the efforts made towards the education of Arabs in Israel, the only reference to *national* background is to the Arab culture and not to the greater Middle East Arab population. The fact that Arabs in Israel are an inseparable part of the Palestinian nation has been consistently overlooked not only in the statement of educational goals itself, but also in the rationale preceding and in the discussion following such a statement.

Another problem in all these efforts and others is that the Arab minority in Israel has always been treated as an object, as a periphery. These committees on Arab education have either been all Jewish or Jewish dominated, and the basic question behind these efforts has been, in effect, how to manipulate the peripheral Arab minority through education in such a way that the central Jewish majority can maintain its interests.

The points outlined in this section can best be summarized by a quotation from Dr. Joseph E. Bentwitch. Though his remarks were published much before these committees were formed, they seem to have had no effect on the way the committees were formed nor on their conclusions.

Jews can assist Arabs, therefore, primarily by advice and, above all, by example. If Jewish education is to be materialistic or chauvinistic, it will be impossible to expect Arab education to be more "spiritual." Nor can a secular-humanist education serve as a model; though it may help to liberate Arabs, as well as Jews, from primitive and narrow conceptions, it has no positive contribution. It cannot show the way to a revival of Arab cultural values, and thus give the Arabs self-respect;

on the contrary, its secularism will merely undermine the foundation
of Arab culture, and so leave it prey to assimilation and levantinism.
Positive assistance can come out if Jewish education can point to
achievements in the revival of Jewish cultural values, or at least
sincere efforts in that direction. "Charity begins at home." A condition
for the successful transfer of ideas from Jewish to Arab education is
that it shall be bilateral: that Jews shall learn from Arabs too.[15]

Statements of goals, whether official or not, are often no more than
formalities in terms of papers and declarations. In many developing
countries there is a great gap between the officially specified goals and
the curricula and practices in the schools. In the Arabs' case, however,
there seems to be a definite consistency between the statements of goals,
on the one hand, and the administrative structure and state-specified
curricula (in terms of subjects, topics and the required class hours) on
the other, especially in those subjects which have national, cultural, and
religious relevance.

ADMINISTRATIVE STATUS

Most government and public bodies in Israel have separate departments
for Arab affairs, all of which are headed by persons of Jewish background. For example, there are Arab departments within the ministries
of labor, religions, and education. Some political parties also have Arab
departments, including the ruling majority labor coalition. The
Histadrut (Israel's Federation of Labor) officially cancelled its separate framework for Arab laborers in 1953, though "it immortalizes
the existence of an Arab Department"[16] and is also headed by a Jew.
In addition, Arab teachers in Israel have a separate division within the
Israeli Teachers' Union. An Arab representative within this division
commented that "the head of this division is not only non-Arab, but he
is the only appointed [non-elected] head in any division of the
Teachers' Union in Israel."
    These directors of Arab departments within the Israeli public and
governmental bodies are often described by the Hebrew Israeli media
as "Arabistim" or "experts in Arab affairs." In other words, they are
identifiable as a group which is supposed to administer Arab affairs in
Israel as well as mediate between Arab communities and the central
Israeli authorities.
    Immediately after the creation of the state the military administra-

tion mediated between Arab communities and the Israeli government. As has already been mentioned, teachers were administratively linked with the military administration. The Department of Interior was also represented by the military administration, and Arab citizens were given ID cards through its offices. These administrative powers were gradually delegated to the different departments for Arab affairs within the government's structure and hierarchy, creating the pattern of separation through special departments. The most popular rationale for the creation of these departments is three-fold. First, the complexity of the Israeli modern political and social structures and organizations, and the "simplicity" of the Arab citizens make it extremely difficult for both to deal with each other. Thus, a facilitating and mediating structure between the two is in order. Second, because the Arab minority in Israel has special problems in culture, education, and economy a separate department in which there are experts would help them receive relevant services. Third, because there were no qualified Arabs to fill the high posts in these departments, Jews who knew Arabic filled them.

The highest of these posts is the advisor to the prime minister on Arab affairs. He is usually involved in "issues related to minorities with regards to initiative, planning, coordination, guidance, and supervision," including "security matters, land problems, local government, agriculture, . . . housing, education and culture, welfare and health."[17]

The attitudes of these advisors towards the Arab minority, however, have been contradictory. Uri Lubrani, the advisor to the prime minister on Arab affairs, in 1961 responded to the fact that Arab students at Israeli campuses were involved in political activism: "If there were no Arab university students it would have been better. If they had remained woodcutters, maybe they would have been easier to control. But there are things which do not depend on wish. There is no escape. . . . One must know how to identify the problems."[18] These comments created an outrage among Arabs and liberal Jewish individuals.

Since 1966, however, Shmuel Tolidano has been occupying the post of the advisor on Arab affairs and is more liberal than his predecessors. He has often urged government and public institutions to provide a better opportunity for Arabs to become integrated within the Israeli economic and social structures, and although representing the majority's interests, he often refers to the possible dangers in the alienation and frustration accumulating among Arab intellectuals in Israel. In December 1975, he declared that "the load of bitterness and frustration of Arabs from the state has reached worrisome dimensions."[19] In the same interview, however, he did not attribute the failure of the Israeli establishment in equitably treating the Arab minority to the Arabists (Jewish advisors, directors, and experts in Arab affairs), but rather to other inevitable factors, namely, Israel's political situation.

As in the prime ministers' office, there are special departments for Arabs in all other government agencies. Arabs and Jews together and independently have expressed their discontent with the separate Arab departments within public and government institutions in Israel. Their criticism is based upon the following points. First, after thirty years of the state's existence, the vast majority of Arabs know Hebrew, thus the language barrier was eradicated a long time ago. Moreover, the Arab in Israel is not "simple" anymore, and his ability to deal with complex bureaucratic institutions is comparable to any other citizen's. Second, the "special problems" attributed to Arab citizens are for the most part a myth, as is the fact that such problems necessitate special departments for their resolution. At any rate, if these aspects of culture, religion, and nationality do make the Arab minority member distinctly different from the majority, then Arabs themselves would seem better qualified to head these departments and administer them. Third, it may have been true in the early fifties that, because of the loss of the educated elite, the Arab minority did not have enough qualified persons to occupy these posts. This has not been the case for a long time, however, and Arabs in Israel are now qualified by the same institutions that qualify Jewish students, that is, universities in Israel. Fourth, members of this group of directors, although some are government employees, are often involved in efforts aimed at influencing the directions in which Arab votes in Israel are cast. The existence of their departments not only reflects a policy of direct and imposed intervention in the cultural, educational, political, and religious aspects of the lives of Israeli Arabs, it also prohibits or postpones the emergence of a political and cultural (not to mention national) leadership within the Arab society in Israel. An Arab Ph.D. candidate at the Hebrew University of Jerusalem has claimed that he is "extremely bitter and frustrated because to serve my own community would mean that I have to obey these Arabists or be fired by them."

This group of Arabists still exists, although pressured and subject to criticism—a situation due probably to the fact that they control a powerful system of rewards and punishments which they operate whenever necessary. They often portray a negative picture of the Arab to the central authorities in order to justify their existence, creating a self-fulfilling prophecy: Through their existence and policies the Jewish advisors on Arab affairs support the negative picture of Arabs; and through the portrayal of such an image they reinforce and justify their existence.

Diab El-'Obeid, an Arab member of the Knesset who has long been affiliated with the ruling party in Israel, tried to bring this issue to the attention of the Knesset members in 1972. In a detailed speech on November 11, he suggested that when the Arabists felt the growing pressure from Arabs as well as Jews,

> they started cooperating among themselves and conspiring and planning so they [could] remain. In their first plan, they controlled all media in order to transmit and publish whatever they wanted against the Arab citizens in a blown-up and exciting way in order to provoke the Jewish people and to make the authorities suspicious. In their other plan, they prohibited the [Arab] citizen from expressing his opinion if it were against the continuing existence of these departments or against their heads, and they opened all the doors to groups formed by them so they can support them. . . . In their third plan, they followed the principle of divide-and-rule. . . . By these plans, they renewed trouble and misunderstanding between the two peoples and convinced the authorities of the necessity of their existence. . . . Their goal is the maintenance of control and power in a form of another government within one state.[20]

In an earlier speech (April 4, 1972) 'Obeid referred specifically to the financing of the Arab Education Department following a speech by the minister of education in the Knesset: "I heard the speech of the Honorable Minister of Education with regard to the budget of his Ministry and I was hoping to hear something with regard to education in the Arab sector. I am sorry I did not hear a thing." He continued to "urge the Honorable Minister of Education to implement his slogans and promises to the educated Arab youth and start by closing the Department of Arab Education and thus take educated Arabs to administer and organize within the Ministry, not within the Department."[21] In his evaluation he also found the department responsible for the fact that education in the Arab sector is lagging much behind education in the Jewish one.

As far as finance is concerned, 'Obeid's comments are symptomatic. Repeated efforts by the author to achieve information with regard to the financing of Arab education in Israel were in vain. While the Israeli Statistical Abstracts present a comprehensive yearly account for the ministry's budget, they are not specific with regard to the financing of

Arab education. Except for the salaries of Arab teachers—who receive the same salary as their Jewish counterparts based on qualifications, years of experience, and number of dependents—there seem to be shortages in the Arab educational system and service indicating a lack of financial resources. As mentioned earlier, 1,500 Arab teachers are needed in order to equalize the average number of pupils per teacher in both Arab and Jewish classrooms, which would require over fifty million Israeli pounds per year.

Clearly, the lack of other ministry-provided educational services to Arab students demands financial resources. For example, if the ministry were to plan for increasing the percentage of junior and high school Arab students in vocational-technological programs from 11 percent to over 50 percent to make the percentages comparable to those in the Jewish schools, hundreds of millions of Israeli pounds would be needed for investment in such programs. Similarly, the creation and development of a special education network in Arab schools, along with necessary psychological services, would certainly require significant additional investments. The same could be predicted for other services such as regional pedagogical centers, laboratories, and libraries—all which demonstrate great gaps between Arab and Jewish sectors.

The problem of school buildings and related physical facilities is a controversial one, especially with regard to the free, compulsory elementary education. The shortage of classrooms in school buildings seems to become more and more acute and detrimental to the development of Arab education in Israel. In 1973 the director of the Arab Education Department drew attention to the fact that 1,720 classrooms were immediately required in order to satisfy the long existing and ever increasing need.[22] Three years later, in 1976, Aharon Efrat, a member of the Knesset, claimed in a query addressed to Aharon Yadlin, the minister of education, that 5,000 classrooms were needed in the Arab educational system and added that in one Arab village of over 10,000 inhabitants there were 62 "classrooms" rented in private homes scattered all over the village. These rooms were not only "old and shaky," but they also lacked the minimal sanitary conditions. Yet over 30 percent of Arab school children were "learning" in such physical conditions. This, he commented, made effective administration and organization an impossible task. The minister, in his response, admitted that 3,000 (not 5,000) rooms were needed in Arab schools. He is also quoted as saying: "There are good intentions but we don't have funds. . . . These rooms should cost one billion Israeli pounds" (approximately $100 million).[23]

Under Israeli law, local authorities (municipal councils) are responsible for constructing, equipping, and maintaining school buildings. This responsibility is usually carried out through various forms of financial assistance from the ministries of treasury, education, and interior. Yet, in more than 30 percent of Arab villages in Israel elected local councils do not exist, making it difficult for these villages to receive loans from the government since they lack a formally responsible body. Other villages, though they do have official councils, do not obtain the assistance necessary for development projects within their villages or towns. When interviewed, Arab mayors often pointed out that on the average their communities receive only 10 percent of what a comparable Jewish settlement obtains from the government. Mahmud Biadsi, an Arab activist in the Socialist-Zionist Mapam Party and the head of the Arab village of Baka al-Gharbieh local council, states that:

> Taxation in the Arab communities is almost as high as in Jewish ones, but discrimination exists in government grants. These grants constitute 30 percent of the total usual budgets of Jewish municipalities, but only three percent for Arab local authorities, whereas local taxes constitute 14 percent of the usual budgets of Jewish local councils and 30 percent of the usual budgets in Arab ones. . . . Up to the time of writing [1975], however, nothing has been done. . . . Righting the inequality in allocating grants and loans, which has been continuing for many years, might have helped the Arab communities solve some of their urgent problems. For example, a large village (15,000), Um al Fahm, receives a grant of seven Israeli pounds per inhabitant and is grappling with a series of municipal problems. Had this village received grants equal to those given Jewish villages over a period of 20 years, it would have overcome the problem of school buildings, and would have solved the onerous sewage problem.[24]

Kupileivitch suggests two reasons for the shortage of physical facilities, particularly school buildings. First, in the beginning the state invested all its financial resources in meeting the urgent needs of Jewish immigrants and neglected the development of physical facilities for Arab school children. Second, although school buildings and maintenance are within the responsibility of the local government, most, if not all, of the necessary financing comes from the development budget of the state. There are plans, he claims, but money should be allocated.[25] Kleinberger states: "In this respect, formal equality before the law has operated to the Arab's disadvantage. No Arab village enjoys the status of 'maintained community' [granted to many new Oriental immigrants and development towns], in which the Ministry of Education defrays the educational expenditure normally borne by local education authorities."[26] Important, too, is that financial assistance, although not readily and equally available, applies only to government schools. The private education system, unless it becomes semi-official, that is, partially controlled, is not able to benefit from even limited assistance.

CHRISTIAN SCHOOLS

As mentioned in the first chapter, Christian schools have existed in the Middle East for over a century. While no Moslem private schools are operating in Israel, Christian schools, sponsored by western european religious organizations, continued to exist after the state of Israel was created. In 1968, 13,204 Arab (Christian and Moslem) students were enrolled in these schools.[27] In other words, more than 10 percent of the Arab pupil population in Israel is enrolled in the private Christian school system, a number which has maintained a status quo with very minor fluctuations over the years.

Because they were nongovernment and autonomous, Christian schools enjoyed an increasingly high status, especially immediately after the creation of Israel. The reason for this was not so much the quality of education they provided as it was of the politics involved. All Arabs, and especially Palestinians, were shocked and frustrated when Israel was established. At first, those who had stayed in the country hesitated to send their children to the government-controlled schools. Christian schools were private and, at that time, completely independent from any influence of Israeli educational authorities. They often served as a refuge for those teachers who were nonconformists. Most of the Arabs in Israel, however, did cooperate with the government schools because of their need for educational services and because the vast majority of them lacked alternatives. Christian Arabs, who lived nearby and who had the means, sent their children to the private Christian schools.

Christian schools were not very popular among rural Moslem communities because Islam was not taught as a religion. Rather, the religion taught and practiced was that of the denomination with which the school was associated. Many Moslems appreciated these schools in spite of this because Christian schools and rural Moslem communities have one important trait in common: traditionalism. Traditional rural Arabs place high emphasis on the value of physical punishment in education, and they insist on the separation of males and females in schools. Christian schools observed both of these practices. Had it not been for religion, Christian schools would probably have been more popular among Moslems than among the relatively more liberal Christians.

The popularity of Christian schools has been declining during the last two decades, not only in Israel but also in the Arab world. After many Arab countries obtained their independence, much of the interest of European countries in Middle Eastern domestic affairs ceased. European governments and religious organizations have consequently reduced both financial and professional support to their schools in the Middle East, and Christian schools in Israel have been no exception. Moreover, the Middle East has been witnessing nationalistic movements and activities which oppose foreign political and cultural interference. These movements typically emphasize their own culture and history and strongly reject foreign cultural interference. This is especially true when the foreign culture belongs to the colonizer or ruler, who is usually the target of these liberation movements.

Christian schools transmitted a foreign set of values and patterns of behavior to the local culture to which communities objected. Although the Arab minority in Israel has no direct political dealings with the Arab countries, it is also true that Israeli Arabs are indirectly influenced by Arab nationalistic movements and want the education of their children to reflect common Arab history and culture and to transmit its values. Thus Christian schools in Israel have been a target of criticism by the communities they serve, regardless of the kind of religion these communities adopt. In an interview a priest serving as director of a Christian school describes the situation: "As far as popularity and status are concerned, our main objective is to maintain a *status quo*. Even that, I am afraid, we can't achieve. . . . We are under fire from both the communities and the local authorities. . . . Even our own countries and organizations do not support us as strongly as they used to."

While the Christian schools have been suffering from budget cutbacks and declining popularity, government schools have been gradually improving. Schools have been built in most villages, textbooks have been translated from Hebrew into Arabic, and most teachers have enrolled in qualification courses, forcing private Christian schools to compete on a qualitative basis. Indeed, for the first time in their history in Israel Christian schools have been challenged. The financial cutbacks in these schools, added to the other factors already mentioned, certainly have not helped them maintain their previous high quality. Because of low salaries, few qualified teachers have been attracted, nor have Christian schools been able to ask for a fee higher than the token one they were charging. Had they done so, they would have lost most of their clientele simply because the government schools, in accordance with the law of compulsory education, provide education free of any charge.

Until the last few years, Christian schools prepared their pupils for a different world from that of Israel. The local languages, Hebrew and Arabic, were not emphasized, the diplomas were foreign, and the educational experiences of the pupils did not correspond with those obtained in the government schools. Graduates from Christian schools faced more difficulties in adjusting to higher educational institutions simply because they were not prepared appropriately for them. This prevented the pupils from continuing their education in an effective manner.

Thus, the Christian schools, which helped provide educational services to the minorities in Israel and which relieved the government of part of the burden of educating large numbers of children, have of late been facing a crisis. Lack of financial support from their mother organizations, lack of support from the authorities because of the schools' autonomy, community complaints on nationalistic and cultural grounds, and unqualified teachers have placed the schools at a disadvantage in competition with the constantly expanding government schools.

To meet this crisis Christian schools have made two major concessions. They have given up some of their autonomy in return for financial help from the educational authorities in Israel, and they have made themselves relevant to the communities and pupils they serve. They have adopted most of the official educational programs and textbooks so that their pupils now have the option of obtaining an Israeli or foreign diploma. This, of course, has made it much easier for students to transfer from one kind of school to another. Teachers in Christian schools are now mostly Arabs (both Christian and Moslem), and in many cases the directors of the schools are no longer foreigners. Christian schools have maintained their existence and regained some of their previous status by adapting themselves to the realities of the political, economic, and sociocultural situations in which they operate. Kleinberger observes that while Christian schools are partially supported by the Israeli government they have had to sacrifice much of their autonomy. The Jewish religious school system, on the other hand, is fully supported by the government and, paradoxically, they are fully

autonomous, demonstrating that while religious Jewish parties have
political power, Christian Arabs in Israel lack the necessary power to
exert in terms of political pressure.[28]

The entire Arab educational system has become government controlled. Budgets, goals, policies, teachers' appointments, curricula, and
textbooks are all dictated by the Ministry of Education through the
Arab Education Department. Like all other Arab departments within
the Israeli government and public bodies, this department is also headed
by a person of Jewish background. One of the two deputies is an Arab,
and the other is Jewish. All supervisors, except a handful of Jews, are
Arabs. School principals as well as teachers are all Arabs, except a
small number of Jewish teachers, most of whom were appointed during
the early fifties. They had immigrated from Arab countries, and because
of their lack of knowledge of the Hebrew language they could not be
employed as teachers in the Jewish school system. Their knowledge of
Arabic, coupled with the great need for teachers in Arab schools,
helped them obtain teaching positions in the Arab educational system.

The Arab Education Department is political in nature and function.
Its politicization "is so abrasive that it permeates every level of that
[Arab] educational system from the elementary grades to the teachers
college. Blatantly and openly, it is a means of political pressure, control
and reward. Furthermore, in his analysis of the politicization of the
Arab educational system in Israel, Khalil Nakhleh suggests that 'political
rather than pedagogic criteria are considered paramount in hiring and
firing on all levels of the system.' "[29] These conclusions support 'Obeid's
comments as to the politically manipulative nature of the departments
for Arabs, particularly the department for Arab education.

As explained previously, all Arab departments within Israeli governmental and public bodies are under severe criticism as to their
existence, staffing, policies, purposes, and the manners in which they
operate. It is especially true that as far as the educational system is concerned, frustration and resentment are rapidly building among Arabs in
Israel. These feelings are probably due not only to the many inequalities
existing with regard to educational opportunities, but also to the increasing sense of competence of Arab professionals in education and
other fields, who feel are deprived of the opportunity of assuming
responsibility for the education of their own communities. As long as
such a demand is not met the inevitable outcome is political activism,
since the threshold level of frustration tolerance has already been
severely violated. Indeed, Arab academics in Israel are emerging as an
eminent and deeply rooted political power.[30]

ALTERNATIVES FOR CHANGE

The existence of a separate department for Arab education is tied to the existence of other departments for Arabs in Israeli government. There is a general policy of maintaining special departments for Arabs within the Israeli government and public administration. It follows that any structural change within one department would necessitate the adoption of an overall general policy concerning all departments for Arabs. One must consider, therefore, the alternatives available for reacting to community pressures and demands and for considering who the decision-making authorities should be. Three such alternatives available for change in the administrative status of Arab education in Israel follow:

The first would be to maintain a separate department for Arabs within the Ministry of Education and Culture but introduce a change in its leadership. This amounts to "Arabizing" the department in the sense that its head and leadership (including the different committees) would all be Arabs. As mentioned earlier, Bentwitch has suggested that the role of Jews with regard to Arab education should not be one of control but of advice when needed. While Arabizing it, the department should become depoliticized as much as possible. Hiring, firing, promotion, and all other administrative decisions should be based on merit only, with no political considerations.

Such depoliticization is expected to help decrease the alienation of teachers from the educational leadership; it will also serve to increase the community support for the schools. Opportunities in education for the available well-trained professionals will be provided, and rather than being frustrated and embittered, they can devote their efforts to constructive involvement in the development of their educational system.

In order that these desired developments and changes can take place, the department should be removed from its ivory tower in Jerusalem, where it has a holiness and mystique which makes it physically, socially, and psychologically distant. In Jerusalem it is close to politics and to the power center, and consequently is more vulnerable to manipulation. The best place to locate the department is probably the Arab city of Nazareth, the geographical, demographic, and cultural heart of Arabs in Israel. This alternative, however, although better than the existing situation, is not without its disadvantages. Because of its separation the department would be identifiable, and prey to manipulation and pressure. Most important of all is that by being *separate,* it may continue to be *unequal.*

A second alternative is to abolish the department, administering Arab education through the District Directorates of Education. Within each of the five districts in Israel (North, Haifa, Center, Jerusalem, and South) there are Arabs and Arab schools. Since the creation of the state they have belonged to the department in Jerusalem and not to the districts, although each district has a director who is responsible to the director general of the ministry. It is, of course, possible to have in each district Arab supervisors and other employees responsible for Arab schools within the specific district. The advantages of such an institutional integration are many. First, the Arab educational system would be diffused and not identifiable as one administrative unit. This would make it difficult to manipulate the system politically. Second, finances would be distributed more equally since the allocation of money would be based on districts rather than nationality. Third, the interaction between Arab and Jewish educational officials is expected to be mutually beneficial. Arab education has much to learn from the many innovations, programs, and efficient services existing in the Jewish educational system. But the adoption of many of these innovations in Arab schools is blocked by the mere existence of the Department for Arab Education. Likewise, Jewish education has much to learn from Arab education, especially with regard to the education of oriental Jews who share a cultural background with Arabs. Fourth, through administrative integration, it is expected that Arab teachers would occupy teaching positions in Jewish schools and vice versa.

Should this alternative be adopted, it would mean the creation of an Arab pedagogical secretariat to decide upon matters relating to curriculum, textbooks, and programs—a job now fulfilled, in many cases arbitrarily, by the Department for Arab Education without a specialized forum. In the Jewish sector, however, there is a secretariat for elementary education, another for postprimary, and a third in the form of a council for the religious sector.

In the early seventies there has been much talk about adopting this alternative of administrative desegregation. In fact, the Druze schools in the Haifa and North districts already belong to respective districts, though desegregation is on a minor scale since the Druze Arabs do not exceed 10 percent of the Arab population in Israel. In addition, the decision to administratively integrate the Druze schools was a political move to separate them from the rest of Arab society in Israel. (They are the only Arab group which serves in the Israeli Army.) Their administrative integration was meant as a reward that their traditional leaders have demanded from the authorities. An Arab scholar from a

Druze group, Nabih El-Kasem, has suggested that the Druze group is demanding administrative desegregation but not for itself only, but does so along with other Arabs in Israel. He also claims that by admitting the Druze schools to the district directorate, the government is trying to "blur and distort" the Arab national identity of the Druze group. After an extensive analysis of the Israeli's government policy aimed at cutting off the Druze group from the rest of the Arab minority in Israel, he demands an immediate stop to the "conspiracy of separating the Druze schools from the rest of the Arab schools."[31]

It seems that in implementing administrative integration, Israeli authorities are following two guidelines: first, to integrate gradually, and second, to integrate on the basis of a subcultural (corresponding to political) basis rather than on a geographic one. In other words, administrative integration is being introduced not only as a possible remedy to the many inequalities existing between Arab and Jewish education in Israel, but also as a differential reward to certain groups. One wonders as to the efficiency of these changes had they started as extremely politicized. While the basic rationale for abolishing the Department for Arab Education is to depoliticize the Arab educational system, it seems that these changes are representative of administrative measures only. Politicization is not only there, but it increases.

A third alternative is autonomy. It is clear that there is direct and imposed state intervention in the education of Arabs in Israel. This alternative amounts to lessening the level of such intervention and granting more autonomy to Arabs in Israel in their educational system within the framework of the Ministry of Education and Culture. It is true that education, like all other services in the state of Israel, is extremely centralized, making the possibility of autonomy within such a system an extremely difficult goal to attain. When the state provides the finances, it has the right to control. It is also the case, however, that both traditionally and legally the opportunity for such an autonomy exists. For instance, the Kibbutz movement and the state religious education systems enjoy a large extent of autonomy in education while financed by the state.

The Kibbutz movement in Israel has traditionally maintained a semiautonomous educational system through an informal, yet not illegal, agreement with the Ministry of Education and Culture. They influence the assignment of principals and appoint their own teachers with the consultation of the regional supervisor. Moreover, they prepare their own teachers in three institutions especially designed for them and also arrange for in-service training. Probably the most important aspect in which the Kibbutz movement practices autonomy is that "they determine their own curricula which in certain respects differ materially from those prescribed for state schools . . . and they insure, in general, that primary education in Kibbutzim conforms to their particular ideals and way of life. This is only logical since education of the younger generation is the chief guarantee of the continuity of the Kibbutz movement."[32]

The other case in point is the religious state educational system which is linked with the religious party of *Agodat Yesrael*. Unlike the Kibbutz, this system enjoys a large extent of autonomy under the state education law. In his comprehensive discussion of legislation and politics of education in Israel, Kleinberger suggests that "the Council for Religious State Education is vested with considerable discretionary powers and may on certain questions overrule decisions of the Minister and his administrative staff." Indeed, the Council may exercise a veto against a minister's decision. Nine of the Council's fourteen members should be nominees of the National Religious Party. It can hire and fire, decide upon policies and regulations, and determine the curricula for the religious schools. All this is "aimed at a religious way of life."[33]

The Kibbutz movement in Israel adheres to a secular-Zionist-socialist ideology, whereas the religious parties adopt a religious-Zionist tone. Both, however, are in harmony with the philosophy of the state of Israel as a Zionist Jewish state. They further its aspirations and revive its background and the rationale for its creation. Arabs, on the other hand, are not only culturally and religiously different (Moslems, Christians, Druzes), but they do not subscribe to the national aspirations of Zionism. In fact, their national aspirations conflict directly with those of Zionism.

In education Arabs do not have the opportunity to choose between a secular and a religious school system. Secularism is imposed upon them by the state. Neither the "aiming at a religious way of life" (as in the case of religious state education), nor the "guarantee for continuity" (as in the case of the Kibbutz movement) has been granted to the Arab minority in Israel through their educational system. Yet it seems only logical and legitimate that these opportunities (necessities) be offered to the Arab minority in Israel by means of informal agreement with the ministry or by legal action. By this action a new pattern will not be created; rather an existing one will be followed and reinforced.

One cannot overlook the difficulties involved in granting autonomy to Arabs in Israel within their educational system. While autonomous educational systems exist in Israel, there is also a pattern of heteronomy imposed on the minority by the majority's institutional structures (i.e., the Department for Arab Education) which controls and intervenes in the lives of the Arabs. Moreover, in light of the continuous conflict in the Middle East Israeli authorities may fear that granting autonomy in education will lead to a demand for political autonomy on the part of the Arab population in Israel. The question remains: Does the deprivation of autonomy in education for Arabs in Israel decrease or increase the demand for political autonomy?

4

Curricula

A COMPARISON OF STATE-SPECIFIED CURRICULA in Arab and Jewish
schools reveals how course content and time are weighted to
comply with the general goals of Israeli education. The neutral subjects,
mathematics and the natural sciences, are not examined in this chapter
because they bear little, if any, significance to the development of the
cultural-national identity of the student. Rather, a special emphasis is
placed on the "culturally loaded" subjects of history, language, literature, and religion. In the neutral subjects, state-specified curricula are
identical in both Arab and Jewish schools from the first to the twelfth
grade. The differences exist in the culturally loaded subjects through
which the inculcation of a national identity and instillment of values are
expected to take place. The differences in these subjects are considered
in this chapter with regard to postprimary education, because of the
significance of this level to the establishment of individual and group
identity through educational contents and experiences in school.

As noted in the previous chapter, Jewish education in Israel had
goals specified by the law of state education in 1953, and goals for
Arab education are in the process of being finally specified through the
Yadlin Document and through the Committee for the Eighties. The
differences between the two educational systems were made clear in
terms of emphasizing identity and active belonging in the case of
Jewish education, and deemphasizing nationality in Arab education. It
is clear that the administrative status and structure of Arab education is
consistent with its goals in terms of majority control over and manipulation of minority education.

70

The state-determined curricula in Israel not only heavily rely on and consistently comply with the general goals of education, but these goals are also broken down specifically with regard to every subject taught in school. The statement that Arab education in Israel has been conducted without general goals for many years is true only to a point, for the teaching goals of each subject were specified with the curriculum. In fact, the curriculum in both Jewish and Arab schools specifies goals for different subjects, determines the amount of classroom hours to be allocated to each subject, and recommends the number of hours to be devoted to each topic within a subject. Therefore, the comparisons in this chapter concentrate on *aims* to be pursued, *hours* allocated, and *topics* to be taught within each of the subjects—history, language, literature, and religious studies.

HISTORY

Aims for Teaching History in Jewish and Arab Schools[1]

Jewish Schools	*Arab Schools*
1. To instruct the students to consider the culture of mankind as the shared efforts of the Jewish people and the nations of the world throughout the generations; to value correctly our share and that of other peoples in the creation of this culture; to strengthen the cooperation, and to develop the will for common action towards peace and good will among nations.	To instruct the students to consider the culture of mankind as the shared efforts of the world's nations throughout the generations; to value correctly the part played by the Jewish and Arabs, and other nations in creating this culture, to strengthen the recognition of cooperation, and to develop the will for common action towards peace and good will among nations.
2. To instill a Jewish national consciousness in the students; to reinforce the feeling of a common Jewish destiny; to instill in their hearts a love for the Jewish people both in their country and throughout the world, and to reinforce their spirit with the nation as a whole.	None.

Jewish Schools	*Arab Schools*
3. To instill an awareness in the students of the importance of the State of Israel as the means of ensuring the physical as well as historical existence of the Jewish people; to instill in them a sense of personal commitment for the consolidation and development of the state; to instill the wish and readiness to serve the state in all ways.	To instill an awareness in the students of the importance of the State of Israel for the Jewish people throughout the ages, to develop a sense of the common fate of the two peoples, Jewish and Arab, in past and present, in order to develop their sense of personal commitment to the state and to instill the wish and readiness to serve the state in all ways.
4. To develop the character of students after the great men of our people and of the world's people.	To develop the character of students after the deeds of the great men of the world and in particular, the Jews and the Arabs.
5. To train and accustom him to deliberate and conclude in general concepts when dealing with social problems and to attempt solving them through independent critical thinking.	Same.

In the evaluation of both sets of goals for teaching history in Jewish and Arab schools it becomes clear that the aims specified by the curriculum for Jewish schools emphasize full identification of the student with his own (Jewish) nation and recognition of its contribution to the world's culture. The Arab student, on the other hand, is required to value the contribution of *all nations* to the world's culture, while his own nation is just one among all these nations. The paragraph which specifies that the Jewish student develop his national awareness, strengthen his active belonging to his own people inside Israel and throughout the world, does not have a parallel in the aims specified in the curriculum for Arab schools. It is worth noting here that a sense of belonging and responsibility seems relevant for the Jewish people and Palestinians both who have populations concentrated in Israel and dispersed throughout the world.

As for the third point, the curriculum requires instilling patriotic sentiments in both Arab and Jewish students because of the significance of the state of Israel to the Jewish people. Yochanan Peres, the first in Israel to study the whole problem of national education for Arab youth in Israel, comments with regard to this point that "this is a logical argument as far as the Jewish pupil is concerned, but how about the Arab pupil? The Arab pupil is thus expected to serve the state not because the latter is important to *him* and fulfills *his* needs, but because it is important to the Jewish people." Moreover, while the curriculum requires molding Jewish students' identity to models of the deeds of the great men in Jewish history, the Arab students' identity should also be molded to these Jewish figures since the great figures of the Arab nation are lumped together with the world's great men. While commenting on this very discrepancy in the goals specified for the teaching of history in Jewish and Arab schools, Peres suggests that "whereas the Arabs are required to take an example from the great men of Israel, the great figures of the Arab world are not deemed worthy of special attention in the Jewish curriculum."[2]

It can be concluded that the goals for teaching history are consistent with and an extention of the general statements of goals for education of Jews and Arabs in Israel. That is, as was demonstrated in the previous chapter, the goals of Jewish education emphasize the inculcation of Jewish consciousness and identity, while the goals for Arab education tend to ignore Arab consciousness and identity. It remains to be seen whether these general and specific sets of goals are consistent with the same theme of developing a national identity for the Jewish student on the one hand, and blurring the national identity of his Arab counterpart while demanding from him "knowledge of the Jewish culture" on the other. In other words, this comparative analysis should be carried a step further to determine whether or not these goals are translated into more concrete specifications in terms of topics and class hours to be devoted to the study of history.

Class Hours

Three general categories exist in the curriculum specified for teaching history in Arab schools: general, Jewish, and Arab history. The following presentation and discussion are of data based on the assumption that the numer of class hours allocated to each of these categories reflects the status and significance the educational planner meant it to have. It is also safe to assume that while allotting time to each of these categories, the planners bore in mind the goals for teaching history.

Table 6 reveals that in Arab junior high schools Arab history is almost completely neglected (only 10 out of 216 class hours). The Arab student in the junior high school studies Jewish history for seven

TABLE 6

Hours Allocated to Teaching History in
Arab Junior and Senior High Schools

	Grade	Total	General History	Jewish History	Arab History
Junior	7	60	48	10	2
high school		(100%)	(80%)	(17%)	(3%)
	8	60	22	30	8
		(100%)	(37%)	(50%)	(13%)
	9	96	66	30	0
		(100%)	(69%)	(31%)	(0%)
Total in		216	136	70	10
junior high		(100%)	(63%)	(32%)	(5%)
Senior	10	64	23	9	32
high school		(100%)	(36%)	(14%)	(50%)
	11	128	98	15	15
		(100%)	(76%)	(12%)	(12%)
	12	128	71	31	26
		(100%)	(56%)	(24%)	(20%)
Total in		320	192	55	73
senior		(100%)	(60%)	(17%)	(23%)
high school					
Total		536	328	125	83
in both		(100%)	(61%)	(23%)	(16%)

SOURCE: Mahmood Me'ari, *A Comparative Survey of School Curricula in the Arab Sector in Israel* (Jerusalem, January 1975) (Hebrew).

times the number of hours spent on his own (70 class hours of Jewish history as compared with only 10 hours of Arab history). In the seventh grade the Arab student learns two hours of Arab history during the whole school year (10 hours of Jewish history), while in the eighth grade he studies only 8 hours. All this reflects a definite bias against the teaching of Arab history in Arab schools which reaches its climax in the ninth grade, where no time whatsoever is allocated to Arab history, and 30 hours are spent on Jewish history.

The total number of class hours allocated to Arab history in high school is slightly greater than the total hours allotted to Jewish history (73 and 55 hours respectively). However, only in the tenth grade do Arab students learn more about their history than about Jewish history. In the eleventh grade the number of hours allocated to each is equal (15), and in the twelfth grade 26 hours are allotted to Arab history and 31 to Jewish history. Thus, in high school there seems to be a slight shift of emphasis. Yet it is really only in the tenth grade, where 50 percent of the hours allocated to the teaching of history is for Arab history and 14 percent for Jewish history, that the single instance in junior and senior high school exists where the Arab student learns about his own people's history more than about the history of the Jews. And even then, in a content analysis of the history textbooks specified for the tenth grade in Arab schools, Mahmood Me'ari has discovered that most of the time is allocated to the history of the Arabs in the Middle Ages, while modern Arab history which tells the story of the development of Arab nationalism is somehow overlooked. In addition, in the history of the Arabs during the Middle Ages, the lives and cultural contribution of Jewish individuals and communities in the Arab Islamic Empire are stressed.

In his content analysis of curricula specified for Arab schools, Me'ari concludes that in Arab junior high schools there is a great emphasis on Jewish nationalism: "In 7th grade the Arab students learn about the relation of the Jewish Diaspora to the land of Israel and in the 8th grade they learn about the Zionist movement and its development, the thrust of Jews to come back to the land of Israel, Jewish immigration, the revival of the Hebrew language and pioneering."[3] Further, while there is a strong emphasis on Jewish nationalism in teaching history to Arab students, Arab nationalism is completely ignored. This is reflected not only in the number of hours allocated to Arab history in junior high school (two in seventh grade; eight in eighth grade; and none in ninth grade), but also in the fact that in textbooks no one chapter is independently devoted to Arab history. It appears as scattered comments incorporated in the chapters about the Turkish Empire and the Middle East in the nineteenth century.

In high school the trend of blurring Arab history through its integration within general topics continues. Modern Arab history and the Arab national movement in general, particularly the Palestinian national movement are completely ignored. Jewish history, on the other hand, appears in well-organized and detailed chapters in the textbooks, and Zionism, the Jewish national movement, is emphasized along with its values and aspirations.

A Comparison Between Jewish and Arab High Schools

Since both Jews and Arabs live side by side in Israel, it seems only natural that each learn about the other's history and contribution to the culture of mankind. However, as mentioned earlier, while the statement of goals for teaching history requires the Arab student to recognize and identify with the value of Zionism (mostly at the expense of the recognition of and identification with his own people's history), the statement of goals for the Jewish schools ignores Arab history.

Table 7 indicates that while in Jewish schools almost 40 percent of the time allotted to history is spent on the teaching of Jewish history, in Arab schools only 19 percent of the time is spent on Arab history. In fact, Jewish history is slightly more emphasized than Arab history in

TABLE 7

Percentage of the Total Hours Spent on General, Jewish,
and Arab History in Jewish and Arab High Schools

	Jewish Schools	Arab Schools
General history	59.8	60.7
Jewish history	38.8	20.2
Arab history	1.4	19.1

SOURCE: Mahmood Me'ari, *A Comparative Survey of School Curricula in the Arab Sector in Israel* (Jerusalem, January 1975) (Hebrew).

Arab schools. Moreover, while Arab schools are required to devote over 20 percent of the time to Jewish history, Jewish schools spent only 1.4 percent of history time on Arab history. Although both devote approximately the same time (60 percent) to general or world history, the remaining 40 percent of the time is unequally distributed, however: in Jewish schools almost all of the remaining time is devoted to Jewish history; in Arab schools it is divided between Jewish and Arab history.

To summarize, as required by the ministry's specified curriculum, there seems to be a striking consistency between the stated objectives for teaching history on the one hand, and the distribution of class hours to the different categories and topics to be taught on the other. In Jewish schools there is a strong emphasis on the development of national identity, active belonging to the Jewish people, and furthering of Zionist aspirations—all with an extremely minor recognition of Arab history. In Arab schools the student is required to develop identification with Jewish values and to further Zionist aspirations at the expense of the development of his own national awareness and a sense of belonging to his own people. The Arab national identity is much less emphasized, and the Palestinian identity goes completely unrecognized. Of course, one would not expect the state of Israel to encourage the teaching of anti-Israel course content in Arab schools. Nevertheless, it seems that the decision-making circles have taken that caution to an extreme and have instead launched a history curriculum which deprives the Arab student of the opportunity to develop a sense of his own cultural and national identity in school. This very deprivation can be expected to bring about results that the educational planner did not hope for. By depriving the students of opportunities provided by the curriculum to satisfy their need to belong the need is not eliminated, it is magnified.

LANGUAGE AND LITERATURE

In Arab high schools in Israel students study Arab and Hebrew languages and literatures; in all but a few Jewish schools, however, Arab language and literature are not required. A comparison of Arabic and Hebrew studies *within* Arab schools and *between* Arab and Jewish schools produces conclusions similar to the preceding look at the history curriculum; simply, in both Arab and Jewish high schools Jewish and Zionist values are pursued, and Arab values are ignored.

Goals for Teaching Language and Literature[4]

Hebrew in Jewish Schools	Arabic in Arab Schools	Hebrew in Arab Schools
1. To impart to the pupil a love of the ideals, outlook, and experience of the nation at its various periods of development, and an awareness of the unbroken historical link between the nation, its country, and its culture. Special attention should be paid to the struggles and achievements of our own as well	1. Correct reading and understanding of the written and spoken language. 2. The clear, precise, and logical expression of ideas and feelings, orally and in writing. 3. The ability to understand and appreciate good literature. 4. To open for the pupil a gateway to a knowledge	1. To give the Arab pupil a basic, comprehensive knowledge of the Hebrew language, an understanding of all reading material, a functional command of the language, both written and oral, for practical and cultural needs. 2. To open the way for the Arab pupil to become acquainted with

Hebrew in *Jewish Schools*	*Arabic in Arab Schools*	*Hebrew in* *Arab Schools*
as of recent generations in the spheres of national revival and cultural and social renewal.	of literary culture, past and present.	Jewish culture and its values, past and present; to facilitate his understanding of the cultural and social life of the Jewish population in Israel.

2. To expose the pupils to the cultural treasures of mankind as an expression of universal human values, and also, as far as possible, to works which express the creative genius of different nations.

3. To develop good literary taste and an appreciation of great masterpieces.

4. To bring the pupils into direct contact with the controversial problems and trends of thought of the world at various periods of its history, and with the Jewish people's way of life throughout history.

5. To develop the pupil's ability to express himself correctly, clearly logically, and accurately, both orally and in writing.

6. To help him acquire an organic understanding of the rules and forms of language and its growth, and the ability to distinguish various literary styles.

7. To equip the pupil with a fund of those idiomatic expressions which mirror the uniqueness of our outlook, of our relationship with the world and with ourselves, and which create a common form of expression among individuals and generations.

It is not illogical to expect that the goals of teaching literature and language should be similar, if not identical, in Jewish schools (Hebrew) and Arab schools (Arabic). However, as the official statements of goals reflect, there is no similarity whatsoever. There are certain parallels in the history goals; in language and literature there is not even a slight resemblance. The curriculum of Jewish schools differs from that of the Arab schools in two basic points as far as goals are concerned. First, while the goals in the Jewish curriculum reach a high level of sophistication, those in Arab schools are rather meager, shallow, and insignificant. Second, while there is a strong emphasis on national identity in the Jewish curriculum, there is not mention of the Arab nationality or culture in the Arab schools' curriculum. In effect, the goals for teaching Arabic language and literature in Arab schools are reduced to the development of language skills in usage, expression, and understanding. It appears as though Arab literature is valueless, at least according to the planner's intentions. Jewish literature, on the other hand, appears quite valuable.

Hebrew is taught in Arab schools as a second language (Arabic is first, and English is third). Thus, one would expect that it would occupy a slightly lower level of importance as far as culture and values are concerned. Surprisingly, Arab culture and values are not mentioned as goals for teaching Arabic, although by studying Hebrew, Arab students are required "to become acquainted with Jewish culture and values" and to understand "the cultural and social life of the Jewish population in Israel." But for the Jewish student, an acquaintance with and an understanding of Arab culture, values, and social life does not seem worthy of pursuit: hence, the curriculum does not require Arab language and literature to be taught in Jewish schools.

In short, state specified curricula for teaching language and literature in Jewish and Arab schools follow the same pattern they set in teaching history: strong emphasis on Jewish nationality and culture for both Jewish and Arab students coupled with a weak, if any, emphasis on Arab nationality and culture for both.

Class Hours Allocated to Arab and Hebrew Language and Literature in Arab Schools

In the following analyses of the hours allocated to Arabic language and literature, the hours devoted to Hebrew language and literature in Arab schools, and the amount of time devoted to Arabic and Hebrew studies, high school is a four-year cycle, as the educational reform in Israel, through which junior high schools are to be created in order to make high school three years, is not fully implemented yet.

Table 8 presents the number of hours devoted to Arab language and literature in Arab schools. The total number of hours allocated to this subject is 732 in all four years (ninth through twelfth grades). There is consistently an equal number of hours in the categories of language and literature. In other words, through all high school years Arab language and Arab literature share an identical status in the Arab school as far as the number of hours allotted to each is concerned. In

TABLE 8

Hours Devoted to Arabic Language and Literature in Arab High Schools

LANGUAGE	9 Grade	10 Grade	11 Grade	12 Grade	Total
Grammar	48	48	48	26	170
	(25%)	(25%)	(25%)	(16.7%)	(23%)
Rhetoric	16	16	16	26	74
	(8%)	(8%)	(8%)	(16.7%)	(10%)
Composition	32	32	32	26	122
	(17%)	(17%)	(17%)	(16.7%)	(17%)
Total language	96	96	96	78	366
hours per	(50%)	(50%)	(50%)	(50%)	(50%)
grade					
LITERATURE					
Poetry and prose	80	80	64		
	(42%)	(42%)	(33%)		
History of	16	16	32	78	366
literature	(8%)	(8%)	(17%)	(50%)	(50%)
Total literature	96	96	96	78	366
hours per grade	(50%)	(50%)	(50%)	(50%)	(50%)
Total hours of	192	192	192	156	732
language and	(100%)	(100%)	(100%)	(100%)	(100%)
literature					

SOURCE: Mahmood Me'ari, *A Comparative Survey of School Curricula in the Arab Sector in Israel* (Jerusalem, January 1975), p. 39 (Hebrew).

the twelfth grade the number of hours decreases from 192 (in each of the previous years) to 156, but the equal division between language and literature remains.

Table 9 presents the distribution of class hours in the different categories of Hebrew language and literature specified for Arab schools. The total number of hours spent on this subject is 768, though they are not equally distributed between language and literature. In ninth grade one-third of the hours is devoted to Hebrew language and two-thirds to Hebrew literature. In the twelfth grade the balance changes to favor literature even more: only 17 percent of the time is allotted to language and the remaining time (83 percent) to literature. (Hebrew grammar is

TABLE 9

Hours Devoted to Hebrew Language and
Literature in Arab High Schools

LANGUAGE	9 Grade	10 Grade	11 Grade	12 Grade	Total
Grammar	32	32	32	—	96
	(17%)	(17%)	(17%)		(13%)
Oral and Written	32	32	32	32	128
composition	(17%)	(17%)	(17%)	(17%)	(17%)
Total language	64	64	64	32	224
hours per	(33.3%)	(33.3%)	(33.3%)	(17%)	(30%)
grade					
LITERATURE					
Bible, Mishna,	64	64	64	64	256
and Agada	(33.3%)	(33.3%)	(33.3%)	(33.3%)	(33.3%)
Prose and	64	64	64	96	288
poetry	(33.3%)	(33.3%)	(33.3%)	(33.3%)	(37%)
Total literature	128	128	128	160	544
hours per	(66.7%)	(66.7%)	(66.7%)	(83%)	(70%)
grade					
Total of language	192	192	192	192	768
and literature	(100%)	(100%)	(100%)	(100%)	(100%)

SOURCE: Mahmood Me'ari, *A Comparative Survey of School Curricula in the Arab Sector in Israel* (Jerusalem, January 1975), p. 39 (Hebrew).

not taught in the twelfth grade. Instead, the 32 hours are added to "prose and poetry.") The overall distribution of hours becomes 30 percent (224 hours) for Hebrew language and 70 percent (544 hours) for Hebrew literature.

A comparative look at the number of hours spent on the teaching of Arabic language and literature (Table 8) and on the teaching of Hebrew language and literature (Table 9) in Arab schools reveals the following:

1. Overall, more time is devoted to Hebrew language and literature than to Arabic (768 hours as compared with 732 hours, respectively). Bearing in mind that Arab is the mother tongue and Hebrew is a foreign (yet important) language, the foreign language is granted more time than the native one.

2. The time spent on Arabic is equally distributed between language and literature and rather consistently so from ninth through twelfth grades. The time devoted to Hebrew, however, is not equally distributed between language and literature. Seventy percent of the total time is spent on literature and 30 percent on language. Thus, in Arab high schools much more time is devoted to Hebrew literature than to Arabic literature (544 and 366 class hours, respectively).

3. In a foreign language the mastery of language skills is at least as important as the knowledge and understanding of literature. Moreover, in the native language it seems only natural to favor literature slightly, if not a great deal, at least as much as it is favored in the teaching of the foreign language. The curriculum specified for Arab schools in Israel, however, proves the opposite. The planner is consistent with the goals specified for teaching Arabic and Hebrew language and literature in Arab schools. Literature is more value oriented; Arab literature is less emphasized whereas Jewish literature enjoys a definite favor and a higher status in the Arab school.

4. The Jewish religious texts (Bible, Mishna, and Agada) are an identifiable entity in the curriculum for Arab schools, whereas Islamic texts are integrated within the category of "history of literature" (see Table 8). Jewish religious texts receive 33 percent (256 hours) of the time allotted to Hebrew language and literature in Arab schools, but Islamic texts occupy only a minor part of the 22 percent of the time devoted to history of literature (64 out of 288 hours in ninth through eleventh

grades; in twelfth grade there is no differentiation. See Table 8).
5. In a content analysis of these curricula Me'ari concludes that while the Arab literature specified by the curriculum is not conducive to the development of an Arab identity, Hebrew literature specified for Arabs emphasizes Zionism and its ideals, such as "the necessity of a Jewish state, the historical rights of the Jews over Palestine, the psychological ties of the Jews with Palestine, pioneering, [and] settlement."[5]

Comparison of Number of Hours Allotted to Language and Literature in Jewish and Arab Schools

Thus far, a comparison of the specifications for teaching language and literature in Arab and Jewish high schools has been drawn for Arab schools only. The following is a comparison of the same subject between Arab and Jewish schools.

Table 10 illustrates the distribution of hours allocated to teaching Arabic and Hebrew in Jewish and Arab schools. It has already been mentioned that Arab is not taught in Jewish schools but Hebrew is taught in Arab schools. A look at this table reveals the following:

1. Native languages are treated differently in Jewish (Hebrew) and Arab (Arabic) schools in two ways. First, the total number of hours allotted to Hebrew in Jewish schools is greater than that allotted to Arabic in Arab schools (768 and 732, respectively). Second, the distribution of these hours between language and literature is also different. In Jewish schools two-thirds of the hours (512) are devoted to Hebrew literature and one-third (256) to language; in Arab schools the hours are distributed equally between language and literature (366 hours each).
2. In Arab schools Hebrew literature is emphasized more than Arabic literature (544 as compared with 366, respectively), and the total number of hours allotted to Hebrew is more than that allotted to Arabic in Arab schools (768 and 732, respectively).
3. The total number of hours specified for Hebrew language and literature in both Jewish and Arab schools is exactly the same (76 hours in each). Moreover, Hebrew literature is more emphasized in Arab schools than it is in Jewish schools (544 hours in Arab schools and 512 hours in Jewish schools).

TABLE 10

Hours Devoted to Language and Literature in
Jewish and Arab High Schools

	Jewish Schools	Arab Schools	
	Hebrew	Arabic	Hebrew
Language	256	366	224
Literature	512	366	544
TOTAL	768	732	768

SOURCES: Yohanan Peres et al., "National Education for Arab Youth in Israel," *Race* 12(1) (July 1970):156; and Mahmood Me'ari, *A Comparative Survey of School Curricula in the Arab Sector in Israel* (Jerusalem, January 1975), pp. 39, 46.

This picture in the revised curriculum for Arab schools (1973) is quite different from that presented in the old curriculum (1965). Table 11 compares both the old and the revised curricula for Arabic and Hebrew language and literature in Arab schools.

TABLE 11

Number of Hours Specified for Arabic and Hebrew Language
and Literature (1965 and 1973) in Arab Schools

	Old Curriculum (1965)		Revised Curriculum (1973)	
	Arabic	Hebrew	Arabic	Hebrew
Language	404	172	366	224
Literature	420	340	366	544
TOTAL	824	512	732	768

SOURCES: Yohanan Peres et al., "National Education for Arab Youth in Israel," *Race* 12(1) (July 1970):156; and Mahmood Me'ari, *A Comparative Survey of School Curricula in the Arab Sector in Israel* (Jerusalem, January 1975), pp. 39, 46.

A look at Table 11 reveals the following:

1. In the old curriculum Arabic, the native language, enjoyed a better status than did Hebrew in Arab schools (824 and 512 hours, respectively).
2. Two-thirds of the number of hours were allotted to Hebrew literature in the old curriculum, and slightly over one-half of the hours were spent on Arabic literature. However, in the

actual number of hours Arabic literature still was favored more than Hebrew literature (420 and 340, respectively).

3. In the new curriculum two changes were introduced. First, the total number of hours devoted to Arabic language and literature decreased from 824 to 732 hours. Second, the total number of hours allotted to Hebrew increased by 50 percent (from 512 to 768 hours). Thus, Hebrew has become more emphasized than Arabic in Arab schools.

4. Although there was a shift of focus in Arabic from more hours spent on literature to an equal number allocated to language and literature, the balance between Hebrew language and literature (one-third and two-thirds, respectively) also changed, but in the opposite direction; Hebrew literature became even more emphasized (from 340 to 544 hours). It seems that because the planner was dissatisfied with the low number of hours devoted to Hebrew in Arab schools, he increased that number at the expense of the total number of hours allotted to Arabic. Thus, Hebrew language and literature are stressed more than the native Arabic language and literature. Thus, in the revised curriculum, Arab students are expected to spend more time learning Hebrew language and literature—in which Jewish and Zionist values are pursued and Arab values ignored—than their own. Here again, the consistency between goals set, hours allotted, and course content specified is even more striking than for that of teaching history.

RELIGIOUS STUDIES

In Jewish schools 640 class hours are devoted to the study of the Bible, Mishna, and Agada; none are allotted to the study of Islamic texts. In Arab schools, on the other hand, only 120 hours are allocated to the Koran, and strangely enough, 256 hours are spent on the Bible, Mishna, and Agada.[6] Furthermore, Jewish religious studies enjoy an independent status in Jewish schools; they are not integrated within Hebrew literature. The Koran is not specified as an identifiable unit in the study of Arab literature, however, the Bible and related texts are independently specified within the Hebrew literature hours in Arab schools.

Additionally, the above data relate to *secular* Jewish schools which, in the religious state education system, heavily emphasize religion. The option of Moslem or Christian state education does not exist in the

Arab schools, and in their secular schools Arabs are required to study Jewish religion for twice as much time as they are required to study their own (Moslem) religion (256 hours for the Jewish religion and only 120 hours for Islamic studies). Christian students in Arab high schools are not required to devote any time to studying their religion.

The aim of religious studies (Koran) in the Arab schools is not religious but literary. Hence, the Koran is recommended by the curriculum as a literary piece rather than a holy book. This emphasis explains two things. First, the curriculum is consistent with the goals for teaching Arabic language and literature to Arabs, which is the mastery of language skills and the joy of literature. Second, if religious studies were specified in the curriculum of Arab schools because of religious related goals, Christians would have a specified curriculum with regard to their religion. However, since these studies are not intended either by the planner or by the curriculum to be of religious relevance, Christians are not required to study their own religion.

The study of Jewish religion in Arab schools, as intended by the curriculum's specified goals, does encompass the amount of time necessary to achieve both literary aims and to provide "a gate to the Jewish culture." But for the Arab student, Arabic literature (including Koranic studies) is not meant to help him investigate his own culture. Indeed, the curriculum in the Jewish schools deprives the student of "opening a gate to Arab culture" because it does not require the Jewish student to study either the literature or the religions of the Arabs.

Recently, under the revision of curricula for Arab schools, more emphasis has been placed on the study of religion in the tenth and eleventh grades. The new curriculum offered, however, is *optional* and is not required for the Bagrout (matriculation) exams.

One can easily observe that the Arab high school in Israel is extremely secularized. A religious state school system does not exist in the Arab sector, contrary to the situation in the Jewish school system. In addition, the religion of Islam is organically tied to the Arab culture and nationality. By depriving the Arab student of a systematic study of his religion, the curriculum makes itself extremely irrelevant to a society which is, by all criteria, uncompromisingly religious. Furthermore, Bentwitch suggests that the secularization of the Arab schools in Israel "merely undermines the foundation of Arab culture and so leaves it prey to assimilation and Levantinism."[7]

To conclude, there appears to be a high level of consistency in the denial of Arab culture nationality in the curricula of Arab schools. This consistency exists on all levels of planning: in goals for Arab education; in the existence of a special majority-nominated department for Arab education; in setting goals for specific subjects; in the specification of the number of hours to be devoted to these subjects; and in the emphasis placed, or displaced, on the different course content categories within each subject. Indeed, Yohanan Peres of the Hebrew University comments that the curriculum in Arab schools "has fallen victim to the tendency to blur Arab nationality and to educate the Arab student towards self-disparagement *vis-à-vis* the Jewish majority. These tendencies are revealed, in the main, in two ways: (a) the goals of various subjects are formulated with a disregard of the nationalist elements in the Arab pupil's consciousness; (b) a wide and profound knowledge of purely Jewish subjects . . . is demanded of the Arab students at the expense of their own culture. This tendency is even more conspicuous against the background of an almost total absence of the Arabic language and culture in the Jewish pupil's education."[8]

It is important to note, too, that Israel's Independence Day is mandatorily celebrated in Arab schools for "appreciating" the achievements of the Zionist movement embodied by the creation of the state of Israel. As a consequence, school principals and teachers become hypocrites in the eyes of their students and communities, for they praise the state inside and severely criticize it outside the school's doors.

THE POWER OF NONFORMAL EDUCATION: A CONCLUSION

While *formal* education of Arabs in Israel has made itself culturally and nationally irrelevant to the students, *nonformal* education has gained special significance. The denial of Arab nationalist content and aspirations by the formal educational system does not, of course, eliminate these aspirations. In fact, it may increase and sharpen them. It is only natural that the lack of culturally and nationally relevant course content and experiences in the schools forces the student to look to other sources to satisfy his needs.

It seems that the educational planners in Israel have overlooked the fact that, at this point in history Palestinian Arabs, like Zionist Jews, are identity hungry. If schools are denying the development of national identity, other sources are readily available to fulfill this need, namely, the many radio and television stations received from neighboring Arab countries. These sources make an abundance of nationality-related materials available to the Arab in Israel even though, in most cases, he is not meant as a major audience for them.

The poverty-stricken Arab villages were full of radio sets as early as the beginning of the fifties, in spite of the fact that for most, if not all of villages, electricity was virtually unknown. A radio set, a luxury under these conditions, was a matter of utmost necessity. People, old and young, made sure to tune in for a few hours a day. Later the transistor radio became everyone's companion. After listening to the news and commentary, or any other political national program conveying a nationalist idea or reporting a patriotic event (i.e., the Egyptian revolution in 1952, the nationalization of the Suez canal in 1956, and the Egyptian-Syrian unification in 1958), villagers engaged in detailed discussions of what they heard. Elementary school children watched and listened to these discussions, and high school youth actively participated if they were not leading discussions.

Moreover, long before Israel had its own television station and programs, the first television sets to be imported for public use were for the Arab communities in Israel. Where there was no electricity, a generator was cooperatively bought to supply power for a few homes so they could watch Egyptian, Lebanese, Syrian, and Jordanian programs. The most popular of these programs had religious, historical, literary, nation-building themes through which the Arab community, particularly adolescents, satisfied their hunger for culturally relevant subject matter. Because of its visual nature, television was of special significance in the satisfaction of the need for developing and enriching the identity of the young Arab in Israel.

Through these programs Arab youth in Israel have been able to re-establish their belonging to the greater Arab population and to reinforce their pride in this belonging. Rather than involving themselves in "self-disparagement *vis-à-vis* the Jewish majority" in the formal educational setting, Arab youth in Israel have undertaken a self-restoring and self-reassuring activity in the nonformal setting. Whereas they had once been glorifying others in the school setting, young Arabs in Israel are now able to glorify themselves in the nonformal educational setting.

These nonformal educational resources available to young Arabs in Israel have been overlooked, or, to say the least, underestimated by Israeli educational authorities as far as their powerful impact is concerned. The authorities have operated under the assumption that *a control over the input of the formal educational setting will assure a majority desired output;* or, the careful specification of goals, course content, and time spent on subjects in the curricula will result in a blurring of the national identity so that the Arab will become loyal to the state. Were it not for the other inputs in the nonformal situation, these curricula might have achieved their goals, at least for a short term. In effect, two processes have been competing with each other, identity-blurring and identity-emphasizing. Apparently the latter has gotten the upper hand, even though it did so in a nonformal setting. It may have not been educationally *desirable* for the Arab national identity in Israel to rely heavily on mass media sources while developing, but socially and psychologically, the need outweighs desirability.

Yet, even though Arab curricula in Israel are designed to deny students the development of their national consciousness, Palestinian Arab national identity is becoming increasingly visible. It is gaining recognition and, in many cases, sympathy from the international community including certain Israeli Zionist circles and political organizations (i.e., the Israeli Council for Israel-Palestine Peace). However, the denial and deprivation of relevant curricula for Arab students seem to be escalating, as reflected in the revised curriculum for Arab schools in the case of Arabic and Hebrew language and literature. Unless curricula in Arab schools in Israel are thoroughly rethought and clearly respecified in favor of the development and encouragement of an Arab national identity which *is not* and *should not* necessarily be anti-Jewish, the Arab educational system in Israel is doomed to a functional death; its curricula will antagonize the Arab community. Neither the Jewish majority nor the Palestinian Arab minority in Israel can expect to benefit from this. Arab schools in Israel should not function in a direction opposing the powerful, nonformal educational resources available, but rather should complement them in a propaganda-free formal educational setting.

The Segregation-Integration Issue

S INCE THE CREATION OF ISRAEL, education has been continuously challenged to become equally relevant to the different population groups. Problems of equality do not exist only between the majority and the minority, but also within the majority itself. Indeed, more than half of Israel's Jewish population are of a non-Western background; these are the immigrants and their offspring from the Middle East and North Africa. The Zionist movement originated in Europe among the different Jewish minorities and has continued to be dominated by individuals and groups of European origin—a trend which has created solid grounds for the "Europeanization" of Israeli society and culture.

In addition, Israel has become a westernized country. Because it has not gained the recognition of its neighboring Arab countries, it remains alienated from the Middle East. This lack of integration within the geopolitical and cultural sphere in the Middle East, coupled with a continuous state of war with Arab countries, has driven Israel toward the West. And the fact that Israel has satisfied economic and security needs by belonging to the Western Block has only reinforced her cultural orientation, in spite of the fact that more than half of her Jewish population are non-Western. This group, often referred to as Oriental Jews, has, nonetheless, had to cope with Western dominance.

From the beginning, Oriental Jews were more followers than creators of Zionism. Drawing its values and aspirations from the old Jewish culture and religion, Zionism has remained a movement beyond the reach of Oriental Jews as far as political and cultural leadership is concerned. As already indicated, the main stream of Western culture within Jewish society has created great gaps in housing, health, income, and education between Western and non-Western Jews in Israel.[1] Most development towns and slums in Israeli cities are populated by Orientals. Although one of the highly emphasized goals of the state of Israel as the embodiment of Zionist aspiration is *mizug galuyot* (the integration and melting of the different geocultural Jewish cultural groups into one unified nation), a semisegregated educational system has developed within the Jewish sector due to the establishment of schools in these towns and slums which are populated by Orientals. A unique case of segregation has therefore emerged. While ideology urges the educational system to play a major role in integrating different groups into the society at large, the reality of that system has played a role in widening the gaps between these groups.

During the last three decades, educational authorities have adopted three major policies in an attempt to lessen or even close the gaps in the level of educational achievement of Jews of a Western origin and the Orientals. Moshe Smilansky traces three distinct phases in the ministry's efforts to address itself to the objective of *mizug galuyot*.[2] First came the phase of *formal equality* (1948–1958), in which the dominant policy was that different populations should be treated equally in the educational setting. It was assumed that recognition by the school of its students' different cultural backgrounds would only hinder achievement of the ultimate goal—the melting of these backgrounds into one unified Israeli Jewish Western culture. In fact, Kleinberger reports that when the minister of education at the time became alarmed at the cumulative evidence of high failure rates among Oriental pupils, he rejected any proposal concerning the revision of curricula, methods, and textbooks which might become relevant to the background and needs of the Oriental pupil population.[3] Instead, it was assumed that by exposing them to the same curricula and methods which were successful with European immigrants, Orientals would soon be assimilated into the normative, Western-type culture.

The second phase was that of *compensatory education* (1958–1968), in which instruction hours in Hebrew and math were added to the Oriental pupils' curriculum so they would reach the level of Europeans. This strategy was adopted after tremendous public pressure was placed upon authorities to address their efforts to the problem of the ever-widening gaps between the two Jewish subcultural groups. The basic assumption guiding this policy was that the differences between the two were quantitative rather than qualitative. Thus, by having more class hours the disadvantaged Orientals should catch up with their Western counterparts. This was merely an administrative measure, however, which, like others adopted then, proved futile.[4]

The third recognizable phase in the efforts of central educational authorities is that of *educational reform* (1968–present), through which the middle (junior high) school has been created. Along with the restructuring of the educational system, there has been a recognition of the culturally *qualitative* differences between Westerners and Orientals, a recognition translated into a few educational measures in curricula, methods of instruction, grouping according to abilities, and streaming into academic and many vocational tracks. Perhaps the most important reform is that of educational integration through which a middle school must consist of students from both cultural backgrounds. The assumption behind this policy is that through such integrated schooling, though limited to the middle school, social contacts will be facilitated and a reduction of prejudices will take place.[5] This process of implementing the reform is ongoing, and projects evaluating the implementations are not finalized.

Whereas problems of integration within the Jewish sector are approached with a rather deep sense of commitment, comparable problems between the Jewish and Arab sectors are not considered an issue, either among Jews or among Arabs. Nonetheless, the few cases and experiments in this direction deserve discussion. Most significant is the political nature of social and educational integration of Arabs in Israeli society.

THEORETICAL CONSIDERATIONS

The issue of desegregation has received worldwide concern and interest in the last two decades. Leaders, policy makers, theorists, and empirical researchers have been involved in effecting a way to induce or even force desegregation in the larger society in general (i.e., through housing), and in education in particular. Desegregation, it is hoped, should create an equal educational opportunity which has been lacking in the segregated social systems (including the school). The ultimate goal is, through education, to achieve a socioeconomic equality by making mobility channels available to minority groups. Moreover, general goals are in many cases extended to the achievement of an ethnically integrated society.

While the "equal right to be similar" rationale has urged many groups to demand integration and thus reverse the discriminatory trend of segregation,[6] another rationale has led to an opposite demand: "An equal right to be different" has urged certain groups (i.e., Chinese and Native Americans in the U.S.) to demand separation.[7] Integration in this case has been perceived as discriminatory because it deprives the group from maintaining its cultural uniqueness.

Integration has usually taken place in two ways: voluntary and forced by law. Voluntary integration has occurred as a decision by individuals or groups from different ethnic groups, reflecting a liberal attitude. Based on the contact hypothesis, it was hoped that integration would almost automatically lead to social and interpersonal interactions which would in time result in the reduction or even the elimination of prejudices and mutual negative stereotypes. Another goal, especially of minority members, has been to achieve equal opportunities and benefits in housing as well as in education.

The increasing awareness of the discrimination involved in segregation and its outcomes has also led to a growing demand to force integration by law, especially when the decision to voluntarily integrate has been limited to a few liberal and committed individuals from the dominating groups. Laws have been instituted by the Supreme Court of the United States forcing desegregation of schools through busing. Findings of evaluative research are conflicting in the U.S. in terms of supporting the hypotheses that integration either reduces prejudice and increases scholastic achievements; has no effect at all; or increases prejudice and causes a drop in achievement. In Israel evaluation is still underway as to the effects of integrating Oriental and Western Jews in educational settings. It is important to note, however, that forced integration in Israel is limited to the middle schools, while in the primary and secondary levels no formal regulations exist to force schools to admit pupils from different backgrounds outside of their neighborhood zones.

Segregation can also be voluntary or forced. The demands of the "equal right to be different" philosophy expressed by French Canadians, Chinese, Native Americans, and Israel's Arabs are just a few cases wherein the urge for separateness is based upon the need to maintain a different cultural or national identity. Although these groups maintain separate residential and educational facilities, they favor economic integration in terms of equal job opportunities. Thus, integration is expected to provide better educational opportunities leading to equal economic ones, yet separation (or in fact segregation), when voluntary, is not viewed as a block to the achievement of economic equality and integration.

Legally forced segregation, a heritage of the past as far as the American black is concerned, still exists in other contexts. The case in point is southern Africa (Rhodesia, and South Africa), where the white minority, still the dominant group, is forcing segregation aimed at maintaining their superior socioeconomic and political status as well as "racial purity." The use of explicit and legally imposed segregation is diminishing, however, leaving in its place hidden socioeconomic and political dynamics and forces which are just as effective. Affirmative action measures can be viewed as a legal safeguard against the effects of these covert social forces which, even though they may not bring about a resegregated situation, produce effects similar to those of segregation.

Although desegregation was and is an all-embracing liberal policy and measure, it does not ensure the desired effects. Social integration, the ultimate goal of these measures, has in many cases been reduced to merely a framework wherein members of different ethnic groups are mixed together. Through such a reduction, however, societies often defeat their explicit purposes. New and relevant educational methods and course content have not evolved for the disadvantaged groups,[8] and improvement in scholastic achievement has not taken place in many cases. Even the contact hypothesis has not proved valid all the time;[9] contacts have resulted instead in an increase in prejudice or have not affected a decrease. In other words, the integrated educational setting, controlled by the already socially dominant groups, has reinforced the existing gaps between groups, if not widened them.

On these grounds a new pattern has appeared, that of voluntary, yet temporary, segregation in the school, also called "segregation in the service of integration." Through this pattern members of different ethnic groups are separated in schools, not to reinforce segregation, but, to alleviate it along with its effects. Professor Carl Frankenstein of the Hebrew University based this pattern upon his theory of cultural relativism and educational relevance and an educational experiment[10] in which a group of Oriental Jewish pupils was separated in a high school. Relevant educational methods and strategies were devised, cooperation with parents was emphasized; and teachers were specifically trained to function within this particular context. In fact, teacher training was based on the principle of educational relevance to the cultural, familial, and personal characteristics of the pupils. As compared with a control group of Orientals who enrolled in integrated classes, the experimental group gained significantly in scholastic achievement, in developing and improving a positive self-image, and probably most important, in socioeconomic mobility. In a follow-up study members of the experimental group were successfully integrated into the Israeli army on equal terms with their counterparts from a Western Jewish background. The control group, on the other hand, did not gain scholastically, improve self-image, nor achieve comparable socioeconomic mobility and equal integration in the armed forces after graduation from the secondary school. In fact, many dropped out before graduation.

Frankenstein's experiment concludes that separation coupled with culturally and psychologically relevant educational strategies, practices, and course content is a better situation for achieving desired outcome in terms of educational and socioeconomic gains and integration. Separation, then, does not and should not necessarily mean inequality. On the contrary, separateness can be a means for the achievement of equality as well as for the maintenance of a distinct cultural and national identity.

However, a policy of separation, even if it is voluntary, might easily be manipulated by the majority or the dominant group in such a way as to reinstitute inequality. This could easily lead to political control, and, in the case of an enemy-affiliated minority such as the Palestinian Arabs in Israel, control of a specific minority group. Erik Cohen concludes that "by manipulating the planning process, a legitimate separation could easily be turned into discriminatory segregation or exclusion of the minority group. The boundary between voluntary separation and enforced—or induced—segregation is by no means clear and unequivocal, as the case analyzed here (Arabs in Israel) clearly demonstrates."[11] The following is a discussion of the few cases in which integration between Jews and Arabs in one form or another has been attempted.

RESIDENTIAL INTEGRATION

Dr. Erik Cohen, of the Levi Eshkol Institute for Economic, Social, and Political Research at the Hebrew University, conducted a comprehensive study of "integration vs. segregation in the planning of a mixed Jewish-Arab city in Israel" in the city of Acre in the northern part of the country in 1973.[12]

Until 1948, Acre was a predominantly Arab city with nearly

15,000 inhabitants, out of whom only a few hundred were Jewish. As a consequence of the 1948 war, however, most of the Arab population fled as refugees into Lebanon and Syria. In 1971, Cohen reported, Acre's population totaled nearly 35,000 inhabitants, out of whom slightly less than three-quarters were Jews, primarily of Oriental (heavily Morrocan) origin. More than one-quarter of the population were Arabs who either remained in the city in 1948, or migrated to it from the surrounding Arab villages and towns afterwards. The vast majority of Arab inhabitants were and still are concentrated in the ghetto-like Old Town of Acre which is surrounded by ancient walls and is characterized by overcrowded, unsafe, and unsanitary conditions.[13] The Jewish inhabitants were settled in the new city outside the walls in modern housing facilities, built by the government to resettle Jewish immigrants who were temporarily housed in camps, and to absorb new immigrants as well.

The Jewish population, however, is facing a crisis. Indeed, Cohen found that most of the educated and relatively wealthy Jewish families leave Acre in order to make Nahariyah or Haifa their new homes. Acre is faced with the problems of the drain on its already limited economic resources and the emigration of the middle class families. Most important is that while the Jewish population is decreasing, the Arab population is growing due to both a high birth rate and to the migration of many Arab families (especially the educated) from the surrounding rural areas. This trend threatens the majority's goal to make Acre as pure a Jewish city as possible, and thus, they are aiming at a significant decrease not only in the percentage of Arabs in the city but also in their absolute number.

While Acre is a mixed city, Jews and Arabs are, for the most part, segregated. Arabs have not been encouraged to own government-subsidized apartments outside the walls. Nevertheless, there are two pressures leading to a serious effort on the part of the authorities to plan for a solution to the crowded, unsafe, and unsanitary housing conditions of Arabs in the Old Town of Acre. One is the pressure of Arabs themselves demanding the improvement of their housing conditions. The other force, evolves from the majority's interests: the solution of the housing problem for Arabs in Acre will bring about definite, even though short term, gains for the majority.

A government company has lately been established under the title of "The Company for the Development of the Old Town." Its goals are twofold: first, "it creates new tourist facilities controlled by Jews . . . taking the tourist business out of Arab hands"; second, "it encroaches upon the low-cost housing market in the Old Town without providing housing outside the walls."[14] While these objectives may seem economic in nature, political reasons are not lacking. In order to turn the Old Town into a tourist attraction with adequate facilities, a reduction in its population is necessary. Thus, a problem is created—the resettlement of the Old Town Arab population.

The solution to this problem which the Arabs prefer is to build and develop housing facilities on the available land resources closest to the Old Town where Arabs have their small businesses and cultural places. This solution would keep the Arabs an identifiable group by maintaining an Arab neighborhood in the city. However, both local and central authorities do not agree to this solution. To begin with, Acre has very limited in land resources, and those resources available cannot accommodate the absorption of Jewish immigrants, whose housing is a top priority. The only land resource left is the one closest to the Old Town and preferred by Arabs, and authorities claim that not only is it not large enough, but it is needed for the development of tourist facilities.

Another solution to this problem is to disperse or integrate Arabs in the housing complexes built by government agencies for the settlement of Jews. Cohen reports that an experiment integrating fifty Arab families was carried out in order to help decide whether or not to aim for integration. While no tensions were created between the Arab and Jewish families, Cohen reports that authorities are not willing to adopt the findings of their own experiment, perhaps because most Jews, he suggests, support a policy of segregation because "some are emotionally opposed to living with Arabs, out of prejudice or political hostility, some are even afraid that the presence of Arabs would affect negatively the value of their property." Although a few Jewish leaders do support integration, they do so "for reasons far removed from a liberal ideology: they consider the concentration of Arabs in their own neighborhoods as a security risk and would feel safer if the Arabs were dispersed into Jewish neighborhoods, which would give the Jews more control over them."[15]

The Arabs' attitudes towards integration in housing and education are no more favorable than those of the Jews. It is their long range intention to keep their national and cultural identity as distinct as possible. As a national minority, the Arabs perceive integration as threatening to their identity and to their way of life. Separation provides them with a feeling of togetherness and security and helps them avoid the dangers and threats to their ethnic identity. As a consequence, a strong tendency towards separation is found in the Arab community. Although "separate but equal" is a preferred principle, Arab antagonism towards integration is not so great as to prevent them from accepting housing alternatives in an integrated setup, out of necessity, not choice. In fact, when a few families were offered this possibility of obtaining modern housing in an integrated context, they did not turn it down but rather competed for it.

Nevertheless, despite the fact that their experiment in integration did not fail, the authorities have neither adopted the possibility of integrating Arab families into the already existing housing facilities built for the Jewish families, nor the idea of a separate, all-Arab neighborhood within the city of Acre. Instead, a plan has been drawn up by which most Arabs will be induced, if not forced, to accept a modern housing alternative which, though it suits their cultural patterns and need, exists *outside the limits of Acre,* namely, in the rural Arab area within the same region. The plan clearly aims at reducing the number of Arabs in Acre to a minimum, turning it into a predominantly Jewish city with a few powerless Arabs (only four out of fifteen members of the municipal council are Arabs). This reduction, in turn, will also help achieve the goal of investment in Acre (Old Town) in the tourist business for the majority's benefit. Most important, the plan, reported on extensively and analyzed thoroughly by Cohen, will help the Jewish majority avoid the dangers posed by an autonomous Arab group within the same city. To the Arabs, on the other hand, the plan means their reruralization, in contrast to the rural urbanization they support. Moreover, it means that they will either be deprived of their living resources or be far removed from them.

The Jewish majority's leaders intend to "purify" Acre by turning it into a Jewish rather than mixed city, however, nationalistic intentions are expressed by Arabs toward the city of Acre as a former all-Arab city, indeed, the very cultural center for the whole Arab population in the area. Arabs in Acre are usually led by individuals who are originally from the city, not by the relatively new Arab migrants to the city. Thus, they identify with Acre as an Arab city, and they remember the period before 1948, when Acre was an all-Arab city. The Jewish majority's intentions to Judaize Acre are clear to the Arab inhabitants. Hence, the city's status as a national symbol in the eyes of the Arabs has tremendously increased as a countermeasure toward the majority's intentions. Therefore, most Arabs uncompromisingly reject the plan by which they are to leave Acre and ruralize, even though, feelings and national values aside, the trade-off is economically worthwhile. By agreeing to leave Acre for the designed rural neighborhood, an Arab family would receive a long-term government loan as well as compensation for their house in Old Town. But this economic attraction is strongly rejected by Arabs motivated by nationalistic feelings comparable yet contrary to those of the Jewish majority.

The policy adopted by authorities in Israel, advocating and ensuring the majority's interest, is quite flexible. In already mixed cities where Arabs are a minority, a policy of reduction of Arabs is adopted to maintain a Jewish predominance. Acre is a case in point. In addition, in places where Arabs are heavily concentrated, as in the all-Arab city of Nazareth, this concentration is counterbalanced by a heavier concentration of Jews alongside Arabs, the newly established all-Jewish city of Upper Nazareth for example. In both cases the ultimate goal is the elimination of culturally independent Arab communities either by ruralizing them or by counterbalancing them with Jewish population.

Another case in which attempted integration failed occurred in the uniting of the municipal councils of the Arab village of Tarshiha with that of the Jewish settlement in Ma'alot, villages very closely located in Galilee. Abraham Benjamin, a professor of counseling and social psychology at the University of Haifa, carried out a study[16] as to the effects of this experiment which clearly points out the disadvantage to Arabs resulting from such a union. Government funds were diverted only to Ma'alot. Strangely enough, since 1963, though the two villages were united officially through a government initiative, only Ma'alot has been defined as a development town and has thus received a tremendous amount of funds to be invested in education (maintained schools which are fully financed by the state), in housing (governmental subsidized), and in industry (governmental owned). The Arab part of the union has not benefited at all from any of these privileges. Indeed, Benjamin reports that the only benefit to Arabs is that they occupy the low ranking and low paying jobs in Ma'alot.

The goal of this union was purely political as far as the majority is concerned: the Arab minority was manipulated to serve the political and economic needs of the majority. Benjamin asks, "How can partners in one joint council be defined differently? Therefore, even by definition, cooperation cannot be symmetrical as resources are not granted to Tarshiha. . . . The lack of symmetry and equality was bound to lead to, and, in fact, has led to extremism among the youth."[17] Indeed, the demand for separation by the youth of Tarshiha is uncompromising, and it is usually only the old traditional and government supported leaders who still favor such a union. Benjamin reports that Jewish leaders in Ma'alot support the union only as a showcase for political reasons inside and outside the country.

Here again the policy of trade-off is clear: a promise of economic improvement to Arabs in exchange for their autonomy resulting from a separation by which the majority gains politically and economically. Benjamin legitimizes such a policy by stating that "the union is beneficial to the Jews of Ma'alot for political and to the Arabs of Tarshiha for economic reasons. Both reasons are valid and legitimate, and can be envisaged as a base to be broadened."[18] He recognizes the economic needs of Arabs—even though they are offered promises rather than actual projects, and even though they become completely dependent upon the Jewish sector—yet he deprives them of the right to have political goals.

However, while Benjamin recommends that such a policy be broadened, Cohen concludes with a rather pessimistic, yet realistic, tone that "the problem facing the Israeli authorities in this, as in other examples of recent policy towards Arabs, is whether they can always achieve a trade-off between promises for economic improvement and socio-cultural autonomy in exchange for Arab readiness to forfeit political power and attachment to Arab national symbols, like, e.g., the Old Town of Acre. The more politically self-conscious the Arab community becomes, the less ready it is for such trade-offs."[19]

One might only add that these very policies towards Arabs in Israel, though not solely responsible for the creation of Arab national and political self-awareness, have a tremendous effect widening and sharpening such an awareness. Clearly, it is a self-defeating policy: The Old Town of Acre turned out to be a national symbol, and the youth of Tarshiha were driven to extremism.

The Arabs usually advocate separateness not only to maintain a sense of security and a distinct ethnic identity, but also, as an important strategy for the achievement of these very goals, to maintain a separate educational system at least as far as elementary education is concerned. This is accepted by both the Jewish and the Arab sectors because, as it seems now, neither is interested in integration and its inevitable threat to his identity and culture.

INTEGRATION IN EDUCATION: AN EXPERIMENT

Haifa is another Jewish-Arab mixed city in Israel. In Acre Arabs constitute more than 25 percent of the city's population, but in Haifa their total does not exceed 9 percent. Aba Hushi, the late mayor of Haifa, often expressed concern for the future of Arab-Jewish relations in

Israel, particularly Haifa. He witnessed and experienced Arab-Jewish cooperation in Haifa before the establishment of the state of Israel, when Arabs were the majority and Jews were the minority. It seems, then, that his efforts to encourage Jewish-Arab relations in Haifa were, at least partly, an extension of the Haifa tradition.

These efforts were expressed mainly in two areas within education. First, as the founder of the University of Haifa, he wanted it to be especially relevant to the population of the North, out of which nearly 35 percent were Arabs. It was explicitly stated that the University of Haifa be open to Arabs as well as Jews. Indeed, the university enrolls 50 percent of the Arab student body in Israel; all other higher learning institutions together have the other 50 percent of the nearly 2,000 Arab students in Israel. Moreover, while Arab faculty and staff members are not a common phenomenon at Israeli universities, Haifa employs six out of the nine Arab professors in Israel. The relationships between Arab and Jewish students at Haifa University is discussed in the following chapter on higher education. These relationships reflect a certain level of cooperation, especially when compared with the scene at other universities, which is usually characterized by almost a complete lack of cooperation and by mutual antagonism.

The second major effort of Aba Hushi was to establish an integrated Jewish-Arab high school. This was the first, and so far the last, effort of its kind in the country. When the school started registration in 1965 for the next school year, Arab students registered enthusiastically. Their main goal was to acquire better educational opportunities and better preparation for the university. Jewish parents rejected the idea of integration with Arabs, however, and expressed their opposition by demonstrations and by exerting pressure on city authorities. The result was that the school's policy was altered from full integration in the classrooms to semi-integration or even false integration, whereby there are parallel separate classes for Arabs within the same high school, and the only possibility for contact occurs during the short time provided for breaks between class hours.

The expressed reason behind the opposition of Jewish parents to Arab-Jewish integration in this specific school in Haifa was that they were afraid of possible future intermarriage: "My father would throw me out of the home if I brought home a Moroccan Jew; what do you think would happen if I brought home an Arab?"[20] a Jewish female student of European origin admits. This fear of intermarriage seems to be in existence in other contexts as well. In the case of Ma'alot-Tarshiha, Benjamin reports that "close contact is greatly feared as it is associated with potential sexual relation and eventual marriage. The Jews are anxious since relations, to the extent that they do exist, are not symmetrical-Arab males with Jewish females."[21] The only Jewish-Arab youth summer camp was not repeated in Ma'alot-Tarshiha because reports came to parents that Arab males were dating Jewish females. This fear, of course, imposes great limits on social, nonsexual contacts.

This problem of social relations between Arab and Jewish youth in a school setting has received the repeated attention of Professor John Hofman of the University of Haifa. In a comprehensive study of the readiness for social relations by Arab and Jewish students of the semi-integrated high school in Haifa, Hofman found that Arabs are significantly far more ready to establish social relations with their Jewish counterparts in the schools than are Jews with Arabs. He concludes: "In view of what seems like an equal opportunity to meet members of the opposite national group, it is difficult to understand why 81% Arabs and only 26% Jews in the mixed high school claim to have the opportunity to meet the others socially. . . . At least in part [it could] be assigned to cognitive functioning: most likely the minority is more aware of the majority than Jews are of Arabs"[22]; and suggests that "peers, parents and teachers are not generally viewed as encouraging contact with Arabs."[23]

The mixed school itself seems to have fallen victim to conflicting forces. On one hand, it has accepted the ideology initiated by the mayor of Haifa with regard to integration. On the other hand, however, it has been under continuous pressure from parents in the majority group demanding separation. As mentioned earlier, this dilemma was resolved by admitting Arab students into separate classes within the school, but it is a most difficult task for the school to take initiative as far as the encouragement of social relations between the two groups is concerned. The task of keeping them apart is somehow easier because that satisfies the majority, especially when the minority lacks the power to resist such policies and, more so, when it is motivated not only by the need to establish social relations, but also by the desire to obtain a better educational opportunity. Hofman quotes a Jewish student of the same school as saying that "the school doesn't know itself whether it wants the contact or doesn't. It does little to provide us with incentives, and, on the contrary, does much to keep us apart."[24] The school has hired three Arab teachers to teach only Arabic language and literature in Arab classes. While the majority of teachers who teach Arab classes are Jews, the school has not been sensitive enough to hire Arab teachers for Jewish classes in order to achieve a certain degree of reciprocity.

Using a wider sample, Yohanan Peres carried out another study concerning Arab-Jewish relations in Israel. He concluded that there are two basic facts with regard to the attitudes of Jews towards Arabs:

1. Social distance from Arabs is big and decisive, and the readiness to intimate relations with Arabs even less than (the level of) marriage, intimate friendships or neighbors, . . . is very low in every stratum, in every status, and in all educational levels. There are differences, but the social distance is very large.
2. Orientals reject the Arabs much more than the Ashkenazim (Western Jews). . . . A large number of researchers verify this finding including a large and representative sample which was studied by the Institute for Applied Social Research under the direction of Professor Guttman.[25]

Peres also found that Arabs are far more ready to establish relations with Jews than are Jews with Arabs: "Arabs reject Jews less than Jews reject Arabs," he stated.[26] He suggested that these findings were compatible with the general theory of intergroup relations: dominant majorities are less interested in allowing the minority to penetrate, whereas minorities are more ready to establish relations with the majority.

Hofman's study was carried out in 1971. Five years later, in 1976, the study was repeated by him to determine possible changes in the readiness of Jewish and Arab students with regard to social relations. The general finding was that Arabs were still more ready than Jews to establish relations. Within this framework, however, a major change has taken place: Arab students' interest in relations had significantly decreased, and Jewish students' readiness had increased.[27] This rather interesting change could be attributed to the political developments which occurred within that period (1971–1976). The war of 1973 in the Middle East awakened Israeli public opinion as to the potential ability of the Arabs. Although each side has claimed victory over the other, one thing is clear: the Arabs have shown a definite ability to fight and threaten Israel's confidence as far as security is concerned. This has meant, among other things, that the Israelis can no longer ignore the Arab whether inside or outside Israel. The Arab, on the other hand, has regained self-confidence and, as far as the Arab in Israel is concerned, the tendency toward favoring close relationships with the majority in order to be accepted has decreased to a large extent.

Furthermore, an increase in Palestinian identity and the international recognition thereof has made the Israeli majority increasingly aware of the Palestinian Arab minority in Israel. Though not overwhelming, this awareness has expressed itself in the formation of political groups and movements (i.e., The Israeli Association for Israel-Palestine Peace); in the demand to study Arab language in Jewish schools; in the demand of Jewish leaders to integrate Arabs more into the Israeli economy; in a more cautious approach to the Arab minority because it may rise as a nationalistically active entity; and in the area of Jewish-Arab relations, including the schools.

The rise of the Palestinian national identity has also had its effects on the Arabs in Israel. They have regained confidence in their national identity, which may represent a significant development for all Palestinian Arabs. For those in Israel, however, the recrystallization of Palestinianhood has a special meaning since they live as a minority side by side with the Israeli Jewish majority. One of the most salient expressions of the re-Palestinization of Arabs in Israel has been that, again, as before the establishment of the state of Israel, they can deal with the Jewish majority as a nationally *equal* group. This means that their rejection by the majority is counterbalanced by a similar response on their part, a decreasing interest in and readiness for social relations.

Social relations in the mixed high school are but one expression of the larger network of Arab-Jewish relations in Israel. These relations, which in some cases are established in times of quiet and relative political ease, can explode immediately when tension increases or when war breaks out. Dan Shivtan of the Shilloah Institute for the Study of the Middle East at the University of Tel Aviv suggests that "the relationship between the Jews and the Arabs, except for the fact that there is a personal element, is basically a relationship between a Zionist and a Palestinian. This national element cannot be neutralized."[28] This very national element imposes itself on every framework in which Arab-Jewish integration and relationships are potentially possible (i.e., housing in mixed cities, joint councils, and schools). Thus, it reinforces the existing separation, a situation which, though it might seem legitimate, is more easily manipulatable by the more powerful majority group to serve its own economic and political interests.

In conclusion, separation rather than integration best describes the social relationship between Arabs and Jews in Israel. Even in mixed cities where integration, at least theoretically, seems possible, the same pattern of segregation is followed. At this point in their history, neither Arabs nor Jews are interested in integration. In fact, it appears that there is a commonly shared anxiety, if not defensiveness, as to possible threats integration poses to the ethnic identity of the groups concerned. It must be clearly stated, however, that behind the negative attitudes towards integration there is more than the fear of identity loss on the part of both groups. Mutual prejudice, mistrust, and even hatred which have accumulated over the past few decades between Arabs and Jews, both inside and outside Israel, are definite deterrents to integration.

If segregation is so overwhelmingly dominant, why have there been a few attempts at integration? These attempts have been induced by representatives of the majority, and the motivation behind their initiative along with the minority's acceptance of the few integrated frameworks in housing, municipalities, and education are very symptomatic. The majority desires political control and economic gains, while the minority is desperately seeking better opportunities in housing and education. Yet, due to the lack of a legal basis for affirmative action in Israel, the majority's efforts at integration often result in manipulation and exploitation. As a consequence, polarization in attitudes and mutual hostilities are greatly increasing. And the most alarming phenomenon is that while in previous years segregation was viewed as a means by which cultural uniquenesses could be maintained it is becoming more and more idealized as an end in itself.

Higher Education

A GREAT NUMERICAL GAP exists between the Arab and Jewish student populations in Israel. Until 1973, the Arab university student population comprised only 2 percent of the total university student population in Israel (1000 Arab and 51,000 Jewish students). But during since 1974 the number of Arab students at Israeli universities has almost doubled and now comprises 3.5 percent of the total student population. Although this increase represents noticeable growth, the gap between the two sectors is still huge; while Arabs comprise 15 percent of the total population in Israel, Arab students are only 3.5 percent of the total student population.

One might claim that the reason behind the imbalance in the ratios of higher education for Arabs and Jews in Israel is the difference in the level of development between the modern, Western, and developed Jewish society and the traditional, non-Western, and less developed Arab society in Israel. This is not necessarily the case. When Arabs in Israel, as a segment of the Palestinian society, are compared with another section of the same society (West Bank), it is minority status which is primarily responsible for the low ratio of Arab students in Israel. This comparison also reveals the social, economic, and political dynamics which govern the opportunities for higher education.

A PALESTINIAN PHENOMENON

Developing societies struggle to make their educational systems serve their national needs. Many nations find it difficult to develop socially and economically. For example, vocational-technical education is often unrealistic in such nations because it trains students for unavailable jobs.[1] Also, higher education is usually recognized as a weak spot in the educational hierarchy and in developing societies is still a privilege of the few. A comparison of the number of students in developing nations to that in developed societies reveals a huge statistical difference. For example, the ratio of students per 100,000 inhabitants in 1968–69 in Iran, Kuwait, Pakistan, and Egypt were 149, 170, 278, and 565, respectively. In developed countries the ratios have been reported much higher; in the United States, USSR, France, Holland, and Israel the comparable ratios are 3,471, 1,830, 1,239, 1,445, and 1,488, respectively.[2]

The second category of needs corresponding to education in many developing countries is nation-building.[3] Many of these societies have emerged lately as independent nation-states whose needs are primarily related to the cultural and national unification functions of the education system, the achievement of a unified national identity, and the actualization of national goals, especially in the painful competition between them and the already developed societies with which they usually have relations as subordinates. Many times education and schooling are isolated from these needs because educational structures and content are usually borrowed and copied from the Western developed societies, especially the former colonizers.[4] Furthermore, the weaknesses in higher education are also manifested in areas other than the ratios of students to population. Quality of educational content is also less relevant to the growing cultural and economic needs in that there is usually an overemphasis on the humanities and social sciences, a lack of good programs in the applied sciences of technology, and which are incompatible with the students' cultural background.

Abdullah Abduldaim, a recognized expert in educational planning in UNESCO and the Arab world, is the author of a book which tries to illuminate some of the problems and issues in the educational systems in developing countries, particularly the Arab world. He overemphasizes the lack of economic resourcs in the developing world as the main reason which leads to the lower student to population ratios of student population.[5] In other words, developing countries lack the necessary economic resources needed for investment in higher education and/or for rewards to graduates, without which an investment in higher education is not worthwhile. Another factor contributing to the low higher education attendance is the absence of a direct relationship between the areas of specialization and the industrial-technological needs for trained manpower.

A deeper look reveals that even more dynamics are involved in such a phenomenon. Although the lack of economic resources and sound efficient planning is an important factor, the processes of selection and screening often perpetuate existing social structures which are feudal, caste, or class related.[6] These processes place higher education far beyond the reach of many candidates, especially those who come from the deprived social classes, often the majority.

The economic rationale may be a valid one, at least partially, in certain socioeconomic contexts in developing societies. But in others it cannot be considered a reason for the lower student to population ratios in higher education. Thus, the Arab and other oil-producing countries where economic resources are certainly not lacking exhibit some of the lowest student to inhabitant ratios (in Kuwait, 170 per 100,000 inhabitants; in Iran 149); while other, less wealthy countries show much higher ratios (in Egypt 565, in Syria 590, and in Lebanon 954). In such cases, the traditions of education and the general level of development and modernization seem to be more influential than economic factors.

However, the economic factor in encouraging higher education cannot be overlooked. In fact, there is a well-known pattern in theory and research on higher education which recognizes the significance of the economic return as a basic motivation for the investment by both individuals and governments in higher education.[7] The decision whether or not to pursue education at higher levels, then, is influenced by economic considerations, namely, the available and possible gains in socioeconomic status.

Harold Howe,[8] recognizing the economic values of education, has strongly defended the noneconomic returns one can expect to gain from higher education. He emphasizes political awareness and social commitment as these basic noneconomic values of higher education and thus adds a very important dimension to its value. Such values seem to have a special significance to developing societies as they try to establish national and political identification with their respective nation-states. Sociocultural commitment is no less important to these societies, because it can be expected to help transfer the sense of belonging from a tribal or caste framework to a broader national sense of belonging.

In conclusion, higher education seems to have two value domains: socioeconomic and sociopolitical. In the first category, higher education becomes more and more popular as long as it promises the individual an upward socioeconomic mobility; in the latter, it is desired as long as it is relevant to the sociopolitical needs and ambitions of both the individual and the society. Both sets of values seem to contradict certain social and political structures in many developing countries, however. The economic return value of higher education in most cases is not assured in those countries which lack the economic resources to reward graduates of higher learning institutions. It is also found that these institutions serve the dominant class or political system and are therefore not relevant to the majority, the unprivileged population.

Higher education among Palestinians does not seem to follow the pattern which is typical in developing societies, that is, unlike most, if not all, developing societies, higher education among Palestinians is following the pattern set by developed Western countries. In a survey of university students on the West-Bank the author discovered that the ratio of students to population exceeded comparable ratios in Western Europe; in fact, in a worldwide comparison it is next only to the ratio in the United States (among Palestinians there are over 3,000 students per 100,000 inhabitants, while in the United States there have been almost 4,000 in recent years).[9] On the macro level, no statistics are available for the West Bank as a separate entity, for until 1967 it was part of the kingdom of Jordan, and the Jordanian official statistics did not differentiate between the western and eastern banks of the Jordan River. Indeed, even as late as 1971 Jordanian statistics included the West Bank, too. In that year the ratio in Jordan was over 1,200, and in Israel it was 1,100.[10] Within the Jewish society in Israel the ratio was 1,300; among Arabs in Israel it was only 130.

The seemingly low student to population ratio in Jordan is due to the fact that it includes both Jordanians and Palestinians, and the vast majority of students who are considered Jordanian are in fact of Palestinian origin, mainly from the West Bank. On the other hand, the ratio in Israel may seem low, too. This is due to the fact that Western and non-Western Jews are included. Among Western Ashkenazi Jews, however, the ratio is estimated to be much higher, as in the case of Palestinians.

A striking gap does exist between Palestinian Arabs on the West Bank and their counterparts, the Arabs in Israel. In 1972–73, when the survey was carried out, in sample rural communities the ratios on the West Bank exceeded 3,000, while among Arabs in Israel the same ratio did not exceed 300 students per 100,000 inhabitants. The ratio was ten times higher on the West Bank than among Arabs in Israel, that is, on the West Bank the ratio was among the highest in the world; among Arabs in Israel it was one of the lowest.

In order to make our statistical survey more accurate, especially in

the comparison between Palestinians on the West Bank and their counterparts in Israel (the Arabs who remained within Israel's boundaries in
1948 when the state of Israel was established), it was conducted on a
micro basis in a controlled situation by using three Arab villages which
were split into two parts by the borderline between Israel and Jordan
(the West Bank) in 1948. They remained separate until 1967, when
they were reunited as a consequence of Israel's occupation of the West
Bank during the six-day war. All villages are Moslem, rural, and have
been in existence as such for a few hundred years. The findings in these
villages are compatible with the macro comparisons which were based
on official statistical publications in both Israel and Jordan. On the
Israeli side of the three villages combined the ratio was 472 students
per 100,000 inhabitants. On the West Bank side, on the other hand, the
ratio was 2,796.

Certainly, one can always claim that the Israeli side of these villages
held a special status under Israeli rule. After all, they are borderline
villages and for security reasons they may have been under special
restrictions, putting higher education beyond their peoples' reach. The
same may not have been the case for the West Bank (then Jordanian)
side of these same villages. Conversely, one may maintain that the
findings are still valid because of their striking consistency with the
overall macro level ratios. However, in order to reinforce the validity of
the findings the survey was carried futher into a comparison between
two nonsplit Arab villages, one under Israeli rule since 1948, and the
other on the West Bank (until 1967 under Jordanian rule).

The Israeli Arab village contained 4,500 inhabitants, out of whom
only 6 individuals were students, making the ratio 133 students per
100,000 inhabitants. In the West Bank village, on the other hand, we
found 530 inhabitants, out of whom 16 individuals were students, resulting in a ratio of 3,018 per 100,000. Moreover, this huge gap (between a ratio of 133 on the Israeli side and 3,018 on the West Bank
side) was discovered in spite of the fact that the Arab village in Israel
was nine times as big as its counterpart on the West Bank. Usually, in
areas with a larger population one would expect to find a higher ratio of
students.

To summarize, higher education among Palestinians on the West
Bank is a unique phenomenon. In fact, it is so unique that one is
tempted to label it as "the Palestinian phenomenon." When compared
with other developing nations, the higher education ratio among Palestinians is the highest; when compared with other Arab nations, it is also
the highest. Lebanon has the highest ratio next to the Palestinians,

though, with a ratio is almost 1,000 students per 100,000 inhabitants; among Palestinians it exceeds 3,000.

When compared with their counterparts in Israel the ratio of students to population among Palestinians on the West Bank is ten times greater than that among Arabs in Israel. Moreover, by international standards the Palestinian higher education ratio is next only to that of the United States, which has always maintained the highest in the world. These findings call for a further study in order to explain this phenomenon in Palestinian society.

DISCUSSION

Higher education ratios in a given society are influenced by many factors, the most important of which are: the efficiency and enrollment rates in elementary and secondary schools; economic return for the investment in higher education; sociopolitical significance of the students in their society; and the availability of institutions and their screening policies and procedures or selection processes. In-depth interviews with graduates, non-graduates, parents, and community and educational leaders on both sides of the border (on the West Bank and on the Israeli side) were carried out in order to determine how the above factors led to these gaps in the ratios in higher education and to delineate the social and structural processes and socioeconomic dynamics which might result in a high ratio of students to population.

Four categories were incorporated in these interviews and surveys: the elementary school enrollment percentages and the secondary school success rates; the uniqueness in the Palestinian experience as it has some influence on the significance of higher education; the economic returns for investment in higher education, or the socioeconomic mobility potential inherent in higher education; and the sociopolitical values of higher education. The following is a discussion of each of these categories in terms of possible contributions to the high ratios in university education.

ELEMENTARY AND SECONDARY EDUCATION

Elementary education in Palestinian society on the West Bank is considered one of the most successful systems of education in the Arab world. Enrollment percentages in school among elementary school age

children there have exceeded 90 percent in the last few years.[11] In the
Arab world, on the other hand, the figure has not exceeded 65 percent.
Among Arabs in Israel the percentage of elementary school enrollment
out of the total school age population reached 80 percent in 1971.[12]
Both populations are very similar in their cultural and educational back-
ground for until 1948, they were united in one sociopolitical entity.
However, the difference in favor of the West Bank society is probably
due to the fact that while Arabs in Israel lost most of their teachers
when they left the country on the eve of the establishment of the state of
Israel, the West Bank educational system remained intact after 1948.

The huge difference between Palestinians on the West Bank and
their counterparts in Israel is not so much in the elementary school enrollment rate as it is in the rates of success in high school, however.
More than 80 percent of the twelfth graders succeed in the Jordanian
matriculation exam on the West Bank, but only 40 percent of the Arab
twelfth graders succeed in the comparable Israeli matriculation exam.

The reasons for this difference in percentage vary. First, curricula
in the Arab high schools in Israel are not culturally and nationally
relevant to the Arab student's background. According to Peres, the
Arab high school curricula in Israel requires more Hebrew and
Zionistic studies than Arab studies.[13] This emphasis in itself lowers the
level of relevance of the educational experience to the point of estranging
the Arab student. The Arab high school student in Israel is also often
pessimistic as to his future possibilities in Israeli society. Thus, although
Benjamin and Peleg[14] have discovered that Arab high school students
have a high level of future aspirations, at least as high as their Jewish
counterparts, it was the Jewish students who were confident that they
would be able to actualize those aspirations; the Israeli Arab high school
student lacked faith in his future. The explanation offered by these researchers for this phenomenon was political in nature: the Arab's non-
equal status as a minority member. This finding further reinforces Ben
Meir's[15] conclusion that Arabs in Israel cannot fulfill their potentials
because of many political and social limitations, a fact which has its
impact on the low ratios of Arab students in Israel and which is reflected directly in the rates of success on the Israeli matriculation exam.

A third reason for the lower rates of success among Arab high
school students in Israel is the validity of the Israeli matriculation exam
for Arab students. A recent study[16] noted that the Bagrout (Israeli
matriculation) is not valid for Arab high school students in that it requires higher levels of intellectual functioning than those required for
success on the regular school exam. In other words, teacher-student

interactions were found to depend heavily on memorization and rote learning and understanding while the Bagrout relied more on higher levels of analysis, synthesis, and application. Thus, the Arab high school student is evaluated for university admission on skills in which he is not trained (the Bagrout certificate is a requirement for admission into a university in Israel).

For the high school student on the West Bank, however, none of these conditions exist. Curricula are culturally and nationally relevant and do not estrange him from the school or his culture. He is not in a minority situation in Jordan, and in fact, he could attain as much as he is qualified to attain in Jordan or in other Arab countries. Finally, the Twajeehi (Jordanian matriculation) is valid for him and thus facilitates his admission to the university.

One can easily see that the quality of high school education among Arabs in Israel is in many ways a complete opposite to the quality of its counterpart on the West Bank. In both situations the matriculation certificate is a requirement for admission to a university in the respective countries. It naturally follows that the potential population of university students is limited among Arabs in Israel much more than among their counterparts on the West Bank . The rate of high school success among Israeli Arabs is 40 percent; on the West Bank it is 85 percent, meaning that for every forty potential Arab university students there are eighty-five Palestinians. Nevertheless, this gap in high school success rates in itself, although important, is not enough to account for the gap in university student to population ratios (ten times greater on the West Bank).

THE IMPACT OF THE PALESTINIAN EXPERIENCE

Prior to 1948 and afterwards, Palestinians have encountered a series of traumatic experiences. However, one could safely observe that while Palestinian society has not disintegrated, it has as a result of such encounters undergone drastic socioeconomic and political transformations. Many Palestinians have become refugees and have helped transform the former social structure into a new one easily characterized by the relative lack of the "fellaheen" class. Moreover, much of the cultivatable land was lost to Israel, and hence, new living resources have emerged, especially in the area of labor. The traditional political leadership has vanished, and a new, nontraditional leadership has emerged, both at the local and the national levels.

These socioeconomic and political transformations are of special significance to the topic of higher education. In other words, the socioeconomic and political dynamics usually recognized in developing (and to some extent in developed) countries as selection or screening processes do not operate as such within the Palestinian society on the West Bank. Our efforts to identify the pattern of correlation between opportunities for higher education and social class were in vain. Instead, it was found that university students in villages and towns on the West Bank are distributed almost proportionately among the different socioeconomic classes.

The deprivation of Palestinians of a nation-state has helped facilitate higher education because the lack of politically determined selection processes has helped many, who would be otherwise deprived, achieve higher education. The Palestinian experience of uprooting and dispersion has helped weaken the traditional social structures which usually are responsible for depriving the majority of a traditional society of achieving education, particularly higher education. Neither is the Palestinian society a self-contained economic entity, nor does it have an independent economic structure which would have been selective as in most other human societies. In other words, the majority of Palestinian graduates are not dependent on internal economic structures; they are dispersed, mainly in the Arab world. Employment opportunities and economic rewards are not dependent upon social class affiliations but on merit.

It is the very Palestinian experience which may have "taught them a lesson." Deprived of land maintenance and ownership and industry ownership and development, Palestinians have learned that the best investment that one can make is in "something which he can easily carry with him wherever he goes." In such a case education is obviously the best area of investment. It is safe in the sense that if for some reason Palestinians have to leave again, they can carry it along. In short, the lack of statehood in terms of a political entity, the deep social structure transformations, the lack of dependence of the educated on internal economic structures, the trauma of repeated, yet forced, physical mobility (dispersion), and the somehow discriminatory policies practiced against Palestinians in their host-affiliate Arab countries in terms of land and industry ownership, have all made higher education the major, if not the only outlet for coping.

Among Arabs in Israel, on the other hand, although some of these socioeconomic dynamics are found, there are differences which account partly for the gap in higher education favoring Palestinians on the West

Bank over their counterparts in Israel. Arab society in Israel has also undergone some of the social transformations observed on the West Bank. Most obvious among these transformations are the following: the society is no longer agrarian; Arabs do not belong to a state of their own but rather to Israel; and they have experienced some aspects of the Palestinian trauma. Nevertheless, these similarities are not enough to produce the same, or a comparable effect. Arabs in Israel have become a ruled national minority which is completely dependent upon the majority, economically and otherwise. The social selection and screening processes take place within the larger Israeli society rather than within the minority's different social strata. In other words, majority-minority dynamics are detrimental to a possible increase in the ratio of Arab university students. Indeed, many educational, political, and socio-economic screening and selection processes have placed higher education beyond the reach of most Arabs in Israel. Likewise, the matriculation and university entrance examinations are a difficult barrier for the Arab in Israel to cross. (Indeed, as will be shown later, the economic re-wards as well as the job opportunities discourage rather than encourage the Arab in Israel from pursuing his education to a higher level.) And. politically, a military administration until 1966, coupled with limitation on admission to the "security" related subject areas of specialization, has blocked the way of young Arabs.

However, it seems that as true as these observations about Pales-tinian society on the West Bank may be, they can be related to motivational factors only. Without the availability of economic rewards and noneconomic relevant values of higher education this motivation would have faded rather soon. Life experiences and the lack of political barriers and social and economic selection processes have created the opportunity for higher education. Yet these factors are of motivational and facilitative significance only, and they may be considered the neces-sary but not the only conditions to account fully for the high ratios of students on the West Bank. Without the economic gains from the in-vestment in higher education these ratios would have not been as high as they were.

ECONOMIC RETURNS OF HIGHER EDUCATION

In a comprehensive study of higher education among Arabs in Israel, Eli Reches found that 74 percent of Arab university students had to work 1–4 years prior to their enrollment in a university; 80 percent worked while studying, 66 percent were partially or fully supported by their families, 14 percent were unemployed for a period of 1–3 years, only 16 percent were offered jobs by employers (high school boards) without asking for them, and the majority of Arab graduates in Israel have expressed dissatisfaction with their income as well as the job opportunities available to them.

On the West Bank, on the other hand, employment is readily available and carries a high economic reward. In order to make the comparison a more accurate one a survey was carried out on both sides to record the average incomes of graduates and non-graduates of the same age group and their parents. The aim of this comparison was to shed some light on "between-generation" and "within-generation" socioeconomic mobility as it relates to higher education. The importance of this was that it allowed comparison, in the case of both the West Bank Palestinians and their counterparts in Israel, between the economic mobility of the graduate as compared with his father as well as with his peer who attended an institution of higher learning. The survey also investigated the extent to which the investment in higher education is economically worthwhile.

On the West Bank side of the three split villages only 30 out of 111 students were available for interviews. Most of the rest did not come for summer vacation to the West Bank from the different Arab countries where they are studying or working. On the Israeli side of these villages 40 out of 54 were interviewed.

On the West Bank the average monthly income of the graduate was 135 Jordanian Dinars, his nongraduate peer's income was 49, and the average income of their fathers was 22 Dinars. Among Arabs in Israel the average monthly incomes were 1,670, 1,527, and 903 Israeli Liras, respectively. To make this comparison easier, these numbers can be converted to percentages, making the average income of the graduate on the West Bank was 285 percent of the income of his peer who did not attend a university, and the average income of the father was 45 percent that of the non-graduate.

On the Israeli side of the split Arab villages, however, if the average income of the non-graduate was 100 percent, as assumed in the former case, then the average income of the graduate was only 109 percent of his peer who did not attend a university. Fathers earned 59 percent of their nongraduate sons' income on the average. Moreover, in both cases, graduates as well as non-graduates earned more than their fathers. On both sides non-graduates earned almost twice as much as their fathers did. Although graduate Arabs in Israel earned twice as much as their fathers did, the Palestinian counterparts on the West Bank earned almost six times as much as their fathers.

A comparison between graduates and non-graduates on both sides revealed a large discrepancy as to the graduate's economic mobility on each side. On the West Bank, the graduate earned almost three times as much as his non-graduate peer did, while on the Israeli side the graduate earned only 9 percent more than his nongraduate peer. It is clear, then, that while the investment in higher education in terms of money, time, and effort is a very worthwhile one for the West Bank student, this is not the case for the Arab in Israel. While the Arab graduate in Israel earned almost the same income as his nongraduate peer, his Palestinian counterpart earned three times as much as his nongraduate peer on the West Bank. This is probably a major explanation for the gap which exists between Arabs in Israel and their Palestinian counterparts on the West Bank in the ratios of university and college students. Mary Ann Bowman,[17] while aware of the methodological difficulties encountered in such an analysis of the economic returns of the investment in higher education, concludes that the decision whether or not to pursue a higher education is basically influenced by economic considerations.

Another important point to note is that all the interviewees on the Israeli side of the villages were elementary and secondary school teachers and administrators (although many of them were trained in fields other than education). All expressed the fact that teaching in Arab schools in Israel was the only job available for them. On the other hand, only 50 percent of the interviewees on the West Bank were teachers and were trained as such; the rest were employed in the many engineering professions. Thus, it is clear that while job opportunities are limited only to teaching for the university Arab graduate in Israel, the opportunities are almost unlimited for his counterpart on the West Bank. Furthermore, 85 percent of the West Bank graduates worked outside the West Bank or even the kingdom of Jordan; they were employed in the Arab oil-producing countries.

In these countries, which suffer a great shortage in the trained labor force, particularly university-trained manpower, Palestinian graduates have a definite advantage. They are preferred by employers on both the government and private levels more than graduates from other Arab countries which are suffering from a surplus of university graduates (Lebanese, Egyptians, and Syrians). The interviews revealed the following reasons behind the apparent preference for Palestinian graduates:

1. Oil-producing Arab countries preferred Palestinian graduates over others out of a feeling of sympathy and solidarity with them. Because of the many traumatic experiences the Palestinians have undergone, governments and private employers often show their sympathy with them by preferring them over others.
2. Because of his life experience and because of the relative lack of other alternatives for him, the Palestinian is more ready to leave his family (on the West Bank) for the major part of a year while working in other Arab countries. Others are less ready to do this, and when they are offered a job they tend to demand more in order for their families to join them.
3. Palestinians are better competitors for these jobs not only because they accept less, but because of their background are found to be more successful and aggressive and harder workers.
4. They are more loyal to their jobs and to their host countries. Others (Egyptians, Syrians, and Lebanese) are loyal to their respective countries, and there is always a fear that they might involve themselves in political activities within the host countries while representing their own. Most of the interviewees referred to Egyptian "cultural imperialism," in the sense that while working, Egyptians also try to impose their cultural background. Palestinians are more neutral in this sense and tend not to interfere in the domestic affairs of the host country, partly because they do not have a state to represent and to be represented by.
5. Because oil-producing Arab countries are trying to limit their population to the "original" one, it is their policy to keep the wealth for themselves. Thus, it is easier to employ a Palestinian and deny him citizenship rights than it is to do this with any other Arab. These countries are often criticized because an employee from their fellow Arab countries may work for ten years or more and still be denied citizenship.

The Palestinian is also denied citizenship but not by the same rationale of keeping Kuwait for the Kuwaitans and Saudi Arabia for the Saudis; rather he is so denied based on the agreed upon principle that no Arab country should grant citizenship to Palestinians so they can maintain their identity. While employing Palestinians, these countries can deny them citizenship and thus avoid being subjected to severe criticism from their fellow Arab countries. In fact, they are encouraged to do so.

All these factors together create a situation in which the Palestinian potential employee becomes extremely popular in oil-producing countries. As an academically trained person he is greatly needed and found to be a most satisfying employee. Moreover, he provides the host country with an opportunity to express its sympathy towards him as well as protect itself from an undesirable increase in population.

Thus, it is clear that the Palestinian on the West Bank has the ability, because of an efficient elementary and high school, the motivation, because of his past experiences, the opportunity, because of the lack of socioeconomic and political screening and selection processes, and the high-paying job opportunity which enables him to move upwards as far as socioeconomic mobility is concerned. His counterpart among the Arab minority in Israel, while having the motivation, nonetheless lacks the needed ability, because of the relative inefficiency of his high school, the opportunity, because of the socioeconomic and political screening and selection processes due to minority-majority dynamics, and the rewarding job opportunity.

The extent to which the investment in higher education is economically worthwhile seems to be a most decisive factor in the decision to pursue education to higher levels. The findings of this study clearly support this notion; indeed, it is a well-known pattern in research on higher education. Bowman suggests that only economic considerations are taken into account in the decision-making process. However, Howe strongly opposes this approach by pointing out that, as far as higher education is concerned, he strongly disagrees with "the tendency of economists to make everyone's affairs fit into their disciplinary system when obviously everyone's affairs don't."[18]

SOCIAL-POLITICAL VALUES

Interviewees on the West Bank and Israeli side of the Arab villages were asked to comment on the following open question: "Keeping the economic values aside, what does it mean to you to become a college educated person?" Of the interviewees on the West Bank 90 percent associated higher education with sociopolitical power, with nation-building, and with Palestinian nationalistic leadership. Although these three categories are closely interrelated, they nonetheless deserve separate treatment.

Higher education for Palestinians on the West Bank is an efficient means for penetrating the sociopolitical structure of the Arab world in general and of Jordan in particular. Since they do not have a state of their own in order to provide them with some kind of protection, they find higher education furnishes the means to occupy highly influential positions in the political and socioeconomic structure of many Arab countries, thereby providing themselves with necessary protection. In addition, the growing need for academically trained leadership in the many fields in Arab countries and the reinforcement of training by tremendous economic resources has motivated Palestinians to "get ready and push themselves through" the different levels of the sociopolitical hierarchy of many Arab countries. They are usually found on the ministerial level (in Jordan) as deputy ministers and ambassadors and in industry, business, finance, and education. Interviewees often referred to the symbolic and instrumental importance of their fellow Palestinians who occupy these positions. As one interviewee put it: "Symbolically, the many people who have made it into the power structure via higher education are a reassurance for us and a proof for others that we are alive, we are not debilitated. Instrumentally, these people are of great help for us in getting jobs, in getting education, and generally, in solving problems."

As far as nation-building is concerned, higher education seems to have a nationally unifying value for the Palestinians. Education, particularly higher education has apparently played a major role in expanding the clan, religion, or region-based identity into a nationalistic one. The following quotations from the interviews illuminate this point: "Higher education helped Palestinians interact with other nations in the world in general, and in the Arab world in particular"; "It helps us understand ourselves and our situation"; "It helps produce unique Palestinian culture in literature and the arts"; "It means that we have met the challenge of Israel and the Arab countries"; "It helped me not only become more aware of, but also more committed to my community"; "It gives all of us a sense of worth . . . a sense of excellence." And finally, a graduate who is a literary critic and short story writer said:

> You see, higher education, while strongly associated with economic mobility and coupled with our unique life experiences, does wonders to the creation of a new Palestinian society and nation. . . . Take literature for example, it is uniquely Palestinian while literature in other Arab countries is less localized than ours. . . . It is a process by which we re-establish ourselves and then move to wider circles. . . . I guess what I am saying is that higher education helps makes us

ethnocentric in a rather sophisticated way, and we need that at this stage of our development."

A comparative look at the Arab graduate in Israel reveals that higher education is not only a relatively worthless investment from an economic point of view, but it also does not have the same political or nationalistic value. As an Israeli citizen, he cannot be involved in Arab (Palestinian) nationalistic activity. Nor are the highly powerful positions in the Israeli socioeconomic and political structure open for him. Thus, unlike the case on the West Bank, higher education for the Arab in Israel is neither associated with power and protection nor with economic gains.

One cannot avoid the conclusion, however, that due to the continuous interaction between Arabs in Israel and their fellow Palestinians on the West Bank (and in the Gaza Strip), and due to increasing political and self-awareness, the Arab in Israel is becoming more and more aware of the opportunities and values inherent in higher education. This awareness, coupled with the improving economic status and the growing efficiency of the Arab secondary educational system, could lead to a significant increase in the number of Arab students in Israel. Nonetheless, this number, while significantly increasing, is not expected to reach the same ratio found on the West Bank, because Israel's economic resources, even if they become fully available to the Arab graduate, are far more limited than those of the oil-producing Arab countries where 80 percent of the Palestinian West Bank graduates are employed.

Nevertheless, the question remains as to the social, cultural, and political impact of Arab university graduates in Israel. How does education in a predominantly Jewish university influence the Arab student, his values, his attitudes, and his behaviors? What role does he play within the predominantly Jewish student community? And, what impact does he have on his own community? These questions deserve special attention, for in answering them one may discover an extremely high level of relevance in higher education for the Arab student in Israel. The following section is devoted to these questions.

SOCIOPOLITICAL ATTITUDES AND ROLES

In spite of their relatively small numbers, Arab students at Israeli universities are probably more active socially and politically than any other student group in Israel. Their presence is felt by the majority in general and by the university communities in particular. From their involvements and activities one may conclude that although they are students, they consider themselves representatives of their society as far as civil rights and other political issues are concerned. They are the educated elite, and thus they are more sensitive to issues and problems related to equality and justice, especially when, as future graduates with a rather high level of aspirations, they are the first to suffer from these problems. Moreover, as a group they assume leading roles in representing their own society, the Arab minority in Israel, because they feel that the traditional sociopolitical leadership is supported, if not created, by the authorities and the establishment in Israel. This traditional leadership is either clan-based or religion-affiliated, both of which are not acceptable as criteria by the students. These reasons, which can be considered internal since they stem from the Arab society itself, are reinforced by external factors.

The Arab student population is the only Arab group which lives amidst the Jewish majority and on a rather equal status, that of university students. From the start they have perceived their role as representing their society's interests and presenting its demands before the Jewish majority, particularly the university community. Of special importance to them has been the achievement of the support of liberal Jewish individuals and groups for their cause. This role of representing their society to the majority has been reinforced by the expectations of the latter. Most Jewish students have never had the chance to interact with an Arab counterpart before the university level. To them, as individuals as well as groups, Arab students represent Arab society and culture. This perception by others has, of course, reinforced the Arab students' self-image as representatives of the Arab minority in Israel.

The study of Arab society and education in Israel cannot be separated from the Middle Eastern conflict. The preceding chapters presented abundant data to support this notion, however, the quality and the intensity of Arab students' activism over the past three decades further reveals a clear expression of this interrelation between sociopolitical behavior of Arabs in Israel and the dynamics and developments in Middle Eastern politics.

It is true that Palestinians have never ceased to consider themselves a nation which has been deprived of a homeland. This awareness has existed at different levels of intensity and has been expressed accordingly. However, it is also true that until 1967, during the first two decades of Israel's existence, the Palestinian issue was treated internationally as a humanitarian dilemma. The international community tried to address itself to the Palestinian issue as one which involved homeless refugees who needed to be helped through all kinds of measures in order to ease their human sufferings. Thus, the aid they received from world organizations was motivated by humanitarian considerations. Until 1967, as a national-political issue the Palestinian problem was relatively vague and almost forgotten internationally. Yet the Arab minority in Israel not only weans its nationalist elements from the larger Arab nation, but it has to cope with Israeli policies in which Palestinians are not recognized as a nation.

After the Six-Day War of 1967, however, the Palestinian issue became political rather than humanitarian, because of the many political dynamics involving the Arab nation, the Palestinians, and Israel, and because of the dangers to world peace inherent in the continuation of the wars in the Middle East, Palestinian national identity was re-established and reinforced, especially after it had gained wide international recognition. As a consequence, the efforts devoted to philanthropic help to the Palestinian refugees has been transformed into local and international activities aimed at the resolution of a national-political problem; that of helping the Palestinians re-establish their homeland on parts of former Palestine occupied by Israel since 1967.

These developments have had tremendous impact on the Arabs in Israel, especially Arab students, who are a rather sensitive barometer of the political dynamics and developments as far as the Palestinian issue is concerned. In correspondence to the two general stages recognizable in the development of the Palestinian issue, before and after 1967, one can clearly identify two parallel stages in Arab students' socio-political activism in Israel. While the political element is common in both stages, it is unquestionably clear, as we shall see in this discussion, that in the second stage the national Palestinian element was most powerful. In the first stage (until 1967), however, the thrust of Arab students' activism was directed towards local causes involving civil rights, causes related more to the status of Arabs in Israel rather than to the re-establishment of a Palestinian national identity.

STRUGGLE FOR CIVIL RIGHTS (UNTIL 1967)

The number of Arab university students in Israel became significant during the early 1960s. Arab students were concentrated at the Hebrew University in Jerusalem, where their number at that time did not exceed a few hundred students (less than 1 percent of the total Israeli student population). In the other two universities existing then (The Haifa Technion and Bar-Ilan University), scant numbers of Arab students enrolled. It was only natural, therefore, that the larger group in Jerusalem would be the leading and most active one. This has become a tradition: the Arab student body in Jerusalem is still a leading one even though the largest number of Arab students is found at the University of Haifa.

In a discussion of Arab students' political activities, Jacob M. Landau suggests that while certain jobs in Israel are not open for Arab university graduates, no carefully designed study has yet been conducted to determine whether or not, and to what extent, discrimination exists against Arabs. Landau determines, however, that a sense that such discrimination exists prevails among Arab students. This feeling determines their political opinions and activities.[19] They usually express themselves "through political activities which are alert and organized. They react to every matter which they see as related to the Arab population in Israel, especially to the government's policy towards them, including political, judicial, economic, and educational matters."[20] Landau lists a few causes to which Arab students were committed through their political activism: the abolishment of the military administration; the abolishment of all kinds of discrimination and the achievement of equal job opportunity; the freedom of expression coupled with a severe criticism of what they considered "the black list" on which an Arab who expresses himself freely is listed and then punished as a consequence in terms of deprivation of socioeconomic mobility; the development of the Arab village in a manner equal to its Jewish counterpart; the abolishment of laws and regulations which allow for the confiscation of Arab land; and the improvement of the Arab education system as well as an emphasis on the historical and national themes in the curriculum.

Another major domain of involvement of Arab university students, was the educational scene. Joined, in many cases, by liberal Jewish colleagues, Arab students volunteered during summer vacations to upgrade the level of Arab high school students through many enrichment programs aimed at increasing the pupils' chances to pass the Bagrout (matriculation) examinations. This effort represented a contribution to the increase of Arab students at Israeli universities, for the Bagrout is necessary to admission to a university in Israel.

Moreover, Arab students have created a reputable tradition through their "orientation and guidance" activities. At the different levels of Arab high schools, Arab university students have always been involved in such activities to encourage and orient and guide the Arab high school pupil as a potential university student. These activities were of special importance during the 1960s when Israeli universities seemed socially and psychologically distant from the Arab high school pupils because of political and sociocultural barriers. Orientation and guidance activities conducted by Arab university students helped high school pupils become familiar with the university, its different requirements and offerings. Thus, by establishing a functional relationship with high school pupils, Arab university students were not only of instrumental help, but they also set an example of committed, successful students. This enabled Arab high school youth to cross many of the political and sociocultural barriers existing between them and the predominantly Jewish universities in Israel.

It is clear that the Arab students' activitism in pursuit of specific causes during the sixties represented a struggle for civil rights which embodied a demand for equality in many areas such as jobs, development, and education. In other words, while being culturally and nationally different, Arab students were fighting for the right to become equal citizens in Israel. In most cases in this stage the national assertion was implicit rather than openly expressed. Yet even so, this assertion did not reflect Palestinianhood as much as it reflected Arabhood. This is a mirror image of the politically dominant force in the Arab world at the time. Arabhood, or pan-Arabism, was the ideal then embodied by the late Gamal Abdel Nasser. Moreover, Palestinianhood as a political-national identity at that time was a relatively silent or at least an unheard of movement in the Middle Eastern scene and more so in the international arena. The Arab minority in Israel, represented in this case by Arab university students, could not raise the Palestinianhood national-political issue because of its special status as an enemy (Arab and especially Palestinian) affiliated minority. Thus, in their activism, Arab students in Israel were addressing themselves to human and civil rights issues. The nationalist element, though hidden, was not lacking, but it was *generally Arab* more than it was *specifically Palestinian*.

THE STRUGGLE FOR POLITICAL IDENTITY

The Six-Day War of 1967 could be considered a turning point in the political behavior of Arabs in Israel. As a consequence of this war three formerly separate sections of the Palestinian nation were reunited. Israeli occupation has made it possible for the Arab minority in Israel, the West Bank population, and the Gaza Strip people, all of whom are sections of the Palestinian nation, to re-establish sociocultural and national-political linkages and interactions. For the Arabs in Israel, this has meant an intense process of re-Palestinization. In his discussion, "Cultural Determinants of Palestinian Collective Identity: The Case of the Arabs in Israel," Khalil Nakleh maintains that "finding company in numbers [more Palestinians under Israeli rule as a consequence of the occupation in 1967], and perceiving a commonality of experience with the recently occupied, the Arab minority, interacting with and strengthened by the rest of the Palestinian segment, transformed the element of identity."[21]

The October War of 1973 and the rise, both locally and internationally, of the Palestinian national-political identity has helped boost this process of the re-Palestinization of the Arabs in Israel. Eli Reches, of the Tel Aviv University Shilloah Institute for the Study of the Middle East, addressed the problem of "changes among Arab intellectuals since 1967."[22] He suggested that:

> There is a common denominator between the different groups of Arab intellectuals [in Israel] in spite of their affiliation with different political currents; it is a great increase in awareness and interlinks with the Palestinian Arab nation. The turning point in this awareness was the war of 1967. . . . Communication and interaction with the population of the occupied territories [West Bank and Gaza Strip] were renewed. At the beginning the interaction was cultural and historical, but after 1973 there was a push towards considering the Palestinian Liberation Organization [PLO] as a Palestinian symbol."[23]

While the demands for equality and the struggle for civil and human rights have never ceased, Arab students in Israeli universities became deeply involved in a national struggle through the means available to them within the framework of the state of Israel. As Reches put it, "in their opinion, students' struggle does not oppose national struggle but complements it."[24] Their means include demonstrations, strikes, and dissemination of information in both Arabic and Hebrew. Their ends are the cessation of Arab land confiscation by Israel, criticism of Israel's policies towards the occupied territories, the return of these territories, and freedom for all political prisoners. Their ultimate goal is the reestablishment of a Palestinian state alongside Israel.[25]

Through their struggle Arab students in Israel are strongly motivated by the intention of re-asserting their belonging to the Palestinian Arab nation. Indeed, Nakhleh has revealed that:

The Arab Students' Committee in Jerusalem has attempted consciously to produce an impact in sectors among the Arab population. Recently [in 1976], they constituted the spearhead in the process to redefine the Arab national existence in Israel. While influencing other Arab student committees, they pushed vigorously against separating the struggle of the Arabs in Israel from that of the people in the territories occupied in 1967. They argued for the Palestinian affiliation of the Arabs in Israel and for the shared destiny with all Palestinian Arabs.[26]

The Arab students' political activism has thus escalated from a struggle for equality and human and civil rights to a nationalist involvement. In this, while opposing Israeli policies they assert their Palestinianhood. This struggle can best be exemplified by the following cases:

1. The Land Issue

Arab students' struggle against land confiscation has never ceased, and they have confronted every incident of massive confiscation. They have demonstrated, gone on strike, published materials, and argued. The nationalist element has been a motivating one: it is Arab land which is confiscated by Israeli (Jewish) authorities. However, the nationalist element in the Arab students' political activism against land confiscation has never been as deliberately explicit as it has been in the past few years. At the beginning (1950s and 1960s) the national cause not only was hidden, but it was also strongly coupled with another cause, that of the land's economic worth. In other words, the land for both Arabs and Jews has two values: symbolic-nationalist as a homeland and economic-pragmatic as a source of living. While the opposition to land confiscation was explained by Arabs as an unjust deprivation of a major source of living, the nationalist element, though strongly felt, was for the most part hidden.

In recent years, however, since the revival and recognition of Palestinianhood as a national-political identity, Arab students who have voiced strong opposition to land confiscation have not only been motivated by nationalist feelings, but have also clearly expressed the idea that land to the Arabs, more than anything else including economic significance, signifies a national symbol, a homeland. After the overwhelming strike of Arabs in Israel on Land Day (March 30, 1976) in which Arab students played not only an active participant's role but a leading one, too, there was much public discussion and argument as to the nature of the strike, especially when six Arabs were killed by Israeli authorities. The university community was deeply involved in the issue. Amidst all this interest, wonder, and questioning, Sa'id Zeedani, an Arab graduate student in the Department of Philosophy, published an article in the students' paper at the University of Haifa concerning the whole issue of land and its significance. He clearly pointed to the symbolic value of land in the eyes of Arabs. His aim was to orient the majority's public opinion to the significance of the issue for Arabs as national rather than a merely economic.[27] In an effort to maintain a balance between opposing opinions, the same paper published a rebuttal by a Jewish student advocating that the strike was a rebellion and should have been crushed because "a fifth column will not rise in our state,"[28] (See both articles in Appendix A).

2. The Issue of Guard Duty

Israeli universities have recently obliged their students to stand guard against the possibility of infiltration and attack by outsiders, especially Palestinian Arabs from outside Israel's borders. As far as the university regulations are concerned, it is the duty of every student, Arab and Jewish, to stand guard. The rationale of the university for setting such a regulation is that every student must take part in the protection of the university and the student body. Arab students, however, opposed such a policy and refused to stand guard. Their rationale included the following: (1) From a humanistic point of view, it was inconceivable, so they argued, that they should guard a university against their brothers and cousins who were refugees in Arab countries surrounding Israel. They maintained that the possibility that they might have to kill and/or be killed by their relatives was beyond their level of human tolerance; (2) They strongly asserted the fact that they were an inseparable part of the Palestinian nation. As such, they could not and would not be involved in any activity in which they related to their fellow Palestinians as enemies. Although Arab university students in Israel, represented by their committees, have not explicitly expressed an attitude which supports or legitimizes violence, terror, and counter-terror, they nonetheless made it clear that these activities were part of an effort aimed at Palestinian national liberation. As Palestinians and, at the same time, citizens of Israel, the best they could do was not to become involved in any violence-related activity; (3) They did not separate themselves from the larger Palestinian Arab nation nor did they separate the issue of guard duty from the larger conflict in the Middle East. They argued that Palestinian infiltration and attacks were a response to Israel's continued occupation of Arab land and of Israel's policy of not recognizing the Palestinians' national rights. By relating the issue of guard duty to the larger conflict, Arab university students criticized the Israeli government's policies and suggested that should Israel change its policies, there would be no need for violence and counterviolence in the area.

In short, motivated by its willingness to apply rules and regulations and pressured by Jewish student groups to implement its regulations indiscriminately, the university was functioning as an institution with its own set of rules and regulations relying on a rationale of equality in rights and duties. The Arab student committees, however, functioned according to a different rationale. Motivated by their Palestinian national affiliation and reinforced by the fact that they, as such, did not serve in the Israeli army, they rejected the university's regulation and refused to participate in guard duty. They asked instead for a substitute activity—spending the same amount of time in any nonsecurity related activity.

Through consistency and perseverance, through demonstrations and sit-ins, which did not occur without clashes with groups of Jewish students (at the Hebrew University), and through publicity and solidarity, they achieved the solution they argued for, namely, that of serving the university in a non-security related way. Arab students at the Hebrew University of Jerusalem took the lead both in refusing to stand guard and in making the concession in 1976, which other major universities followed.

CONCLUSION

It seems that the most intensive phase of political socialization of Arab youth in Israel takes place at the university level. This phenomenon of active political involvement of university students appears to be common in both developing and developed countries. The case of political activism of Arab university students in Israel, however, has its own uniqueness and significance. Compared with all other public and government institutions in Israel, the university provides a more liberal environment in which the Arab student can become involved in political activism without being punished by the university authorities. Thus, the university atmosphere has provided the Arab student with an opportunity for expression of his feelings stemming from his national affiliation and status as a minority member. To illustrate this point, in the governmental-controlled all Arab Teachers' Training Institute similar opportunity does not exist. In this institute an Arab student is not allowed by the institute itself to become involved in political activism.

In a predominantly Jewish institute (the university) Arab students enjoy a democratic atmosphere and observe a freedom of expression. On the other hand, in similar institutions of higher learning which are all Arab, the democratic atmosphere does not exist. This leads to the conclusion that when separateness prevails, even if it is voluntary, it is easier for the majority to manipulate and control. The all-Arab Teachers' Training Institute is a case in point. When integration prevails, as in the case of the university, it is far more difficult to apply double standards of democracy. For the Arab student in Israel, then, the investment in higher education may not be economically worthwhile, however, from a political perspective, higher education is of great value.

Student Variables

THE PSYCHOLOGICAL VARIABLES examined in Arab youth in Israel are *scholastic achievement, vocational aspirations and future perceptions, intellectual abilities,* and *active coping ability.* The common denominator of all these variables is that each is influenced by and dependent upon the fact that Arabs in Israel comprise a national minority whose status has a great effect on the environment within which their children grow. The status of the minority and its interaction with the majority has brought about substantial changes in family atmosphere, the school environment, and the larger social, political, and economic contexts in the Middle East in general, and in Israel in particular.

A comparative cross-cultural approach has been adopted for this discussion in which minority samples are compared either with majority groups in Israel or with samples drawn from another section of the Palestinian Arab nation, which until 1967, did not live as a minority under Israeli rule. These comparisons were not made simultaneously; nor were they made in both directions (Arabs with Jews in Israel, and Arabs in Israel with Arabs on the West Bank) in every variable. Nevertheless, despite this limitation these studies are still unique in context, for rarely in cross-cultural research in the social sciences has there been a situation wherein a minority was compared with two majorities: one different (Jewish majority in Israel); the other similar (Palestinian Arab majority in Jordan). The Arab minority in Israel "belongs" in between as far as research is concerned. On one hand, it is expected, at least theoretically, to meet standards and test norms achieved by Israeli Jewish groups because it is exposed to similar influences within Israel. On the other hand, Arabs in Israel are expected to have similar

131

characteristics to those found in the West Bank society because both belong to the same nationality and culture.

Another characteristic of the variables discussed in this chapter is that, while influenced by political, social, and cultural factors, all are psychological in nature. Through these variables Arab youth express the psychological impact on themselves as members of a national minority which is undergoing intensive processes of modernization. That is, they express the effects of being a minority at the crossroads of cultures. Thus, this chapter can be looked upon also as a study in the psychology of a minority.

SCHOLASTIC ACHIEVEMENT

Before the introduction of educational reform, creating the middle school, there used to be a national scholastic achievement test (Seker) given to all eighth grade pupils in the country. The Seker was used for two purposes: to screen those who should be allowed and encouraged to continue in secondary school and to enable those who passed at a satisfactory level to obtain financial aid, an opportunity which was also based on the economic situation of the pupil's family.

It soon was discovered that eighth graders from Sephardic (Oriental Jewish) background as well as Arabs scored lower on the average than their Ashkenazi (Western Jewish) counterparts. Thus, norm B, a lower standard, was introduced for the former groups. Not only was admission to high schools much more difficult with a norm B, but also there was strong opposition to the stigma attached to it. As a consequence of the inequalities which were produced by the culturally biased Seker, and as a result of the efforts of educational authorities to increase the number of compulsory years of schooling (to nine instead of eight years), the Seker was abolished and the reform was introduced in 1967–68. This reform in education was not created in order to add one year to the eight already compulsory years of schooling, however, though it was, and still is, expected to achieve integration between the two Israeli Jewish subcultural groups (see Chapter 5).

Another effect of the reform was the postponing of the screening and selection procedures until the end of high school at which time pupils are tested nationally on a matriculation exam (Bagrout). In most subjects the exam is identical for both Arab and Jewish students, differing only in languages and social studies. Yet in the past five years the average rate of success has been 80 percent in Jewish schools, but in

Arab schools it has not exceeded 30 percent. A look at the success rate of Arab twelfth grade students on the West Bank reveals a significant difference; it is 80 percent, or comparable to the rate found in Jewish (not Arab) schools in Israel.

To explain the large discrepancy in test scores between Arab in Israel and Arabs on the West Bank, it might be argued that the Bagrout and the matriculation exam used on the West Bank do differ. After all, the first is an Israeli test and the latter is still Jordanian. However, functionally both tests are similar. Both are considered in their respective contexts as a criterion for admission to higher learning institutions as well as other institutions outside the university which train for a wide range of jobs (i.e., teacher training seminaries, nursing schools, technical jobs, and positions in the armed forces). Therefore the striking gap between rates of success for Arab twelfth graders in Israel (30 percent) and their Jewish counterparts (80 percent), and between them and their Arab counterparts on the West Bank (80 percent) does need explanation. Our surveys[1] revealed the following threefold explanation:

1. Lack of relevance. As mentioned in Chapter 4, state-specified curricula in Arab secondary schools lack relevance to the cultural and national background of students. However, this factor holds only with regard to the "culturally loaded" subjects such as language and literature (in both Arabic and Hebrew) and history, in which state-specified curricula in Arab schools overemphasize the Jewish majority's cultural values and national aspirations while ignoring the Arab culture and nationality. As a consequence, Arab students are often antagonistic to these courses and to the goals behind them, whether implied or explicitly stated. This antagonism often leads to rejection on emotional grounds that the subject matter is in opposition to Arab students' values and national background. The result is often lack of involvement and active participation in the learning process. Thus, when evaluated on their achievement in these subjects, Arab students do not show a level of mastery similar to that found among Jewish students for whom curricula are far more relevant.

2. Lack of motivation. Although lack of relevance is bound to bring about a lowering of students' motivation as far as learning and achievement are concerned, it is nonetheless limited only to those subjects which bear cultural and national significance. Lack of motivation of Arab high school students involves more than these culturally oriented subjects, however. It has been found that twelfth graders become less motivated to achieve on tests for a greater number of reasons. Arab students maintained approximately the same level of scholastic

achievement measured by school-administered tests from the eighth to
the eleventh grade (the average level of achievement in these grades
was 75 percent), but scores for the same group of students dropped
significantly to an average of 65 percent in the twelfth grade.[2]

In an effort to explain this phenomenon Arab twelfth graders in
Israel were compared with their Jewish counterparts and with Arab
twelfth graders on the West Bank. While the average level of achievement on school tests dropped from 75 percent to 64 percent in Arab
high school between the eleventh and the twelfth grades, Jewish students
maintained a similar average (76.5 percent) in the twelfth grade, and
Arab high school students on the West Bank even gained 2.4 percent
(from 74.5 percent in the eleventh grade to 77 percent in the twelfth).

These findings are explained by the fact that Jewish students in
Israel and Arab students on the West Bank are motivated and optimistic
as to their future after the twelfth grade (end of high school). Arab
students in Israel, as they approach the end of high school, become less
optimistic as far as their future in Israel is concerned. Indeed, when
asked whether or not they have a future in Israel, more than 50 percent
felt free to claim that young Arabs do not because of the perceived
discrimination in job opportunities.[3] (For a more detailed discussion of
this point, see the section on vocational aspirations and future perceptions in this chapter.) It becomes clear that, unlike Jewish students and
Arab students on the West Bank, Arab students in Israel are influenced
by their perception of a dim future for themselves in Israel, an outlook
which may have many consequences. In the context of scholastic
achievement, it is almost inevitable that while approaching the future
beyond high school they become discouraged and despaired, with the
result that their level of achievement is significantly lowered.

3. Problems of validity. The matriculation tests (Bagrout in Israel
for both Arabs and Jews, and Tawajihi in Jordan and the West Bank)
were analyzed and evaluated in a pilot study,[4] in terms of the levels of
intellectual functioning they demand. This evaluation was conducted
according to Benjamin Bloom's taxonomy of educational objectives in
the intellectual domain.[5] Also, student-teacher interactions as observed
in classroom sessions were analyzed according to Bloom's scale in order
to find out whether or not the intellectual levels demanded by the tests
were compatible with those developed in the students through their interactions with their teachers. It was found that the Tawajihi was compatible with the quality of student-teacher interaction on the West Bank.
The test demanded primarily memorization and rote learning of required materials. For Arab students in Israel, on the other hand, it was

found that the Bagrout was *not* compatible with the quality of student-teacher interaction as far as the required levels of intellectual functioning were concerned. The test relies not on memorization and rote learning as much as on understanding, analysis, and synthesis. Yet, it was observed that there was heavy reliance on memorization as required by the teachers' questions to their students.

These findings, although tentative, indicate that while the matriculation exam (Tawajihi) on the West Bank tests abilities relied upon and developed in the classroom, the Bagrout is not valid for Arab students in Israel. It relies on intellectual functioning levels which are higher than those developed in the classroom. Furthermore, it tests understanding, while the students surveyed learned through memorization for the most part. This incompatibility between student preparation and evaluation measures is related to cultural differences. Although the Bagrout is designed by Westerners to test the heavily Western Jewish high school population, it is also applied to Arab students in Israel without consideration of the poor quality of teaching in Arab schools. Thus, the invalidity of the Bagrout for Arab students in Israel stems from the fact that Arabs in Israel, as a minority in a cross-cultural situation, are evaluated on criteria dominant not in their schools but in the Western Jewish high schools. One, of course, would advocate that the Bagrout standards be changed, reinforcing reliance on memorization and rote learning which is dominant in Arab schools. It also seems logical to advocate that a serious effort be undertaken to improve the quality of teachers and teaching in Arab elementary and secondary schools. Furthermore, as a temporary measure, those cultural biases inherent in the Bagrout should be taken into consideration when preparing the test and/or when scoring it.

Although improvement in the quality of teaching coupled with a temporary policy of compensating for the cultural biases of the test are necessary, these conditions are not enough to increase the rates of success of Arab students in the matriculation exam. Rather, a change of curricula toward more meaningful and relevant course material is required in order to attract and motivate pupils to become involved and actively participate in the process of learning. This change, in effect, would help provide a situation which is very conducive to the improvement of the quality of teaching and learning in Arab schools. Antagonistic course content is not conducive to the development of higher levels of intellectual functioning.

In addition, the political and social blocks which hinder Arab high school students from the actualization of their socioeconomic and professional aspirations must be removed if the rates of success are to improve. As will be shown later in this chapter, the pessimism of Arab high school students is increasing rather than decreasing with time despite the following three developments. First, the quality of education in Arab schools in Israel is improving because young Arab university graduates are joining the teaching teams in Arab schools. Second, educational authorities are replanning the Bagrout test to make it more suitable to the different cultural and personal characteristics of Arab and Jewish students in Israel. Third, universities in Israel are becoming more and more aware of the disadvantage at which Arab university student candidates are operating because of the poor quality of their high schools and are looking for ways to compensate for it.

Despite these positive steps, economic and status opportunities for the Arabs in Israel are no more available. On the contrary, as perceived by Arab students themselves, the more they become potentially socially and economically mobile, the more they are deprived of opportunities through which they can actualize their aspiration for mobility.

VOCATIONAL ASPIRATIONS AND FUTURE PERCEPTIONS

In a comparison of Arab and Jewish high school students in Israel as to their respective structure of vocational interests, Elhanan Meir, Saul Solberg, and A. Barach found that while the range of Arab students' vocational interests is more limited than that of their Jewish counterparts, they nonetheless expressed vocational interests which were Western in nature.[6] This is understandable in light of the following observations. First, there is a general and widespread trend towards Westernization among developing societies, a trend which is due to introduction of technology and industry and urbanization. Second, because the Arab minority in Israel lives side by side with the predominantly Western Jewish majority they are aware of the opportunities and possibilities which exist in the majority society.

In a study of vocational aspirations of Arab high school seniors and their social implications, Abraham Benjamin and Rachel Peleg discovered similar results.[7] Arab twelfth graders expressed vocational aspirations far beyond their parents' occupational range. The authors hypothesized that because opportunities for mobility are blocked for Arabs in Israeli society, Arab high school seniors would have a lower level of educational aspirations than that of their Jewish counterparts. The findings not only did not support their hypothesis, but the level of vocational and status aspirations was as high as that of the Jewish group. In yet another study, Benjamin and Peleg uncovered similar results with regard to Arab university students.[8] It may be concluded, therefore, that Arabs in Israel have a level of vocational interest and status aspirations comparable to that of the Jews. This has been found to be true not only in different studies, but also at different levels of the educational hierarchy.

While a high level of vocational and status aspirations on the part of students is a necessary condition for success and socioeconomic mobility in the future, it is not enough. A high level of aspirations assures the existence of enough motivation and a positive self-concept which are needed in the pursuit of a successful future, however, an individual must also have positive and optimistic perceptions as to the possibilities of actualizing those aspirations. Indeed, the question is whether or not Arab high school and university students think they can actualize their aspirations in the larger context of Israeli society. That is, do Arab students believe that they have a future in Israel?

In 1972 John Hofman discovered that more than 50 percent of Arab high school students (N = 213) thought they had no future in Israel.[9] In a later study Hofman found Arab high school students becoming increasingly pessimistic as far as their future in Israel was concerned. After four years, in 1976, over 90 percent of the Arab students he questioned (331 out of 367) did not perceive a future for themselves in Israel. It is interesting that 40 percent of the Jewish students questioned (123 out of 306) reached the same conclusion regarding their Arab counterparts' future.[10] In both cases the reasons given by the subjects were: "discrimination in jobs and education against Arabs, lack of trust, alienation, resentment of the Jews, and other political and personnel reasons."[11]

Benjamin and Peleg concluded that higher education does indeed increase the status aspirations of Arab university graduates, but these high status aspirations are not parallel to the perceived chances of actualization.[12] They also found that Arab high school seniors who majored in science considered their chances for future socioeconomic success practically nil.[13] However, those students who majored in humanities considered their chances at least as good as those of their Jewish counterparts. It seems, then, that those who major in humanities have more chances to actualize their aspirations because in order to succeed they are not dependent on the majority, rather they are usually absorbed within their own social contexts as school teachers. But those who major in science and technology are dependent on the majority because the Arab sector lacks the industrial framework which can absorb such students. Indeed, the latter group of Arab high school seniors stressed political and socioeconomic factors as responsible for the lack of opportunity for future success in the larger Israeli society.

It is important to note here that all of these studies were concerned mainly with the manner in which Arabs perceive their chances for future success. Because these perceptions are subjective in nature, the students' pessimism may be unrealistic and exaggerated and the perceptions do not necessarily correspond to objective factors and situations which may or may not promote discrimination against Arabs. However, the differences found between Arab high school seniors whose major was humanities and those whose major was science seems to corroborate perceptions which are somewhat objective. Had Arab students exaggerated in their perceptions of their future in Israel, the clear difference between the perceptions of humanities students and their counterparts in the sciences would not have existed. It seems that where their aspirations can be realized, the students are optimistic.

Benjamin and Peleg determined that "as it is today, Israeli social reality appears to block the Arab's way for vocational-social-political integration."[14] The Arab minority group "unfortunately does not participate in the social institutions in an equal manner for the moment because of the blocks activate against it, in this way or another, in society."[15]

During the past few years, quite a few studies have been conducted by Israeli social psychologists as to the attitudes of Israeli Jews towards Arabs. In all of these studies a clear pattern exists: Arabs are rejected by Israeli Jews on the basis of the latter's prejudices and unconscious feelings which were internalized at an early age and which will remain fixed unless there is a planned and directed effort to change them.[16] Thus, while political and socioeconomic reasons are not lacking, psychological factors are also a reason for depriving equal opportunities to Arabs in Israel.

INTELLECTUAL ABILITIES

Social-psychological research concerning Arab-Jewish interaction and mutual perception is abundant, but the topic of intellectual functioning abilities of Arab samples has not received similar attention. In fact, research of the intellectual abilities of Arab youth in Israel is limited to a few studies on creative and critical thinking abilities.

In general, when compared with samples drawn from Western developed societies, Arab samples tend to lag behind. For example, Lindgren and Lindgren in a comparative study of creativity, both through individual and group brainstorming techniques and test situations, found that Arab university students (enrolled at the American University of Beirut) achieved significantly less than their American counterparts (enrolled at San Francisco State College) on measures of creativity.[17] Similarly, in a comparative study of creative abilities the author discovered that American rural youth significantly outscored Arab rural youth in Israel. In the American group there were no significant sex differences, but boys excelled over girls in the Arab sample.[18]

The Lindgrens attributed American-Arab differences to the dichotomy existing in Arab language between spoken (informal) and literary (formal) forms. (They used English as the medium of testing.) It seems that while such a dichotomy in the linguistic background of Arabs may have its effects on certain intellectual qualities, the use of English as a testing medium is certainly not conducive to the detection of these effects. The author attributed the differences in creativity scores between American and Arab samples to differences in the sample's respective home atmosphere and school environment as well as to general sociocultural levels of development.

In a recent study the author compared samples drawn from the Israeli side of three formerly split villages with samples drawn from the Jordanian (West Bank) side of these same villages. Each of these villages was divided into two parts by the borderline between Israel and Jordan from 1948 until 1967. As a consequence of the 1967 war, through which Israel occupied the West Bank, these villages were reunited. All seventh and eighth graders on both sides were the subjects of the study and were compared on creative and critical thinking abilities.[19] The Torrance Tests for Creative Thinking[20] were used for creativity variables after they were translated in Arabic; and for the critical thinking variable a test was constructed based on Ennis' theory of critical thinking.[21]

Results of this study show significant differences on both creative and critical thinking measures which favor Arab samples in Israel over their counterparts on the West Bank. The differences between mean creative and critical thinking scores for males and females within the Arab group in Israel were significantly smaller than sex differences on the West Bank. In other words, the gaps between males and females within the Arab group on the Israeli side were significantly smaller than the gaps between males and females on the West Bank side. In both groups, however, the gaps were in favor of males.

The results of this study clearly show a definite gain by Arabs in Israel who have undergone a cultural discontinuity over their counterparts on the West Bank who have maintained cultural continuity. In an effort to explain these differences, the student-teacher interactions on both sides were explored with the hypothesis that on the Israeli side these interactions would be more conducive to the development of creative and critical thinking. The rationale behind this effort was that Arab teachers in Israel have absorbed some modern Western values because of their interactions with the Western Jewish society, educators, and educational concepts.

When analyzed according to Bloom's taxonomy,[22] however, the observations of teacher-student interactions on both sides did not show any major difference. Rather, on both sides the interactions between students and teachers relied heavily on memorization and did not require higher levels of intellectual functioning. It seems, then, that while Arab society in Israel is undergoing intensive processes of modernization and change, the educational institutions (i.e., Arab schools in Israel) are last to be affected by these processes. They were found to be as traditional and as authoritarian as the schools on the West Bank.

As a second effort to explain the differences between Arabs in Israel and their counterparts on the West Bank with regard to their respective levels of intellectual functioning, the researcher looked into parent-child interaction with the expectation that if the school environment has not changed, home environment may have become more democratic as far as Arabs in Israel are concerned. In the presence of their parents thirty randomly sampled Arab children on each side ranging from four to eight years of age were asked to perform the task of classifying a few circles according to size and color. Whether or not the child performed the task successfully was not of any importance to the objective of this experiment. What was of relevance was the manner in which parents behaved while their child performed the task. When the observations were given to four judges who were graduate students in education at the time, without knowing where the case belongs, they were asked to determine whether or not the parents' behavior reflected authoritarian or democratic attitudes towards their children.

Twenty five (83 percent) out of the thirty cases observed among Arab families on the Israeli side were classified as reflecting democratic home atmosphere. Parents were encouraging and emotionally supportive if they interfered with their child while he performed the task. Only five cases (17 percent) were judged authoritarian: parents directly intervened and performed the task instead of their children in order to show them how to do it, or threatened the child who failed. On the West Bank, however, twenty (67 percent) out of the thirty cases observed were classified as authoritarian, and only 10 (33 percent) of the cases were judged as democratic.

It is, of course, difficult to establish a cause-effect relationship between the differences in home environment and those in creative and critical thinking scores. However, positive correlations between democratic home atmosphere and high creativity scores, and correlations between authoritarian home environment and low creativity scores have already been established by Getzels and Jackson in their famous study of creativity and intelligence in American youth.[23] Paul Mussen reported that children who grew up in a permissive, democratic atmosphere were active, curious, original, and creative and expressed themselves freely and creatively, and often in nonconforming ways.[24] And in his cross-cultural theory of creativity, the author lists eight assumptions pertaining to the differences in socioeconomic and cultural factors which affect children's creative ability, highlighted by the ideas that to encourage creativity, a society must provide sufficient rewards for the creative person, and the type of socialization to which individuals are exposed affects their creative performances both qualitatively and quantitatively.[25]

One may conclude, then, that the differences in creative and critical thinking scores between the samples drawn from the two sides of the villages are attributable to differences in home environment. It is worth noting, however, that while Arab schools were not affected by change and modernization, Arab families in Israel have become less restrictive and less authoritarian. The agents of change in this case have been Arab workers in the Jewish cities who continuously interact with their fellow Jewish workers. In other words, while Arab teachers are confined to their cultural context due to the lack of educational integration between them and their Jewish counterparts, the carriers of change are those who interact with members of the Jewish modern society. In such a situation the educational institution, though expected to lead as a change agent, plays a conservative role, and schools are challenged to accompany the changes which have already taken place within the family. As a consequence, the schools' relevance lies at least partly within their complementing such changes rather than within their resistance to change.

ACTIVE COPING ABILITIES

The same subjects used in the study of intellectual (creative and critical) abilities also took part in another study, one on active coping abilities. On both sides of the divided villages, subjects were administered the Shanan Test for Active Coping (STAC), which was developed by Joel Shanan and his staff at the Hadasah Institute of Mental Health, The Hebrew University of Jerusalem. As defined by Shanan, "active coping is a tendency (which, of course, assumes ability) to mobilize psychic energy; first, in order to direct attention to focal points of difficulty so as to identify them; and second, in order to cultivate the external and internal fields so as to disperse the focal points of difficulty, in such a way as to enable coordination between the objective reality and the feeling of selfhood."[26] The concept of active coping which is relatively new, testifies to overt as well as covert behavior in the attempts of the individual to actively, rather than passively, adjust to the various situations he encounters. Active coping involves two basic abilities; first, the ability to set goals and detect difficulties; and second, the ability and readiness to invest the necessary energy in pursuit of these goals.

Coping ability as a dependent variable was tested and found to be affected by age.[27] mental disturbance,[28] sex, degree of integration into the social framework,[29] and ethnic and cultural factors.[30] The study reported here with regard to coping behavior of Arabs in Israel and on the West Bank focused on the investigation of the propensity for coping so influenced by sex, exposure to processes of modernization, and integration into the wider society.[31]

STAC was translated into Arabic and administered to 234 seventh and eighth graders (128 from the Israeli side of the divided villages and 106 from the West Bank side). Results showed that with respect to males on both sides were superior in coping to females. However, as in the intellectual abilities study, the gap between males and females on the Israeli side of the divided villages was smaller than that found within the West Bank sample. Mar'i and Manna' explained this result by the notion that modernization processes, which are more intensive on the Israeli side of the villages, are bound to gradually narrow the gap between the sexes.

Although the differences between the larger samples were inconsistent, there was a clear pattern in their inconsistency: Arabs in Israel outscored their counterparts on the West Bank as far as goal setting and problem detection were concerned, but they expressed a significant inferiority in their readiness to invest energy. This finding can be explained by the degree of the influence of processes and agents of modernization. The accelerated processes of modernization operating within the Arab minority in Israel, along with their continuous contacts with the Jewish, predominantly Western society have helped the Arab recognize the many potential opportunities inherent in modern industrial society, a recognition which has been transformed into an increased ability to define and set goals. The restricted opportunities and goals offered by traditional West Bank society were expressed in a poorer ability to recognize, define, and set goals. However, the restricted mobility in socioeconomic status of the Arab minority in Israel was reflected in an inferior readiness to invest energy in the pursuit of their goals. When there are no restrictions, as in the case of the West Bank society, a superior readiness for energy investing was expressed.

Based on this study one may conclude that exposure to intensified processes of modernization presents new opportunities and potential which are contained within the conditions of the new life. But the segregation of minority status delays and sabotages an individual's efforts to cope with these goals, despite his awareness of their existence and his desire to achieve them.

On the other hand, the findings of this study show that in political, cultural, and social contexts in which there is a great deal of active integration in the wider society, an individual's ability to cope is increased. This is the case among the subjects from the West Bank who were much less exposed to the processes of social alienation. The obvious conclusion is that in order to increase active coping ability as an essential variable in the personality of the Arab in Israel it is not enough to set the various possibilities that exist in modern Israeli society before him. Instead, these goals must be made available and obtainable by him through the elimination of the objective conditions which are liable to place him on the margins of society.

CONCLUSION

The variables of scholastic achievement, vocational aspirations, future perceptions, intellectual functioning, and coping ability are interrelated in the life of Arab students in Israel. The definite gains in the level of vocational aspirations, in intellectual functioning levels, and in the ability to recognize, define, and set goals are of little help to the

Arab minority member in Israel. He not only lacks the motivation to succeed in school, but also optimism and encouragement from the Jewish state.

In short, Arab youth on the crossroads of cultures benefit from both intercultural and intersocietal influences. However, the more he benefits in terms of gains in intellectual abilities and vocational and status aspirations and goals, the more the Israeli Arab becomes frustrated. As he recognizes the opportunities existing in the larger Israeli society, the more he realizes that these opportunities are not meant for him, but are open mainly, if not only, for the Jewish majority in the Jewish state. Thus, as the Arab in Israel tries to develop a sense of belonging, he becomes alienated from the state and its institutions—a condition reinforced by other rather powerful forces, the continuation and escalation of the Israeli-Palestinian conflict, for example. In the case of a settlement of the Israeli-Palestinian dispute, therefore, the Arab in Israel is expected to become more active than ever before in his struggle to attain equality in what he believes is his land, no less than any fellow Jewish citizen.

8

Changing Socioeconomic
and Political Conditions

ONE OF THE MOST CONSPICUOUS INEQUALITIES between Arab and Jewish education in Israel exists in the area of vocational-technological education, an inequality leading to, among other things, inequality in economic opportunities. In the cases of both education and jobs, a thorough analysis reveals that the status of Arab society and education in Israel is no longer determined by political issues and forces stemming from the Middle Eastern conflict as much as it is by internal Israeli social and economic forces. In addition, even the issue of security is manipulated to serve the majority's social and economic needs. Indeed, many researchers and scholars who belong to the majority in Israel have observed that the security rationale is often utilized to manipulate the Arab minority and deprive them of equal opportunity. This maintains superior opportunity for the majority which, in turn, has its own problems of inequality between the two major Jewish subcultural groups. Arieh Luva Eliav, an eminent Zionist and political leader in Israel, claims that Jewish society manipulates and controls the Arab minority to maintain superficial socioeconomic stability and avoid confrontation with problems of social unrest.[1]

The Arab minority in Israel is vulnerable to such manipulation because it lacks the political and economic power necessary to express any opposition to the majority's control. Moreover, the little opposition that Arabs in Israel are capable of expressing is automatically perceived by the authorities as subversive activity directed against the state and its existence. This rationale makes it easier for them to suppress any opposition by Arabs or any effort on the Arabs' part to organize politically to defend their rights to be equal citizens of the state of

145

Israel, and thus make better educational and job opportunities available to themselves, too.

THE ISSUE OF TECHNICAL EDUCATION

This study originated mainly as a consequence of a disagreement between educational authorities and Arab community representatives, all of whom were members of a committee formed in 1973 by the director general of the Ministry of Education in Israel. The task of this *ad hoc* committee was to define the goals and needs of Arab education in Israel during the 1980s. One of the major issues the committee found itself dealing with rather intensively was career (i.e., technological) education for Arab youth in Israel.

Through its surveys and data collection activities, the committee discovered a huge gap between Jewish and Arab educational systems in Israel; for example, in the Jewish educational system about 50 percent of the middle and high school pupils are enrolled in vocational-technological educational programs either in vocational schools or in vocational streams in comprehensive schools. In the Arab educational system, on the other hand, less than 10 percent of the middle and high school students are enrolled in such programs.

A few observations could be offered as possible explanations for this astonishing gap, each of which seems to have some validity. One of the explanations used most often by the central educational authorities is that Arab society in Israel is a developing rural one, and as such has a long history of placing a negative value on manual labor and a very high value on white collar jobs, even those jobs which are not highly prestigious (i.e., elementary school teachers, clerks, secretaries, and civil servants). This position may have basis because, as mentioned before, the basic role of secondary education during more than three decades of the British Mandate over Palestine was to prepare qualified personnel as elementary school teachers, civil servants, and clerical employees, not only to serve their own communities, but also to mediate between the British government and the Arab communities in Palestine.

This tradition of linking high school education and the attainment of a white collar job, goes the argument, is deeply rooted and still exists. Thus, the educational authorities are not ready to risk a fairly large investment in vocational-technological education in Arab schools because, based on the assumption that Arab parents would prefer academic over vocational training, such an investment would be in vain.

Those parents who express such a preference have already placed their children in a few available vocational programs in Arab schools in Israel. Indeed, the small percentage (10 percent) of pupils enrolled in such programs is a reflection of such parental attitudes. Moreover, no demand for such educational programs has been reported by the field representatives of the official educational authorities. Nor has there been a demand from communities or local organizations (municipal councils or parent associations). This lack of demand, again, supposedly proves that Arab society in Israel does not hold the kind of attitudes which favor manual labor, even though it is skill based.

A twofold assumption underlies this position. First, the Arab society has been for a long time associating postelementary education with the achievement of a job which does not require manual labor. Second, the first part of this assumption continues to be considered valid unless a community's demand is reported to the educational authorities by its field representatives for a different option of educational quality, a course of action which in itself assumes community awareness and involvement that is basically a Western type of community characteristic.

Another explanation is usually presented by Arab community representatives, however, for the gap between Arabs and Jews in the vocational-technological educational network. They maintain that the gap is due basically not to negative parental attitudes towards this kind of education, but rather to discriminatory policies which are being practiced against Arabs by Israeli authorities, particularly educational authorities. Vocational-technological education is costly, at least more so than the academic type of schooling, because it demands more personnel, updated equipment geared to the different technological vocations, and an adequate physical set-up to contain such equipment. And this is only one reason why educational authorities are not willing to invest in Arab technical education.

But, the argument goes, in the eyes of the Arab communities the educational authorities' assumptions as to the negative attitudes of Arabs toward labor, though erroneous, are of minor importance. The community representatives claim that the attitudes of central educational authorities in Israel towards Arab education are an extension of a larger policy towards the socioeconomic status of Arabs in Israel. With the academic trend increasing in importance, the relevance of postelementary education is gradually being lessened since it leads nowhere except to the university. With regard to university education, still other problems exist. The ultimate outcome is that more and more Arab pupils either drop out earlier or graduate, and in both cases they join their fellow

Arab cheap, unskilled laborers to serve the majority's economy. Thus, the Arab educational system in Israel helps keep the young Arab at the lower level of the country's socioeconomic spectrum which, in turn, insures that the opportunities for skill-based jobs remain exclusively to majority members.

This feeling, whether justified or not, on the part of Arab community leaders as to the attitudes of educational authorities, implies a few assumptions. One is that a discriminatory policy exists against the Arab minority with the educational system as the perpetrator of such a policy. Another assumption is that although the Arab community may have held attitudes which were not favorable to educational programs involving preparation for a future manual job, those attitudes were operative in the past. A third assumption is that Arab society, due to changes in the economic and social aspects of its life, has changed tremendously in that it has realized that one of the best ways to insure an economically secure future is through learning skills useful in the different technological jobs available in the Israeli job market. "The experiences which an Arab laborer gains in the Jewish society while working or hunting for a job, is that unless he owns the skills necessary, he is forced to accept lower paying and lower valued jobs out of necessity. When he interacts with his Jewish boss or fellow workers, he soon discovers that they had learned a job, or at least useful skills at high school. The first question which comes to his mind is why his high school did not have those helpful programs. . . . Is it because the authorities want him to serve in the lower unskilled jobs?" This is an excerpt from an interview with a young Arab journalist who is associated with a majority party's newspaper. During the interview he often referred to his many talks and experiences with Arab workers in the city of Tel Aviv. He was quite positive that a favorable attitude towards vocational-technological education exists among Arabs in Israel. "It is a necessity out of the continuous daily reality," he said.

A third explanation for the rather large gap in vocational programs and enrollment between Arab and Jewish educational systems, which is usually expressed by moderate professional Arabs and Jews in Israel, is that the Arab Education Department within the Ministry of Education is built in such a way that it is difficult for it to see the emerging needs of Arab society in Israel. Not only does this department not have a history of trying to make itself relevant to the needs of the society within which it functions, but also it is basically run by Jews and Arabs who are either remainders from the British mandatory educational system in Palestine or the products of it. Thus, the Department of Arab Education fails to recognize the changes which have taken place rather rapidly in Arab society in Israel, and as a consequence, fails to adapt curricula to the needs which have emerged from changes in the economic life of the Arab in Israel.

These shortcomings become more detrimental to Arab education in Israel in light of two conditions. First, the Israeli educational system is very centralized, and the quality of education, innovations in curricula, and goals are the responsibility of the centralized educational authorities, not the communities. Second, from an administrative point of view, the Arab educational system is an integral part of the overall Israeli system of education. It is anticipated that the subsystem for Arab education should approach planning and implementation with a rather high level of sophistication, at least as high a level as exists in the Jewish educational system in Israel. As far as vocational-technological education is concerned, it is maintained by Arab community leaders that the gap between Arab and Jewish educational systems is due to false or outdated assumptions concerning values of Arabs in Israel towards manual labor and vocational-technological education.

Apparently, in the argument between Arab communities and educational authorities, there are two central and opposing positions, each of which may have a certain validity. One is a position of hesitation and restraint on the part of the educational authorities from investment in vocational-technological education in Arab schools because of the fear that the very small number of pupils who will decide to choose this program does not legitimize the relatively large investment. The second more decisive position is pressing for just such an investment in vocational-technological education for Arabs. Under circumstances so wrought with contradictions, it is not easy to arrive at a decision in one direction or the other, when such a decision may necessitate large amounts of money for investment or when a lack of investment can be interpreted as supporting a position of neglect, deprivation, or even discrimination.

In an attempt to solve this dilemma and supply the educational authorities responsible for making decisions in this matter with dependable data, a survey was undertaken as to the attitudes of Arab society in Israel towards postelementary education in general and towards manual, skill-based labor and vocational-technological education in particular. This was done under the assumption that such an educational program corresponds to the changing values and needs of Arabs in Israel.

This study was requested by the Research Authority of the Ministry of Education in Israel and carried out within the framework of the Institute for Research and Development of Arab Education at the University of Haifa. The research report was published in Hebrew in 1975, and the data provided in this chapter are based on the report. Because of the sensitivity of the issue involved and its background, two researchers, one Arab and one Jewish, carried out this study, and the report was originally published under their names.[2] Since the study is expected to be used as a basis for decision making by the educational authorities, the combination of the researchers' backgrounds is also useful as a safeguard against any complaints of slantedness and subjectivity.

In addition, the secretary of the Research Authority of the Ministry of Education, the director of the Arab Education Department, and the chairman of the Ad Hoc Committee on Arab Education during the 1980s, all of whom are majority members, asked to preview the questionnaires which were to be used in the study. The latter two did complete the preview and made appropriate comments. The questionnaires were then revised accordingly, and when the revised edition was previewed again the reviewers had no objections. These individuals also approved of the subjects and methods of the study.

There were two reasons for this preview procedure. First, it is a general rule in the Israeli Ministry of Education that any research project which has to do with entering schools, whether sponsored by the ministry or not, be approved by the ministry's Research Authority. This study, of course, was not, and should not have been, an exception to the rule. Second, because of the controversial nature of the subject and because of the opposing claims and accusations, it was the wish of the authorities to make sure that the study tools and plan were not inappropriate as far as the level of desired objectivity was concerned.

A SURVEY OF ATTITUDES TOWARD
TECHNICAL EDUCATION

Three hundred ninety-six eleventh grade pupils, 210 of their parents (fathers), and 67 teachers were administered the questionnaires which were constructed for this study in order to determine their attitudes towards technical education. The pupils were chosen from the eleventh grade Arab pupil population in Israel because at this level pupils have to make decisions concerning their future after the twelfth grade. Fathers were chosen because in a traditional patriarchal society, such as the Arab society, they influence decisions more than mothers as far as the future of children is concerned. More than 50 percent of the fathers were given the questionnaires on an interview basis on the assumption that some of them might have difficulties in reading and writing? Finally, all of the pupils' teachers were given the questionnaires based upon the assumption that they influence the decision-making process as far as their pupils' future is concerned by being consulted by the parents and the pupils as well.

The following were the points of emphasis in this study: attitude toward continuation in postelementary education; the identity of the person(s) who takes the major part in the decision making as to the continuation of education; attitudes toward work in general and manual skill-based labor in particular; differences as to attitudes toward the sexes; effects of occupation upon status; and finally, attitudes toward vocational-technological education in light of changing economic realities.

1. *Attitudes Toward Secondary Education in General*

The researchers tried to learn something about parents', pupils' and teachers' attitudes toward secondary education because such information would indicate how the society relates to secondary education, which includes both academic and vocational streams. The assumption is that to the extent that there is greater approval of secondary education one can expect the differences in attitudes towards academic and vocational education to be more discernible. In other words, the greater the approval, the greater the effort will be to exhaust all the possibilities and potentialities in secondary education.

Table 12 shows in percentages the attitudes of parents, teachers, and pupils to the statement: "It is preferable that a pupil with no chance of achieving his matriculation certificate should start working earlier." The three groups examined expressed themselves as very much in favor of secondary education. The issue was purposely put strongly: a pupil with no chance of achieving his matriculation certificate had better leave school and go to work early. Only 13.3 percent of the parents agreed that the youngster should drop out and go to work if he had no chance of getting his matriculation certificate. The same feeling was expressed by the teachers. However, almost 20 percent of the pupils examined agreed that in this given case the pupil better drop out and start working.

TABLE 12

Attitudes Toward Continuation in Secondary School

	Agree	Disagree	Undecided	N
Parents	13.3%	86.2%	0.5%	210
Teachers	13.4%	86.6%	—	67
Pupils	19.9%	78.0%	2.1%	396

SOURCE: Sami Khalil Mar'i and A. Benjamin, "The Attitudes of Arab Society Towards Vocational Education" (Haifa: The University of Haifa, Institute for Research and Development of Arab Education, 1976).

Apparently, the small gap between the position of pupils and that of the parents and teachers can be explained by the notion that the school experiences of the unsuccessful pupil are not particularly pleasant. Therefore, he finds it better to drop out and thereby escape frustrating experiences and make better use of his time. Despite acknowledging this possibility of dropping out, most of the pupils were still in favor of continuation of high school regardless of the absence of any significant chance of achieving the matriculation certification at the end of the twelfth grade. In conclusion, Table 12 illustrates that all the groups together and each one separately favored secondary education because of its intrinsic educational and its pragmatic values in a changing society, such as the Arab society in Israel.

2. The Decisive Factor in Decision Making

One of the important variables in the issue of attitudes toward vocational-technological education is the relative significance of the factor most affecting the decision in all matters touching on the continuation of studies and the type of studies to be undertaken.

Table 13 shows the distribution of the responses to the following item: "In your opinion, which of the following most determines the decisions in matters of study?" As shown in the table, in most cases both parents and pupils feel that the decision was arrived at by the pupil himself. Here also a small gap between parents and pupils in terms of the identity of the decision maker was found: 80.9 percent of the parents left the decision to their children, the pupils, while 72 percent of the pupils reported making the decisions independently. This gap can be explained by the fact that 14.4 percent of the pupils felt that decisions

TABLE 13

Determining Elements in the Decision to Study

	Parents	Pupils	Both	N
Parents	15.7%	80.9%	3.4%	210
Pupils	13.6%	72.0%	14.4%	396

SOURCE: Sami Khalil Mar'i and A. Benjamin, "Attitudes of Arab Society Towards Vocational Education," (Haifa: University of Haifa, Institute for Research and Development of Arab Education, 1976).

concerning their future education were reached by both parents and children.

In conclusion, a situation clearly exists in which the pupils themselves were primarily responsible for making the decisions in all matters having to do with their studies. The intervention of parents and other elements was minimal. This finding is interesting and even strange in the light of the fact that the society under discussion is a traditional and patriarchal one in which the father has ultimate and almost sole authority in everything connected with his family and its members. Because of rapid sociocultural change, however, it is difficult for those same parents—who, for the most part, studied in only the first few grades of elementary school—to keep abreast of the various developments in the fields of study and education and the opportunities these fields offer the pupil. In other words, the difficult conditions of a period of transition have resulted in many parents losing their ability to decide in matters about which they have insufficient knowledge and in which they have relatively little previous experience. In addition, in the transition from a traditional to a modern society there is also a change of values toward granting greater autonomy to children to make decisions and bear responsibility.

3. Attitudes Toward Work

There are in general two popular categories of occupation: the first, clerical work and other white collar jobs, and the second, an occupation which involves manual labor. It seems very important to clarify the positions taken in regard to these categories because of their direct influence on the positions taken with respect to vocational-technological education.

The position of parents interviewed toward the future occupation of their children was, in general, that they favored work in some trade and preferred it over clerical work or other office jobs. Thus, when parents were asked to state their reaction to the statement: "A good trade is better than a desk job," 65.2 percent (N = 210) answered in the affirmative and 30.5 percent didn't agree—that is, they preferred a desk job and clerical work to a trade. Of the parents questioned, 4.3 percent answered that it was difficult for them to decide. It is clear, therefore, that most of the parents preferred a good trade for their children to a desk job.

Another question attempted an examination of the degree of differentiation existing in the attitudes of parents towards their children of each sex. It is necessary to keep in mind, of course, that we are dealing here with a traditional society which had formerly preferred white collar work to manual labor even for their sons. How much difference was there in parental feelings towards the occupational future for their sons on the one hand, and for their daughters on the other? It was expected that their attitudes towards their daughters would remain more conservative.

Table 14 shows the distribution of parents' responses to the item concerning the kind of occupation considered desirable for their sons

TABLE 14

Parents' Attitudes Toward the Future Occupations of Sons and Daughters

	Trade	Clerical/nonmanual	Undecided	N
Parents toward their sons	64%	32.0%	4.0%	100
Parents toward their daughters	15.2%	77.3%	7.5%	110

SOURCE: Sami Khalil Mar'i and A. Benjamin. "The Attitudes of Arab Society Towards Vocational Education," (Haifa: University of Haifa, Institute for Research and Development of Arab Education, 1976).

and their daughters. The interesting point is that the parents held contrary opinions concerning the future of each of the sexes. Whereas most of the parents (64 percent) were interested in a future in some trade for their sons, most of them rejected this kind of occupation for their daughters. They were interested (77.3 percent) in clerical work for them, and only 15.2 percent were interested in a future job for their daughters which would involve manual labor.

In this item the parents were divided into two groups: those who had sons in the eleventh grade and those who had daughters. This method of division was in itself significant: the sample included 210 parents who had a son or a daughter, each in the eleventh grade at the high school level. One would expect, based on many statistics concerning developing societies, that males would outnumber females in high school. However, among Arabs in Israel the ratio is also balanced at 50 percent each.

Two conclusions can be drawn from the analysis of the responses to this item. First, the parents questioned agreed to the notion that a skill-based job was far better than a lower ranking white collar job (clerical and desk jobs). This finding supports the notion that the society under discussion has indeed changed in the direction of accepting manual, skill-based labor over other usually nonmanual occupations. The second conclusion is that parents had opposing attitudes with respect to the sexes. For their sons they (64.0 percent) preferred a trade over clerical jobs. However, more than 77 percent of the parents interviewed objected to the idea that their daughters might have a manual job. They preferred clerical jobs for them. The expectation of conservative attitudes of parents towards the quality of jobs for their daughters was confirmed by the data.

It is worth examining this finding on parental attitudes toward female employment still further. A closer examination of interviews with parents reveals that this position on the future of their daughters was in no way a rejection of vocational-technological education for them. On the contrary, the parents viewed this type of education favorably on the condition that it would lead to clerical work rather than to manual labor. An effort to pursue this point in depth was made. In the city of Acre there are 37,000 inhabitants; 30 percent are Arabs, and the rest are Jewish. Acre has an Arab comprehensive school, one of the very few Arab schools in the country that has vocational training streams. For female pupils, it has two streams: one is home economics and the other is office management. However, the latter was introduced only in 1975, and is also very weak. The training does not exceed basic typing skills in Arabic and Hebrew.

In the city there are four Arab schools; most of their secretaries are Jews with a background in Arabic. This is not so much due to policy as it is to necessity. In the city there are more than twenty-five Arab lawyers' offices serving basically the Arab citizens of the city and the Arab population in the many villages surrounding Acre. Only 3 of the 25 lawyers have Arab secretaries in their offices. Office managers and chief secretaries are mostly of Jewish background, again out of necessity. Moreover, among the hundreds of clerical employees of the city municipal council, there is only one Arab female secretary.

In such a situation one wonders why a school which already has the minimum basis for establishing a quality training program for a needed vocation such as office management does not provide it. By doing so, the school would make itself relevant to its pupils' and community's needs. In a discussion with members of the parent organization it was learned that what is needed is money and good teachers. "Without having the first, we can't have the second; and money should come from the Department for Vocational-Technological Education in the ministry through the city government."

The discussion with fifteen eleventh grade girls was most enlightening. All of them attended the Arab Comprehensive School in Acre and at the same time enrolled in the vocational streams of both home economics and typing. Although they enjoyed the nice dishes and tasty cookies and cakes they learned to prepare in their home economics classes, they nonetheless felt resistance to such learning. "We don't need a class that reinforces our already inferior status in our society; we are sick of our role as housekeepers. We want some good quality vocational program, like office management, which would help improve our status by becoming independent. . . . This also will help us compete for the many secretarial jobs available in our city." Apparently, school was perceived by them as perpetuating their traditionally inferior status as females instead of improving it in their very male-dominated society.

4. Vocation Contributing to Socioeconomic Status

An attempt was made to find out to what extent, in comparison with other factors, vocation was viewed by parents and pupils as likely to contribute to raising a person's socioeconomic status. Six factors were listed and the subjects were asked to arrange them in order of importance in terms of their possible contribution to upward mobility in a person's socioeconomic status. Findings here show that both among parents and pupils technical occupation was listed in second place after higher education.

Ranking by Parents	Ranking by Pupils
Higher education	Higher education
Technical occupation	Technical occupation
Government connections	Government connections
Money	Money
Property (land)	"Hamoula" (clan) distinction
"Hamoula" (clan) distinction	Property (land)

A number of interesting points stand out in this ranking by parents and pupils. In fact, the marked congruence between the order of priority given by parents and that given by pupils is quite amazing. The parents and pupils related to these factors in a similar way in all but two cases. *Property* took fifth place and *"Hamoula" distinction* sixth place among the parents, while there was a reversal of this order among the pupils. However, these two factors were ranked at the bottom of the scale by both groups.

Another outstanding point is the value placed on *government connections* as a factor in mobility and social status; this factor was ranked in third place by both groups. It can therefore be said that not only were the two groups unified in their opinions, but also *government connections* were perceived as significant in an individual's attempts to rise on the social ladder. This attitude reflects the individual's feelings that it was not enough to succeed in studies and training, but that in many cases there was a need for association with government (the ruling group) for studies and success to become significant factors in social mobility. This supports Benjamin and Peleg's findings[3] that Arab high school pupils felt they couldn't actualize their aspirations because of political reasons.

It is interesting that in a society which only a few years ago feudalistic wherein the landowners almost automatically enjoyed the highest social status, *property* was now not considered a significant determinant of a person's social status. Similarly, *"Hamoula" distinction* was considered unimportant in determining social status in this society in which status is ascriptive rather than achieved. The transition from a traditional-feudalistic society to a more modern one has apparently required relinquishing feudalistic life patterns and abandoning class membership as important factors in consolidating social status; this transition has thereby allowed greater personal achievement and responsibility.

There was an attempt to examine further the variable of family position (the Hamoula distinction variable) as a factor considered important in contributing to a person's social status in which the following statement was presented to parents, teachers, and pupils for their reactions: "A good trade gives no honor to a man without position."

Table 15 shows that the decisive majority of parents, teachers, and pupils rejected the statement that a good trade grants no honor to a man without family position. This finding again strengthens and even confirms the contention that the processes of modernization are at work in Arab society in Israel, processes which gradually bring

TABLE 15

Hamoula Membership Compared to a Trade as Potential
Contributors to the Individual's Social Status

	Agree	Disagree	Undecided	N
Parents	15.6%	82.0%	1.5%	210
Teachers	13.4%	83.6%	3.0%	67
Pupils	21.2%	72.2%	6.6%	396

SOURCE: Sami Khalil Mar'i and A. Benjamin, "The Attitudes of Arab Society Towards Vocational Education," (Haifa: The University of Haifa, Institute for Research and Development
of Arab Education, 1976).

about cultural and value changes as well as structural alterations
within the society. The values have changed in that a man is not
automatically seen in a positive way just because he is a son in an
important Hamoula. Instead, his work is measured by his achievements
and not by the position he inherited. There are, of course, various
influences on the structure of Arab society in Israel. Its traditional
class structure is being transformed in a way that is gradually replacing
the traditional Hamoula which existed for so many years and continues
even now to exist alongside of social systems more characteristic of
modern rather than traditional society. To mention one example, a
working class has emerged to replace the traditionally known fallaheen
class which is Hamoula based.

5. Attitudes Toward Vocational-technological Education

The attitude toward the type of education given to children in
school is determined, to a large extent, by the value system prevailing
in the society, by the attitude of the society toward work of various
kinds, by its conceptions of status and the connection between status
and a given type of occupation and by the opportunities such an
education offers.

Of course, the quality of vocational-technological education and
the resources provided for it determine to no less a degree the attitude
of the society towards this type of education. However, in this study
there was an effort to differentiate between the actual situation which
exists in regard to vocational education and the opinions of those
questioned, regardless of the poor quality of the limited technological-
vocational programs in Arab schools. In other words, subjects were

asked to express their opinion regardless of the situation which exists in the school with which they are familiar.

From the attitudes expressed toward work and the contribution of trade to social status, it can be concluded that Arab society in Israel not only does not reject vocational training in the school, but in fact favors it. This conclusion can be reached indirectly on the basis of the findings mentioned above. It would seem, though, that this is not enough to ensure a conclusion of scientific credibility and pragmatic significance. Rather, the conclusion must be directly derived from data which make its formulation unavoidable. The survey, therefore, posed direct questions to parents, teachers, and pupils to determine their positions in relation to vocational-technological education. Table 16 expresses the difference in percentage frequencies in the reactions of

TABLE 16

The Position of Parents, Teachers, and Pupils
in Regard to Vocational Education

	Agree	Disagree	Other	N
Parents	67.1%	30.5%	2.4%	210
Teachers	74.6%	22.4%	3.0%	67
Pupils	58.0%	39.9%	2.1%	396

SOURCE: Sami Khalil Mar'i and A. Benjamin, "The Attitudes of Arab Society Towards Vocational Education," (Haifa: University of Haifa, Institute for Research and Development of Arab Education, 1976).

those examined to the statement: "It's not so terrible if a good student in the academic stream continues in the vocational stream."

In a general way, most of the parents, teachers, and pupils agreed that there is nothing wrong in a good student in the academic curriculum transferring to a technological-vocational course emphasis.

It should be pointed out that the teachers were the most favorable to technological-vocational education (only 22.4 percent did not agree to a good student in academic studies transferring to vocational studies). On the other hand, the position of the pupils was less affirmative than that of parents and teachers (about 40 percent did not view with favor a change from an academic to a vocational curriculum on the part of good students). Apparently, the other two groups, particularly the teachers, were more aware of the potential and the implications inherent in vocational-technological education than were the pupils, who were inclined to identify the pupil in the vocational stream as relatively weak in academic studies.

In order to bring out a clearer and more unequivocal position, the question was made more rigorous, and the subjects were asked to react to the following statement: "A good student in academic studies would be making a serious mistake if he were to switch to vocational-technological studies." Table 17 reveals the distribution of the frequencies of the subjects' responses to this question in percentages. And, in fact, there is a shift to the affirmative. Only 2.5 percent of the parents and 25 percent of the pupils agreed that a successful pupil in academic studies would be making a serious mistake if he were to switch his studies to a vocational course. The teachers, on the other hand, remained unique in this case, too, in that they were even more in favor

TABLE 17

Attitudes Toward Vocational Education

	Agree	Disagree	Undecided	N
Parents	25.2%	72.4%	2.4%	210
Teachers	7.5%	89.5%	3.0%	67
Pupils	25.0%	70.5%	4.5	396

SOURCE: Sami Khalil Mar'i and A. Benjamin, "The Attitudes of Arab Society Towards Vocational Education" (Haifa: University of Haifa, Institute for Research and Development of Arab Education, 1976).

of vocational education than the parents and pupils. Only 7.5 percent of the teachers agreed that a good student in the academic program would be making a serious mistake were he to switch to a vocational program. Here again the teachers demonstrated greater perception and awareness—because of their broader education—than the other groups questioned toward the problems which could stem from an overemphasis on academic studies on the one hand, and the advantages and possibilities of vocational education on the other.

It is noteworthy that although the two items concerning the attitudes toward vocational-technological training in the school differ in their wording, they have a common factor. It was the purpose of the researchers to draw the subjects' attention toward considering a successful student turning from academic to vocational-technological education, for, in general, vocational-technological education is identified with the low-achieving pupils. In this way, an attempt was made to reveal the attitudes of subjects towards vocational education in its broader sense, namely, as an educational quality which offers opportunities other than just providing a framework for the absorption of under-achieving pupils.

A third item in the parents' questionnaire probed their attitudes toward vocational-technological education in a direct personal manner: "What would you advise your child who is in the ninth grade before entering high school?" Four alternatives were provided: to continue in the academic stream; to continue in the vocational stream; to drop out and start working; or undecided yet. Of the parents questioned, 59 percent would advise their children to continue in the academic stream, 34 percent in the vocational-technological one, 5 percent to quit and start working, and 6.5 percent undecided yet. We see, then, that one-third of the parents would advise their children to continue in the vocational stream. This seems a very high and promising proportion considering that vocational-technological education in the Arab schools in Israel is in its beginnings and is still struggling with the most difficult problems of scope, equipment, quality, and diversification.

So far, the subjects' attitudes towards vocational-technological education have been revealed without any consideration, at least not an explicit one, of the current status of the economy and job opportunities. The following is an analysis which was specifically designed to evaluate parents' and pupils' attitudes when they were instructed by the questionnaire/interviewer to consider job opportunities and the economy as far as the Arab in Israel is concerned.

It is clear from Table 18 that when the job opportunities for Arabs in Israel are considered, 42 percent of the parents preferred

TABLE 18

Distribution of Responses of Parents and Pupils as to Attitudes Toward Vocational vs. Academic Programs

	Vocational-Technological Training	Academic Stream	Undecided	N
Parents	42.0%	18.5%	39.5%	210
Pupils	65.7%	28.5%	5.8%	396

SOURCE: Sami Khalil Mar'i and A. Benjamin, "The Attitudes of Arab Society Towards Vocational Education," (Haifa: University of Haifa, Institute for Research and Development of Arab Education, 1976).

vocational-technological training over an exclusive academic program; 18.5 percent preferred academic, and surprisingly, 39.5 percent of the parents could not decide. This is apparently due to the fact that many parents find themselves in a situation wrought with contradictions when it comes to decision making. On one hand, they favor academic programs because of the opportunity for the continuation of their children's education in higher levels and/or because of the possibility that an academic program may lead to an affiliation with office type of work. On the other hand, they are familiar with the difficulties involved in achieving a job such as this and with the many job opportunities available in the technological field. Thus, they found it difficult to decide. However, more than 40 percent of the parents in this study preferred vocational-technological education for their children.

The attitudes of the pupils are expressed in their responses to this item were much less equivocal and more fully appraised. The percentage of those who could not decide was very low (only 5.9 percent). Two-thirds of the pupils questioned preferred a vocational-technological stream over an exclusively academic one when asked to take into consideration the job opportunities available to them after graduation from high school. This fact is important in light of another finding in this survey, namely, that in the opinion of most parents (80.9 percent) and most pupils (72 percent), this decision was in the hands of the pupils themselves (Table 13).

It is worth noting that when parents asked what advice would they provide for their elementary school children, 59 percent responded in favor of the academic stream. These parents were then placed in a position where they had to take existing conditions into account. At that point, their support for academic studies decreased from 59 percent to only 18.5 percent. On the other hand, their support of vocational-technological streams increased. These observations clearly testify to the fact that society's attitudes are not static, but vary by degrees in accordance with living conditions and the possibilities that these conditions allow the individual.

In a summation of the findings of this study, it can be concluded that:

1. Secondary school education in general is highly advocated. The percentage favoring a "drop out and go to work" position is almost zero.

2. The pupils in secondary school (eleventh grade) are the ones who decide about their education, its continuation, and the stream to be chosen.

3. There is a clear preference for work in a trade which is skill based over work in clerical occupations.

4. Parents prefer trade to an office job for their sons, while they prefer an office job and clerical work to a trade involving physical work for their daughters.

5. The acquisition of a trade takes second place (after higher education) as a factor contributing to the improvement of the individual's socioeconomic status.

6. Property owning and Hamoula affiliation are least important among the factors contributing to upward socioeconomic mobility. Moreover, a person's lowly social origins are not thought to hurt his status if he has acquired a good trade.

7. About one-third of the parents are still torn between the heritage of the past and conditions of the present. They are struggling with a situation wrought with contradictions in that their attitudes of esteem and preference towards white collar work are in conflict with the existing conditions of the economy.

8. Both parents and pupils are sensitive to and aware of the present conditions of the economy and the job market, conditions which require a change from positions giving priority to academic studies to those giving priority to vocational-technological training.

9. Overall, not less than half the subjects of this survey preferred vocational-technological streams over exclusively academic ones. If the situation in the Jewish sector is taken as a model, it follows that half of the pupils in the Arab secondary school system should turn to vocational-technological programs provided that these programs are available for them at a comparable quality.

SOCIOECONOMIC CHANGES AND EDUCATIONAL NEEDS

The findings of this survey point to some of the indications of sociocultural change which Arab society in Israel is undergoing. One of the indisputable indications of transition from a traditional to a modern society is the existence of a state of conflict engendered by forces pulling towards the past and forces pushing toward the present and the future. In the case of the survey, the conflict was revealed in the uncertainties of many parents (almost 40 percent) when their traditional values conflicted with existing socioeconomic conditions.

Another indication of sociocultural change reflected by the findings of this study is that society emphasizes the achievement aspects of status more than the ascriptive aspects. Feudalism and Hamoula position were the outstanding indications of socioeconomic status in Arab society until a few years ago when, in general, the distinguished Hamoulas were also the feudalistic clans and the large land owners. However, these are no longer the exclusive or even the principal tokens of socioeconomic status in an ascriptive society. Higher education and the acquisition of a trade have taken the place of feudalistic affiliation and family position, and the two variables of education and occupation are the outstanding status tokens in a modern achievement-oriented society.

A third indication of modernization in Arab society in Israel is expressed in the right and freedom practiced by the youngsters to make decisions concerning their education and their occupational future. In the decisive majority of cases Arab youngsters are the main decision makers, an indication of modernization in the development of a more democratic family atmosphere and interpersonal relation. All this is taking place in a society in which family has traditionally been extremely patriarchal and strictly authoritarian. The father once almost exclusively determined everything concerned with his children, but today apparently he determines the decisions in a relatively minor percentage (15.5 percent) of the cases.

The agreement by most parents to let their daughters work outside the family and the home is also an indication of modernization, since women working outside the family domain is a relatively new development. The type of work preferred by these parents for their daughters testifies to the fact that the changes in attitudes are not uniform and equal in all cases. There is a certain degree of restraint affecting such changes. Thus, when living conditions necessitate changes in attitudes which are in sharp contradiction to a particular value, the attitudes change in a moderate and considered way. Arab parents, then, are opposed to their daughters working at various occupations which are incongruent with the value placed on white collar work. In other words, if a girl goes to work, it is preferable that she be employed in a job within the limits of traditional values, i.e., clerical work.

The high value placed on secondary education by the subjects questioned in this survey is in itself indicative of modernization. There has been a shift in the way education is viewed: in the past, if it was necessary at all, it was only for the sake of acquiring the "three Rs" and some religious training; now the whole process is extended and viewed positively not only as instrumental but intrinsic to the growth of the youngster. Moreover, it can be deduced from this position that the period of adolescence is prolonged. This is an obvious character-istic of a modern complex society, for it is well-known that the more traditional the society, the sharper and more abrupt is the transition from childhood to adulthood.

Finally, the positive shift in attitudes towards skilled labor and vocational-technological education is the most conspicuous indication that Arab society is going through accelerated processes of sociocul-tural change. And these attitudes, in conjunction with the opportunities available in the job market, will sooner or later bring about some far-reaching changes in the occupational structure of the Arab society in Israel, provided that the educational authorities are aware of and responsive to those attitudes expressed in this survey.

It is difficult to establish beyond any doubt why the gap in voca-tional-technological education between Arab and Jewish educational systems in Israel exists. It could be related to the fact that the edu-cational authorities in charge of this educational sphere hold outdated assumptions about Arab society in Israel. If this is the case, one can't avoid the conclusion that should these false assumptions and miscon-ceptions continue to be held, the outcome will be a gradual lowering of the level of relevance of education for Arab youngsters in Israel. And as the educational system becomes outdated, it will become iso-lated from the society it is supposed to serve. Whatever the case may be, one thing is obvious: the need is great and the attitudes are positive for Arab vocational-technological education. As a consequence, in-terest is assured. Therefore, an investment in a vocational-technological educational network in the Arab educational system in Israel is indeed a worthwhile one, at least from the minority's point of view.

The need for quality education in the vocational-technological sphere is becoming more and more intensified as a consequence of two separate yet related trends. The first trend is an external one: job opportunities, in terms of those jobs which necessitate specialized former training in school, are available in the larger Israeli job market. Arabs in Israel are aware of the many opportunities available in the Israeli industrial society, and they are motivated to enjoy them. Through relevant vocational-technological programs schools are an important means by which young Arab can make use of those oppor-tunities. Because they are untrained, however, the masses of Arab youth and adults in Israel are occupying the less prestigious, lower paying, and less secure jobs in construction, restaurants and gas stations.[4] Moreover, these jobs occupied mainly by Arabs are the most sensitive to economic fluctuations in the country. For example, the first to be affected by an economic slowdown is the area of construction, both public and private, thus Arabs are the first to be jobless. By demanding a vocational-technological educational program, Arab parents are expressing a need for employment and economic security for their children.

The other trend is within the Arab society itself. The subordinated class in Arab society, traditionally known as *fellaheen* in the feudalistic days, awakened a long time ago. The society is no longer feudalistic, and farming is no longer the basic source of living. The fellaheen have become workers in the predominantly Jewish cities. They are not dependent on their former masters (landowners) anymore and have a strong ambition to develop and compete with the formerly distinguished class. Occupation is the arena for this competition. An occupational-technological educational program will not help them compete in the job market with majority members, but it is expected to help reinforce the improvement in their socioeconomic status as compared with their former masters within their own society. These internal tensions are being transformed into educational needs—needs which are magnified, of course, by the economic realities in a country where the Arab worker in the Jewish society observes and learns through the cross-cultural situation that a promising way to move upwards on the social ladder is to acquire a technical vocation.

By being at the crossroads of cultures, Arab society in Israel is undergoing many changes and transformations. The Arab educational system in Israel is at these same crossroads and, like the society within which it functions, is being challenged to become more relevant by being more responsive to the needs of the society, represented by a young generation which, for the first time in a few hundred years, is spending thirteen years or more in school. Whereas Arab society in Israel is affected by the cross-cultural situation as revealed by the many cultural and structural changes and transformations, the Arab educational system has been less responsive than Arab society to possibilities for changes. A major part of the reason for this rigidity is that the Arab educational system *is* on the crossroads of cultures, and, as such, the decisions are not made by the recipients of education from the system but by the representatives of the majority culture. And their decisions are based on the way they perceive Arab society and on their convictions and beliefs which are conditioned to a large extent by their background.

One could, of course, observe that majority domination over minority education is universally true. Examples are provided by the cases of black, Indian, and chicano minorities in the United States; the French minority in Canada; the Catholics and Asians in India; the North Africans in France; and the Basque people in Spain. Moreover, this is true to a large extent within Jewish Israeli society itself, which is dominated by the Western-oriented Ashkenazi culture though the non-Western Sephardic Jews are the majority. Like Arabs, Sephardic Jews are also thrown into a cross-cultural situation where another culture is dominant. Consequently, their younger generation constitutes the culturally disadvantaged group in the Israeli Jewish school.

It is clear from the findings of the study reviewed earlier in this chapter that Arab society in Israel is indeed interested in vocational-technological education, not as a substitute for, but as an alternative to academic education. Yet these attitudes in favor of vocational education may not seem consistent with the pattern of preferences among parents, i.e., their preference for academic over technical training. Nevertheless, because of the special situation of the Arab minority in Israel and because of the opportunities existing, yet not available in the Israeli job market, Arab parents and students would prefer to have the option of vocational training in order to avail themselves of such chances for advancement.

Furthermore, this preference for vocational programs expressed by at least 50 percent of Arab parents, is also due to the fact that many academics turn out to be simple workers without any helpful technical skills. The accumulation of frustrating experiences arising from this trend has helped endow education with a pragmatic value in the sense that it should prepare one for a future job rather than be irrelevant and lead nowhere for the many who cannot make it into higher learning institutions. As one Arab parent put it: "If the investment of 13 years in schooling does not lead a person to the university, it should lead him somewhere and not turn the high school graduate into a simple construction worker. . . . Even at this, he cannot compete with those who have not had as much education as he did because they are tough and he is soft for such a job."

TOWARDS AN EQUALITY IN JOB OPPORTUNITIES

The establishment and development of a vocational-technical educational network in the Arab educational system in Israel—both on the qualitative and the quantitative level—is of utmost importance. Such a network would not only contribute to solutions for educational and socioeconomic problems in the Arab sector in Israel, but would also strengthen the processes of integration of the Arab labor force into the wider Israeli economy on an egalitarian basis. Furthermore, development and enrichment of the vocational-technological educational network in the Arab sector would to a great extent prevent the intensification of those dangers which could accompany the appearance of a surplus of academics—a surplus which would be difficult for this society or any society to absorb satisfactorily because of their lack of specific vocational skills.

However, vocational education is often referred to as a "fallacy" in many developing societies.[5] Indeed, it has been discovered that this type of education, while thought of as the solution for the lack of relevance in many educational settings, is a creator of another, possibly more severe social problem. Through vocational education many expectations are created and raised as far as the achievement of jobs which require skills. But soon graduates of technical programs are faced with a frustrating reality: there are no jobs available due to the fact that the process of job creation through industrial development projects has not accomplished the establishment of vocational programs in the schools.[6] In other words, educational planning and industrial and economic development have not been compatible and mutually complementary.

Although in Israel industrial development is blooming and jobs are available for the trained, it is naive to assume that a quality vocational-technological education will solve the Arabs' socioeconomic problems and will meet their aspirations as far as socioeconomic upward mobility is concerned. Although such training is a necessary condition for the Arab in Israel to become integrated on an equal basis into the Israeli economy, it is not sufficient in itself. The equality of educational opportunities is just a necessary step towards equality of job opportunities.

It is this principle of equality in job opportunities between Jews and Arabs in Israel which is so difficult to achieve, for two reasons. One is the often used rationale of *security*. Because Israel and the Arab countries have been involved in a continuous state of war and because Israeli industry and other employment frameworks are involved with security, it follows that an Arab citizen cannot obtain a job because he belongs to the nation with which Israel is at war. This rationale, though it may be understandable, is nevertheless so broad and so fluid that it can be applied to almost any position. Moreover, as justifiable as it may or may not be, the security rationale gives rise to some definite absurdities as far as employment of Arabs in "security loaded" jobs is concerned. An Arab engineer or technician is often barred from obtaining a job in a factory because of security reasons, while the same factory is being guarded all night long by an Arab worker with a gun. It seems, then, that lower ranking jobs are available for minority members even though these jobs are "security loaded." Higher ranking jobs, on the other hand, are less attainable.

While discussing this problem as it negatively affects Arab-Jewish relations in Israel, Dan Shivtan of Tel Aviv University has suggested the following: "Take an Arab engineer for example. After he graduates, what can he do? Can he enter the ultra-modern industry of the State of Israel? Nowadays every modern industry in the State of Israel produces for the needs of defense. Maybe it is not written that in order to be accepted for a job you must not be an Arab. But, after all, if you are an Arab you will face many difficulties in being accepted for a job."[7] Aharon Kleinberger elaborates on the consequences of this apparent inequality of job opportunities and states that:

> The Arab sector itself has no industry and few social and administrative services of its own which can offer white-collar jobs to Arab graduates of secondary schools or universities. In the Jewish sector, social and cultural distance as well as alleged security reasons (which are not infrequently unfounded) and suspicion of Arab loyalty and reliability prevent their employment in any substantial number. In consequence not a few of the educated young Arabs remain unemployed or are forced to accept employment in manual labor. . . . This results in feelings of frustration, bitterness, and reinforced animosity against the State of Israel.[8]

A most inclusive as well as conclusive study of the Arab's economic situation, particularly job opportunities in Israel's economic structure was carried out by Yosef Waschitz of the Kibbutz Giv'at Haviva Institute of Arab Studies. He determined that the Arab labor force in Israel has started and remained as "guest workers" and "commuters." He concluded that:

> The higher we rise in the echelons of employment, the less we find Arabs: in civil service, in the Histadrut administration, on university

staffs. The Advisor for Arab Affairs has made a large effort to open middle and higher echelons of civil services to Arabs. But in general, the government and Histadrut have set the example for the private sector in their reluctance to employ Arabs in key positions in which Jews would be their subordinates. Openly, the reasons given are usually "security considerations". But the reluctance to employ white-collar Arabs in general and the fact that Arabs are employed in constructing security installations, seem to indicate a problem of status, not of security.

To sum up: Arabs are climbing, exasperatingly slowly, the institutional ladders of public institutions. They compare the snail's pace of their advancement with the avenues open to Jews—quick advance, taking part in decision-making, self-fulfillment. All this is denied to most Arabs, especially the well educated ones.[9]

It is clear that the security rationale is applied indiscriminately to "security loaded" and to "security free" positions, thus depriving Arabs of the many existing job opportunities for which they qualify. The results of such deprivation are usually expressed in an estrangement from the state and its institutions, more polarization between the Arab and the Jewish sectors, and, most important of all, a feeling of despair as far as Arab-Jewish coexistence in Israel is concerned. As an indicator of this feeling, more than 50 percent of Arab youth, questioned in a late study by John Hofman, thought that they did not have any future in Israel.[10] They felt that because of existing inequalities and trends the possibilities of fulfilling their future professional aspirations were dim.

These economic, social, and political dynamics usually operating under the "security" considerations rationale are reinforced by another, yet no less powerful element in the process of depriving Arabs of equal opportunity. Indeed, Arieh Luva Eliav, a Knesset member of the majority ruling labor party, claims that due to a continuous and extensive reliance on Arab labor in Israel, Jewish society is becoming a society of bosses. The very basic values upon which the pioneers created the state of Israel are being neglected and reversed as younger Israeli Jewish generations relinquish the idea of labor to become masters of laborers. Eliav claims in *Land of the Deer*[11] that this is the most poisonous thing that could happen to the Jewish society in Israel. It is not only inhumane and unjust, but it is also harmful to Israeli society itself.

Moreover, Eliav in a later book[12] suggests that the Arab minority in Israel, through its labor force in the Israeli economy, is being manipulated in such a way as to solve some inconsistencies within the Israeli Jewish society. Thus, with Arab labor forces at the lower level, the Israeli Jewish Sephardic labor force occupies the middle, and the Ashkenazi maintains itself in the highest level of the occupational structure. The minority is being manipulated to serve as an outlet for the lowering of tensions existing within the two Israeli Jewish subcultural groups. Any noticeable changes in the direction of more equality of job opportunities between Arabs and Jews in Israel, although not expected to bring back the pioneers' values, would certainly shake the structure of the Israeli Jewish society and mean a reorganization of the occupational structure so that more Arabs could move up likely to be from the Sephardic group, a result which would intensify the job hierarchy. Fewer Jews would be privileged, then, and those are the already existing tensions within the Jewish society in Israel.

Nevertheless, although it may be difficult to implement the principle of equal job opportunities, it does not seem impossible. Lessening tension and conflict within Israeli Jewish society opened up and magnified the conflict between Arab and Jewish societies in Israel—a conflict by no means isolated from the larger one in the Middle East. Moreover, the maintenance of relative stability within Jewish society by reinforcing the status quo might quiet down potential social conflicts between the two Israeli Jewish subcultural groups. However, a situation of relative, yet superficial stability would not eliminate these tensions and conflicts caused by inequalities within Jewish society itself. And it is not illogical to expect that any sense of political stability, in the case of peace or even the absence of war, could help excite conflicts within Israeli Jewish society.

Finally, although some of the difficulties encountered by Arab society and education in Israel are attributed to the existing conflict between the Arab nation and Israel, it is also true that other conflict-independent socioeconomic forces within Israel are contributing to the amount and scope of the problems encountered by the Arab citizen in Israel. It seems that Arab minority status is becoming more and more dependent not only on political dynamics in the Middle East, but also on internal socioeconomic dynamics within Israel. And these problems are most likely to continue even when a Middle East peace settlement becomes real.

In conclusion, it is clear from the discussion presented in this chapter that Arab education in Israel is at the crossroads of cultures. It is influenced by the socioeconomic forces and cultural transformations which are taking place within Arab society itself; it is affected by political and socioeconomic dynamics operating within Jewish society; and it is sensitive to the cultural and political movements in existence within the Arab world in general and among Palestinians in particular. Arab education is caught in the middle of this triangle. The quality and direction of change in any of these dimensions will not only influence Arab education in Israel but will also, to a large extent, determine the political, cultural, and socioeconomic conditions in the lives of Arabs in Israel.

Education
at the Crossroads of Cultures

EDUCATION AND SOCIAL CHANGE

CHANGE IS probably the most profound yet commonplace characteristic of our time. As it contrasts with prevailing tradition, however, change is most apparent in developing societies and takes place in two forms: *intentional* and *unintentional*. In its intentional form change is introduced by social and political agencies and institutions in developing societies as they aim at modernizing their industry, agriculture, social and health services, and political institutions. In developing societies, represented mostly by new nation-states, intentional change can be easily observed in the offensive and defensive functions of the military institution as a strong token of and extension to nationhood and statehood.

Change may also be unintentional. These subtle, mostly invisible forces of change penetrate deeply into the structure and culture of a society, in spite of the barriers of politics and ethnicity. These forces are found mostly in the framework of human relations on both the interpersonal and intergroup levels. It is also elicited through other means, most important of which are the mass media, especially those which utilize the audio-visual form. When people from a traditional background interact with others from a more developed one, change is bound to take place. While both are affected by such interaction, sociocultural change is more noticeable among the less modernized group.

In its intentional form change is planned and highly publicized. It is usually imposed, or at least forcefully induced, by the social planner. Indeed, change is direct intervention with the cultural values and lifestyles of the communities to which it is introduced. Because of its purpose and planning, this form of change—which may range from technical assistance to family planning—has been repeatedly studied in order to understand its dynamics and to evaluate its impacts.

In its unintentional form change is not only unplanned and not imposed, but also subtle and spontaneous. As such, it takes place without much self-awareness, it simply happens to people. It is this very spontaneity, or the lack of direct intervention from forces of government and social agencies in the lives of people, which makes the unintentional forces of change penetrate gradually yet powerfully into the culture and structure of society. Change which is unintentional has received much less attention from social scientists than intentional change, because of its lack of purpose in terms of predefined objectives, the unspecific nature of such change, and to the fact that, unlike planned change, it takes place at no cost in terms of investments. Nonetheless, a careful investigation of the unintentional forces of change and their impact is expected to reveal more effectiveness of and less resistance to change and its manifestations than has been consistently reported in situations of intentional change.

Arabs in Israel demonstrate a case of the power of unintentional forces of change. It is found in the framework of Arab-Jewish relations and interactions which take place on a day-to-day basis. Tens of thousands of Arab workers commute daily to and from the predominantly Jewish urban centers where they are employed in construction, services, and industry. More than any other factor these workers are agents as they carry the seeds of change to their communities and families. While mutual hostilities, prejudices, and stereotypes are rarely reduced or even weakened through such an interaction between Arabs and Jews in Israel, change does take place. Spontaneous forces of change are powerful in spite of the hostile framework of the interaction. The forces of change penetrate and deeply influence Arab society in Israel in spite of political and ethnic barriers.

In such a sociopolitical setting change takes place not *in spite* but *because* of the hostilities and tensions existing between the Arab minority and the Jewish majority in Israel. A deep sense of competition—national, cultural, and economical—seems to be emerging among Arabs in Israel. This driving force to "make it," a motivating factor to prove a point politically, economically, and educationally, demonstrates the organic link between modernization and nationalism. Indeed, while the less modern Arab society becomes more modern by borrowing the agricultural techniques and adapting the values and patterns of behavior found in the more modern Jewish society, the Arab national identity becomes more crystallized and distinct. The process of cultural adaptation is counterbalanced by a process of cultural and ethnic differentiation. This can also be observed among non-Western Jews in Israel, the more modernized they become, the more they appear a distinct social and political entity within the pluralistic social framework in Israel.

The unintentional forces of modernization have a great impact upon the culture and structure *within* Arab society in Israel: Interpersonal relationships within the family are far more democratic than before; the level of intellectual functioning is improving; females are becoming more independent; the extended family is fading out; status and power are being redistributed in favor of the formerly oppressed farming class, now the working class; social and cultural tensions are commonplace; the culture is dynamic rather than static; a sense of nationalism is being re-established; and, more than at any time in its history, the educational system is challenged to be relevant and functional in the sense that it must accompany, if not lead, this overwhelming and all-embracing process of modernization.

The educational institution seems locked into the traditions of the past however, and it appears to have lost the ability to step out into the drama of changes in culture and structure. This can be observed in the extreme rigidity of the pattern of authoritarianism which governs all relationships in the educational hierarchy: in supervisor-principal relationships; in principal-teacher relationships; and, most important of all, in teacher-student interactions, whether in the traditional, obsolete teaching methods or in other modes of interaction.

It is universally true that the educational institution, by nature, is usually a conservative more than a modernizing force. One of its basic functions is passing on tradition and cultural values, as well as perpetuating existing structures and distributions of power and privilege. As such, the educational institution enforces tradition rather than promoting change, and the Arab school in Israel is no exception.

Those young teachers who are university graduates and have interacted with members of the more modern majority on both individual and group bases are also a force of change. Unlike Arab workers in Israel, Arab university students are more aware of change and are committed to modernization. Those who become teachers, however, are hardly recognizable as change agents, for they often reduce their commitment to change the whole system to better ways of transmitting more information. Here a political factor intervenes, blocking those elements from producing a noticeable change in the educational system. To function as a committed and effective modernizing force in the school setting, Arab teachers in Israel have to devise ways through which they can deal with issues relating to nationality and national identity— issues which are inseparable from the dynamics of modernization. These issues are within the realm of taboo in the Arab school in Israel, and the expression of nationalistic feelings endangers the teachers' job security and chances for mobility, as they are government employees. Teachers often find refuge and security in tradition, embodied in this context by the educational institution. As Dean McCannel suggests, in its deep structure modernity is a totalizing idea.[1] This means that to be modern and to promote modernization is to be placed in a position which totally opposes the forces of tradition. The political dynamics and pressures at play in the life of Arab teachers in Israel condone tradition, thus while the teachers are indeed at the crossroads of cultures, a tendency towards traditionality rather than modernity prevails among them.

Modernity as a totalizing idea does not only place modern man in opposition to traditional forces and entities, it also brings about a whole new mentality which touches every institution in a society. Tribalism is transformed into individualism, and then into nationalism. Like other social institutions among Arabs in Israel, the educational system is influenced by these forces. Yet in terms of a modernizing force this influence is not carried to the school through the central educational authorities; neither is it borne by teachers. Arab students themselves, on both the elementary and secondary levels, are emerging as a driving force of modernization in the educational institutions.

In the elementary school, where corporal punishment is commonplace, the active and in some cases violent refusal to be punished is commonplace, too. More than any time in the past, children are expecting to be treated and respected as individuals. As their individuality is encouraged in their modernizing families, they expect the school to relate to them as individuals worthy of respect. Secondary school students, often guided and encouraged by their parents and community leaders, are demanding curricular quality and relevance from their teachers. Through their national executive committee Arab secondary school students are emerging as powerful groups which exert pressure upon the educational institution. The latter, however, not only fails to recognize and support them, but also opposes them as a force which threatens the myth of stability and status quo. It is expected that in due time young university educated male and female Arab teachers will be the first group to depart from the traditional force in order to join the modernizing one to achieve personal and professional fulfillment. The totalizing effect of modernization for the students who are current consumers and future providers of educational services, more than any other group, will have a great impact in the liberation of education from the bonds of traditionalism.

MULTICULTURALISM AND EDUCATION

Multiculturalism is a process through which a person develops competence in several cultures.[2] In culturally heterogeneous societies such as Israel, multiculturalism is necessary as individuals move in and out of the varying cultural contexts. Multicultural competence should involve the ability to communicate with, understand, and participate in cultural frameworks other than one's own. It implies the development of linguistic proficiency and the acquisition of knowledge about other cultures within the same sociopolitical framework. It is only natural to assume that the school is the ideal place where multiculturalism can and should be undertaken.

Israeli society is heterogeneous. Its heterogeneity stems not only from the existence of the Arabic and Jewish cultures side by side, but also from the existence of the rich cultural variety of ethnic Jewish groups who immigrated from different countries. Israel has the background and the potential for multicultural education. In fact, for society in Israel multiculturalism in education is not only appropriate, but it is also necessary. This necessity arises from the need for cultural competence within the different Jewish cultural frameworks and the Arab and Jewish cultural entities. In general, other benefits of multiculturalism in education are not lacking: It greatly increases the relevance of educational content and experiences; it fosters cultural democracy; it is a safeguard against racism, cultural chauvinism, and misplaced ethnocentrism; and it eliminates the chances of cultural imperialism.[3] Indeed, multiculturalism is prescribed as the most desirable form of social organization.[4]

While Israeli society is highly suited to multiculturalism in education, the Jewish educational system has fallen into the trap of monoculturalism which overlooks the cultural variations within the Jewish society itself. A careful investigation of the cultural origins of teachers and their distribution within schools, communities, and the educational hierarchy, coupled with an investigation of curricula and the school culture in the Jewish educational system, reveals a definite bias favoring Western Ashkenazi culture over that of the non-Western Sephardi group, which comprises more than half of the Jewish population in Israel. Furthermore, while curricula in Jewish schools tend to overlook Sephardic Jewish culture, history, and contributions, these curricula also ignore Arabic language and culture at a time when Arabs in Israel have to study Hebrew language and literature as well as Jewish history and culture.

The basic goal of Jewish studies in Arab education is not the development of cultural competence as much as it is to make Arabs understand and sympathize with the Jewish cause. The ultimate outcome is undoubtedly the acquisition of cultural competence by Arabs not only in the Jewish culture, but also in their own. The extensive study of the Hebrew language helps the Arabs communicate with majority members, and the study of Jewish history and culture, which is heavily an extensive ethnography of the Jewish minorities and their struggle in their diaspora, is being transformed by Arabs into effective strategies in their own efforts to cope with their status as a national minority. While the goal is to blur the Arab national identity in Israel, Arabs are achieving multicultural competence, and at the same time their national identity becomes more and more distinct, for multiculturalism does not lead to assimiliation nor does it blur ethnicity and nationality.[5]

Why then has the Jewish educational system fallen into the dangerous trap of monoculturalism? Israel is not alone in this trap; it is joined by many developing countries and newly created nation-states. In our times, dramatic examples of monoculturalism can be seen in the newly created nation-states in Asia and Africa. Furthermore, Arturo Pacheco suggests that "mass schooling and the development of loyalty to the newly formed nation-state via the idea of citizenship seem to go hand in hand, especially in those cases where new political boundaries enclose regions marked by tribal, ethnic, and language diversity."[6]

After thirty years of existence, the Jewish educational system has helped create a linguistic amity among the different Jewish ethnic groups. Now, more than at any time in its history, the Jewish educational system in Israel is challenged to step out from the narrow limits of monoculturalism into the drama of cultural varieties in and around Israel. Through the promotion of multiculturalism in Jewish education the potential dangers inherent in the emergence of cultural supremacy can be avoided. Jewish young generations will instead enhance their competence in a heterogeneous cultural setting. The Jewish educational system can learn from the experience of multiculturalism in Arab schools that it did not blur the national identity even though it meant to do so. As peace becomes imminent in the Middle East, if Israel wants to integrate into the area culturally and socially and make the peace meaningful and lasting, it has to provide its young generation with competence in the Arab culture.

By the same rationale, eliminating Jewish studies in the Arab school curricula in Israel is *not* advocated. However, the aims of such studies should be changed from blurring the pupils' identity to the achievement of competence. This, of course, necessitates changes in the Arab school curricula. Instead of celebrating monoculturalism, education in Israel should emphasize multiculturalism in a sensible balance and a harmonious manner. If "there is no one model American," it is equally true that there is no one model in Israel.

EDUCATION AND THE POLITICS OF PLURALISM

Multicultural education is an educational philosophy transformed into policies, strategies, practices, and learning contents in school settings which promote competence in more than one cultural context. Cultural pluralism refers to social structure and organization. Multiculturalism and pluralism are interdependent in the sense that both refer to a heterogeneous society; the first implies cultural differences, and the second connotates structural gaps parallel to those cultural differences. Culturally different groups are often distributed differently on the social ladder on a group (or cultural origin) basis.

Pluralistic societies try to achieve what Toqueville has labeled *democratic pluralism,* a process through which political participation takes place on a group, rather than individual basis. Democratic pluralism also implies that a balance of power exists between different ethnic groups as they participate in the political and decision-making processes. In the United States, the legacy of democratic pluralism has existed for over a hundred years without fully achieving its promise of a balanced political and socioeconomic power. Indeed, democratic pluralism has recently come under severe criticism as fallacious,[7] colonialistic, and exploitive in nature.[8] Norris Brock Johnson suggests: "Plural societies do not evolve through collective effort and socio-cultural consenous . . . [they] are the product of conquest. . . . Plural societies are neither integrative, representative, participatory, nor democratic."[9]

These criticisms have led to the emergence of the concept of multiculturalism as a more positive and more promising principle because it implies cultural quality rather than structural gaps. While pluralism implies limited cultural sharing and interaction, multiculturalism fosters those without placing culturally different groups on lower or higher steps of the social ladder. As appealing as it is, however, multiculturalism alone can not be expected to solve problems evolving from the pluralistic nature of a society. The organizational and structural dynamics in a society are at least as important and influential as its cultural composition in determining the extent to which equality prevails. In societies where minorities are not legally and ideologically excluded or deprived, there are groups which are still in a position best described as a subordinate.

For a variety of reasons, the Arab minority in Israel has very little, if any, political power. The authorities, through direct or indirect measures, have suppressed the minority's efforts to become politically organized, and most Israeli political parties do not accept Arabs as full members. As a consequence, the Arab minority cannot exert political pressure to achieve a better status and influence the decision-making process to lessen existing gaps in educational and economic opportunities. Political decisions are made for the Arab minority by majority members and/or institutions. The Arab Education Department is directed by members of the Jewish majority, and curricula are decided upon by the authorities with little, if any, participation of Arabs. Arab participation does not exceed writing or translating books and materials according to carefully specified guidelines, nor does it extend beyond implementing the majority's policies.

Arab education is a victim of Israeli pluralism not only in that it is directed and managed by the majority, but it is also a tool by which the whole minority is manipulated by a powerful reward and punishment system, based on the quality of political behavior rather than the merit of Arab teachers. The Arab educational system is not only an example of the Israeli pluralism by which Arabs are denied power, it is also a means through which the lack of power can be maintained and perpetuated. Arab citizens are marginal, if not outsiders. While the religious, secular, and socialistic sociopolitical trends in the Jewish society have resulted in autonomous educational systems, the Arab educational system in Israel is fully controlled by the majority's representatives. This is due to the peculiar nature of pluralism in Israel.

De jure, Israel is a Jewish state; *de facto,* it is not. Fifteen percent of the population is Arab. Within the Jewish sector there is a fair share of political power and a satisfactory level of educational autonomy. Although most education is secular, the religious and the Kibbutz educational systems, while separate, are neither underfinanced nor controlled by members from outside their respective groups. Unlike Arab education, these systems are equal within the majority's society.

The inconsistency between the legal and ideological conceptions of the state of Israel as Jewish and Zionistic and the existence of an Arab minority puts the Arabs in a rather peculiar position. By definition Arab citizens are alienated culturally and politically from the state and its institutions. While such an inconsistency is not expected to disappear, it affects the quality of Jewish-Arab relations in Israel.

When peace becomes a reality in the Middle East, Arabs in Israel can be expected to demand more relevance from the state and its institutions. In times of peace they are expected to be the first to interact economically and culturally with the Arab peoples around Israel. The Arabs in Israel are expected to step out from their alienated, excluded, and relatively passive position to share power and become active in the cultural, economic, and sociopolitical life in Israel. In order to do that, however, pluralism in Israel has to be legally and ideologically redefined to include the Arab group on an equal footing.

APPENDIX A

An Arab and a Jewish Student Argue
on "Land Day"

BLOOD IS THE RANSOM OF THE LAND

A Voice Calling in Sakhnin

by Sa'id Zeedani

THE "LAND DAY," March 30, is engraved deep in our memory; a day that is impossible to pass over in silence. This is a day that took thought out of the shell of the daily routine. This is a day in which blood was spilled. On this day, the language was stones and shots. A day in which blood is spilled in a different day, absolutely different. When you hear somebody talking furiously, this is one thing. When you see a human being lying without a spirit, this is another thing. The difference is not only in your stream of thought—it is in what you sense, in what you feel about the whole matter. Logic is paralyzed. Feeling speaks. The tongue becomes dumb. The hand, and what is in its reach, speak!

The "Land Day," as planned, was a day of a general strike. People did not go to work, did not leave their homes if possible. Stores were closed. Obviously, it was a difficult day. This is a *strike,* not a party or a formal ceremony. Such a day is difficult even for those who did not buy cigarettes before. This was an exceptional day. A strike is to emphasize, to draw the utmost attention to the center of pain, to the limb from which pain spreads to the other parts of the body. A day of strike is a day of general groan, a silent one. Politically, this is a protest against a wrong that has been, or might be, done. This is what was planned for the "Land Day."

THE OFFENSIVE OF THREATENING

However, theory and practice are different things. Threats were heard. Painful declarations were heard; declarations like needles. This hurt the Arabs. When you are convinced that your cause is just and, at the same time, you hear all sorts of threats, your rage is multiplied twice or three times. Con-

SOURCE: Both articles from *Pesek Z'man*, May 5, 1976.

183

tractors, ministers, chairmen of local councils, inspectors of the ministry of education, labor councils' officials—all of them took part in the offensive of threatening and frightening people who believed in the justice of their cause. Threats are not effective, persuasive arguments. Those who threatened have to reconsider how to deal with a problem which touches the heart of a nation.

OCCUPATION FORCE

They scattered salt on the wounds. The frontier guards entered the villages. In fact, this took place after the demonstration; their function was to restore order; to prove the existence and strength of democracy. In principle this is true. But what I cannot accept is: why make the citizens feel (even if they are Arabs) that the frontier guards are a hostile force? When they entered the village, people felt that they were occupational forces. "Occupational forces," this precisely describes the feeling of the Israeli Arabs as they caught sight of the tanks and the police forces that entered the villages. The caravan began to move slowly (for those who have not seen weapons this was their opportunity!), exactly like an occupational force—this was the general feeling. Hypothetically speaking, had the frontier guards not intervened nothing would have happened. No blood would have been spilled. The frontier guards provoked the people who were on strike, who demonstrated and gathered. This is the whole truth. Besides, the very presence of security factors itself constitutes provocation. This is because it was the first time that they entered the villages in such magnitude. The villagers are not used to such a sight.

THE THEORY OF THREATS

The intervention of the security forces was the armed actualization of the theory of threats (written as well as oral) which preceded the day of strike. In this respect, at least, the policy was very consistent! The logical reasoning was, without the least doubt, valid. The inevitable practical conclusion was the use of force. However, we have to remember that consistency is not always a guarantee for truth, and does not validate any moral argument. In brief, the policy (in theory and in practice) was consistent but mistaken and immoral.

OBSTINACY VERSUS MORALITY

The theory of threats was not only supported by weapons but also by another doctrine, the doctrine of lying and forgery. They claimed that most of the Arab workmen appeared in their workshops; that the silent majority are against the strike. They talked a lot about "incited" and "inciters" who belong to the minority camp. The mass media took part in the ritual of throwing dust in the eyes, in the ritual of falsifying facts, all of this to justify the rightness of a policy that is nearly bankrupt. In order to deceive, they talked about the major role of RAKAH, (Communist Party) about the role of the extremists (by the way, this term requires a redefinition in the light of what has occurred), who heated the atmosphere, to be more precise, who damaged the "texture of the relations" between Arabs and Jews. What is this unceasing stream of deception an evidence of? It is an evidence either of naivety or of adherence to obstinacy even at the expense of morality and truth. When the police minister talked before and after the strike, as an Arab, you sensed that he belongs to the camp which advocates a consistent policy more than a moral one.

THE MORAL

In the press, in the cabinet, they try to analyze what has happened, they try to learn the lesson. They contend that the extremists had the upper hand. We have to strengthen the positive camp and to outlaw RAKAH. This was the advice of Mr. Amnon Leen. There are those who advise to stretch the long arm of security even more, and simultaneously, to cure minor wounds in the Arab sector. The significance of what happened, sirs, is simple, very simple. The Arab became aware of three basic things: (1) the game of democracy; (2) never to give up his rights, in particular when this concerns his lands; and (3) a more profound apprehension of the axiomatics of conflict. This means the Arab understood that he had to take risks, to sacrifice, in order to get what he deserves or to keep what he has.

LAND-NATIONAL SYMBOL

In addition to these three principles that were present to the consciousness of the Arab, he started to realize that his relation with the land is a relation of life, of dignity, of nationality. The land is not only an economic treasure. The economic value is not the crucial constituent in the attitude of the Arab toward the land. The land is the highest value. It is a symbol of the first grade, a symbol for remaining in the country, a symbol for his identity with a broad nation. In the eyes of the Arab, the land is a national symbol, rich in life; perhaps one of the richest symbols that he knows in his history. How did the land become such a symbol? This is a different story.

EXPROPRIATION AS MONSTER

This is a story that involves the modern Arabic literature; this is a story which is connected with a vocabulary of occupying Arab lands, of settlements, of annexation, of Judaizing, and of expropriation. Each of these terms has its own history. But collectively they contributed to the constitution of the symbol of the land. "Expropriation!" This is the ugliest monster in the eyes of the Arab. This is the Greek "Medusa" in his eyes. He must, once and for all, break it; cut off its head at any costs. The Arab understood this symbolism. For this reason he was on strike, he demonstrated, and threw stones; and for this reason he was ready to die. This symbolism escaped the attention of the government officials. Their basic mistake was they confused the land as an economic concept with the land as a symbol. The necessary conclusion is: the leadership (in the language of Romanticism) lacks some imagination!

THE LAND DAY IS NOT A REBELLION

What occurred on the Land Day was not a rebellion. "Rebellion" contains not only description but also evaluation, exactly like the term "extremist." What happened in the Land Day is, simply, a genuine emotional response, an overflow of an emotional feeling, a sincere and furious expression of a feeling that existed; which was hidden in the inner recesses. What happened was the discharge of the burden of pain and suffering. The Arab wanted to say explicitly, openly, and directly, even though rudely: Stop! The land is mine; I am hers, and it is impossible to separate us. Between me and the land there is an eternal vow. If blood is the price, with blood she will be ransomed. The land is my bride; I am her bridegroom!

Realize this, sirs. This is the significance of the events in Sakhnin and the other villages. This is the meaning of the oracle of Sakhnin. This is the implication of the voice that cried in Sakhnin.

A FIFTH COLUMN—NOT IN ISRAEL

Sakhnin, Araba, Tayba—The State of Israel or Fatah-land?

by YOVAL PELEG

More than a month passed since the "Land Day." A short period has been devoted for summaries and evaluations by the two sides. Articles have been written, speeches have been delivered, and everything in a logical manner and in pure thought. Then "A Voice Calling in Sakhnin" comes and takes us back to that day. To that day in which feeling, anger, and plain, and unfortunately, the hand and all that was at hand, spoke.

I give myself leave to raise some thoughts about that day. I admit that I wasn't in Sakhnin on that day. I did not see anybody lying dead before my eyes. But I saw by means of the mass media the violence which celebrated the existence of a wide gap between Jews and Arabs.

I saw the "desire for murder" in the eyes of children and adults. I heard the "battle cries" of the incited crowd, and the savage desire to break, to destroy, and to damage everything Jewish, and, for the sake of change, also moderate Arabs who cooperated with "the enemy." Yes, this is the appropriate word. The state, the government, the military, every Jew was an enemy on that day. In the name of the "holy land" and the stable democracy, the Arabs were called upon to hit the enemy mercilessly.

Opposite them, I saw the young policemen and soldiers, standing, excited because of what they saw. There was no desire to kill within them. The will to damage was not in their hearts. I saw the hesitations of the commanders, their attempts to rescue people without causing damage, the tremendous desire to prevent bloodshed. I saw the great pain which accompanied the order to fire in the air.

I saw thousands of rioters running after a small group of soldiers who were looking for a place to hide between the rocks. I wondered in my heart how great the moral strength which prevents them from acting feelingly in the way that anger dictates.

I understood that they did not consider these people "enemies." They were not in the battlefield, they were not an "occupational force," and not a hostile power, they were the men of the law and they considered the people as citizens of the state. They were the arm which was put to action against citizens of the state who put themselves out of the state for one day.

A strike is a democratic weapon, but the "Land Day" was not a day of strike. It was a day of riots, a day of hatred on a national basis, a day of attempting to take the Arab minority out of the body of the state. The Galilee, the Triangle and every footstep of land in this country, whether under Arab or Jewish ownership, is a part of the body of the state. Whenever an intentional attempt is made to damage the integrity and sovereignty of the state, the government must act, and it acted rightly. It acted in the only way that the rioters left for it to act.

The police forces and the military had no choice to act otherwise, they did not initiate the incidents, they did not burn tires, they did not enter the villages in processions of victory. They came in order to prevent bloodshed, in order to rescue the soldiers who were attacked by thousands of demonstrators. They used their weapons only when their lives were in danger.

They did not "occupy" villages, they recoiled. They were distant from any touch with the rioters. Is this the way of an "occupational army?" They did not come as an occupational force, because there is nothing to occupy. Sakhnin, Araba, Tayba, and the rest of the villages are the state of Israel.

They are neither the south of Lebanon nor Fatah-land. Any attempt to disturb life, to harm order, necessitates intervention. If words, persuasions, the appeal to logic are rejected, nothing is left but to use force. This is painful. This is cruel, but it is necessary.

The shout "All of us are PLO" which we heard on that day has still its echo in my ears. This was not only a shout from the mouth but a wish in the heart. The organization of the murderous terrorists will not exist in the State of Israel. We won't let this vicious octopus wave its flags in our state. Anyone who joins its lines risks his own life.

The land is a symbol, as you say. March 30 was also a symbol; a symbol of hate, a day in which the mask was removed, the veil was removed from your faces. It is good that such a day, a day of truth, has come. No more hate in the eyes, no more curses in the back, but proudly and violently, the Arabs, the citizens of the state, expressed themselves. If this is the prophecy in their mouths, our answer will be accordingly—a fifth column will not exist in our state.

I am not accusing RAKAH. But without your readiness and that of your friends, its malice would not have succeeded. It gave the reason, it supplied the instruments to inflame the feelings, but you, and only you, chose violence to express your feelings.

You might reject what I have said on the ground that this is falsification of the facts. But I have testimonies of Arabs, the citizens of those villages, who say that the security forces were self-restrained, and that the policemen acted neither against those who worked nor against those who were on strike, but only against those who rioted, those who damaged public property, those who provoked.

I also think that they acted with great self-restraint. Maybe a stronger hand, a hand which would suffocate violence, is the only appropriate response against inciting and unrestrained rioting. If, after all, you are ready to be my friend, the way is still open for a life of cooperation and brotherhood, and the "holy land" can be transformed to a meeting place for Arabs and Jews. But this was not the way you took on that hurried and bitter day, the day of feeling and revenge.

The Study of Minority Education

A MINORITY is an ethnically distinct group which is outnumbered by another within the same political framework. As such, the minority is usually weaker than the majority, regardless of the sociopolitical philosophy prevailing in a country at a given time. The minority is also more vulnerable to control and manipulation by the majority, which usually controls the power structure whether by democratic vote or by totalitarian doctrine.

Problems of minorities are especially acute in liberal democracies where their expectations stemming from an ideological framework of equality and freedom are usually not fulfilled because of the socioeconomic and political forces which function in a direction opposed to that of the ideology. It is this very contradiction between ideology and reality which makes minority-related problems so serious in liberal democracies. Ideology is transformed by the minority into expectations and aspirations related to socioeconomic equality. These aspirations, in turn, are translated into behaviors aimed at the achievement of such equality and its attendant mobility. The need for cheap labor and, in any industrial society, for untrained or semitrained manpower to perform certain tasks which are physically hard and psychologically painful, become conscious or unconscious forces which often limit minority group members to the lowest standards of achievement.

Because of their inherent lack of power to dominate or to successfully resist domination by others, minorities are usually manipulated to fulfill the needs of the majority. Manipulation takes place, for the most part, within the frameworks of economy, education, and politics—frameworks which are not isolated from each other but are interdependent. Efforts by the minority to improve its status should take into consideration not only these frameworks, but also their interdependence. For example, a minority's struggle for equality in educational opportunities is often inseparable from its quest for equality in economic opportunities and political power. A strength or a gain in political power or in economic situations will, in turn, bring about further improvements in education. It follows that any effort to thoroughly understand one aspect of a minority group's life, (e.g., education) should necessarily include a comprehension of other aspects (i.e., political status, cultural values, and economic situation).

Historical perspective is of special importance to the study of minorities, especially if both the majority and the minority were once involved in a conflict resulting in the domination of one group by another. When such a conflict is not resolved (by a mutual settlement or even by voluntary or forced concession of one group to the other), much of the quality and dynamics of intergroup interaction can be attributed to the lack of resolution. In this case the minority is defined by the majority as a potential, if not actual, enemy.

When the existence of a minority implies a potential or actual threat to the majority and its institutions, behavior and attitude towards the minority are shaped by the majority's need to establish a sense of security. This sense of security is weakened when the minority is enemy affiliated. Manipulation of and control over the minority becomes intensified, and socioeconomic and educational deprivation and inequalities are rationalized in terms of security. The majority's need for such security along with its need for reliance on the unskilled labor provided by the minority reinforce each other in a vicious cycle. In a situation where control for the sake of security and manipulation for the sake of economic advantages are prevalent, interdependent, and often interchangeable, it is difficult to explain many aspects of minority existence in terms of cause-effect relationships.

These difficulties often manifest themselves in education since the minority group member and the majority group member are ethnically different, and each reflects and expresses a unique perspective. This poses a methodological problem with regards to the explanation of findings in studies which compare a minority and majority on different variables: Are the differences found a function of ethnic differences or the result of the respective status of the majority and the minority in a given political framework? Ethnic uniqueness and status are undoubtedly interrelated. A minority's status often becomes an integral part of its culture, and self-concepts, values, attitudes, and behaviors appear which are difficult to differentiate from "original" cultural manifestations.

Minority status is not determined solely by the majority's policies and behaviors; it is a function of the interaction between the minority's internal characteristics and the majority's intentions. A group's original culture determines to a certain extent its status as a minority, and that status exhibits perceptions, attitudes, and beliefs which have been internalized to become part of the minority culture. Cultural strength and political solidarity of the minority are extremely helpful in maintaining a better status. The very interrelation, and even interchangeability, between ethnicity and status of a minority makes it difficult to explain phenomena in the minority's life.

The study of minority-related variables does not only require an understanding of other aspects of the minority's life, but it should also rely on a knowledge and comprehension of the majority's cultural, socioeconomic, and political dynamics and structures. The mere terms *minority* and *majority* imply that each is relative to the other not only numerically but culturally, socially, and politically. In any pluralistic society there are patterns of interdependence, even though direct interaction might be minimal. Thus, any study of a minority must be *cross-cultural* in nature, or it is not a study of minority.

A minority can be studied without comparison to the majority. In this sense, the minority is treated as a "closed system," and when treated as such the objective is not the study of those variables related to the fact that a group is a minority; the objective is rather to study nonminority-related variables of an ethnic group which happens to be a minority. When this is the case it is very difficult to isolate and separate variables in a minority's life which are not influenced by the group's minority status; though it is still possible to study the effects of minority status or the impacts of interaction with the majority on processes (i.e., socialization and child rearing) and structures (i.e., family or social class). The minority group is not treated here as a *minority* (in relation to the majority) as much as it is dealt with as an *ethnic* group interacting with another. The significant aspect of a group studied from this perspective is its ethnicity and its interaction with other groups, rather than its minority status in relation to the majority's situation and conditions. This approach in studying an ethnic group, which happens to be a minority, as a closed system is called, in Pike's terminology, the *emic* approach.[1] Berry and Dasen have elaborated on this approach by suggesting that it studies behaviors, processes, and structures from within the system; it examines only one culture; and criteria by which evaluations are conducted are relative to internal characteristics only.[2]

It has already been stated that a study of an ethnic group as a minority, emphasizing this very characteristic as an independent variable upon which many others are dependent, is cross-cultural or cross-ethnic and comparative in nature. This statement does not mean that all cross-cultural research deals with minorities in relation to their respective majorities. Nevertheless, it seems that minority-majority comparative studies do tend to satisfy the methodological conditions for cross-cultural research set forth by Berry and Dasen, who suggested that in order to be methodologically sound, cross-cultural research must meet three conditions. First, there must be functional equivalence, which means that the functions or goals of the systems and/or behaviors studied should be similar at least to a degree which allows comparisons. Second, a conceptual equivalence in the concepts and tools applied or used must be established. And third, metric equivalence of the evaluation of the variable studied across cultures must be achieved. This last condition applies only to quantitative studies, for qualitative research and analysis necessitates phenomenological (essential or structural) equivalence, a condition which is difficult to satisfy.

In the study of minorities in relation to their respective majorities within the same political context it is easier to satisfy these conditions than it is to compare Western and non-Western cultures, which is the dominant pattern of cross-cultural research in the social sciences. This ease in establishing the different kinds of equivalence in the case of minority-majority comparisons is due to the fact that, while each group is unique, both live within the same political and socioeconomic frameworks. In other words, as Berry and Dasen have suggested, it is only after certain common characteristics are established that the detection of differences becomes methodologically possible. A minority and a majority share common characteristics in the functions and goals of institutions (i.e., educational, economic, political) and in their exposure to certain stimuli and/or situations (i.e., common familiarity with objects to be used as testing tools).

In contrast to the emic approach which focuses on the internal characteristics of a culture, the approach of studying certain variables across cultures was termed by Pike as *etic*. Comparing two or more cultures, this approach studies institutions, behaviors, and processes from a position outside or between the systems. Phenomena are measured and evaluated by criteria which are relatively universal or common to the two or more cultures being studied. While this approach allows for generalizations and strives for universality in the conclusions reached by research, it is also expected to be appropriate, from a methodological point of view, in the evaluation of minority status and achievements in relation to the majority. What makes the etic approach appropriate for the study of minorities is that it is comparative and cross-cultural by definition. As such, the etic approach uses common rather than relative or internal criteria.

The study of minorities increases the understanding of majorities. Many of the dynamics, processes, and ideologies of the majority influence the minority, and in a pluralistic setting, the structure and culture of a majority can best be exposed, analyzed, and evaluated through the study of the minorities' status in relation to the majority. Immediately after the creation of Israel in Palestine, Dr. Chaim Weizmann, the first president of Israel, emphasized this point when he warned that the world will judge the newly created Jewish state on how it treats its Arab minority.

Notes

Chapter 1—Background of Arab Education in Israel

1. Jacob M. Landau, *The Arabs in Israel: A Political Study* (Tel Aviv: Ma'arochout, 1971) (Hebrew). I have preferred to rely on the Hebrew version of this book, although it was published in English under the same title by The Royal Institute for International Relationships and Oxford University Press, London, 1969. The Hebrew version is improved and updated and was published by Ma'arachout, the publishing house of Israel's Ministry of Defense, in 1971.

2. *Ibid.,* p. 19.

3. Sabri Jeries, *The Arabs in Israel* (Haifa: Al Ittihad Printing House, 1966). Jeries quotes many Knesset (Israeli Parliament) members and decisions of political organizations opposing military administration, including the right-wing Cherout party and many Israeli Jewish lawyers' opposition to the philosophical basis of the "emergency law" from which military administration draws its legality.

4. Aharon Cohen, *Israel and the Arab World* (Tel Aviv: Sifriyat Po'alim, 1964), p. 510 (Hebrew).

5. Rustom Bastouni, "The Arab Society in Israel," *Hamizrah Hehadash* (The New East) 15(1 & 2)(1965) (Hebrew).

6. Landau, *The Arabs in Israel,* p. 18.

7. *Ibid.,* pp. 18–19.

8. *Ibid.,* p. 91.

9. Sami F. Geraisy, *Arab Village Youth in Jewish Urban Centers* (Ann Arbor: University Microfilms, 1971).

10. Aharon F. Kleinberger, *Society, Schools, and Progress in Israel* (London: Pergamon, 1969).

11. J. A. Beegle and R. Rice, "Some Demographic Characteristics of Rural Youth"; and C. E. Black, "Family Backgrounds of Rural Youth," *Rural Youth in Crisis,* ed. L. G. Burchinal, (Washington, D.C.: U.S. Department of Health, Education, and Welfare, 1965).

12. Louis Wirth, *On Cities and Social Life* (Chicago: University of Chicago Press, 1964).

13. Yousef Waschitz, "Commuters and Entrepreneurs," *New Outlook* 18(7) (1975).

14. Jeries, *The Arabs in Israel*, pp. 70–75.

15. Landau, *The Arabs in Israel*, p. 19.

16. Abner Cohen, *Arab Border Villages in Israel* (Manchester: Manchester University Press, 1965), p. 20.

17. E. Stock, *From Conflict to Understanding* (New York: New York Institute for Human Relations Press, 1968), p. 20.

18. Jeries, *The Arabs in Israel*, p. 143, Table 4.

19. Geraisy, *Arab Village Youth*, p. 82, Table 9.

20. Cohen, *Israel and the Arab World*, p. 532.

21. This section on education in Palestine during the last few decades of the Turkish Empire is based on Butrus Abu-Manneh, "Some Aspects of Ottoman Rule in Syria in the Second Half of the 19th Century" (Ph. D. diss., Oxford University, 1971).

22. Sami Khalil Mar'i, "The Education of Minorities in Israel," *Journal of Christian Education* 14(2)(1971).

23. This section on Arab education in Palestine is based on the extensive study of Abdullatif Tibawi, *Arab Education in Mandatory Palestine* (London: Luzac and Co., 1956).

24. Kleinberger, *Society, Schools, and Progress in Israel*, p. 14–15.

25. Dr. Khalil Totah's views are presented in Abdullatif Tibawi, *Arab Education in Mandatory Palestine* (London: Luzac and Co., 1956).

26. Moshe Smilansky, ed., *Child and Youth Welfare in Israel* (Jerusalem: Henrietta Szold Institute, 1966), pp. 71–72.

27. Kleinberger, *Society, Schools, and Progress in Israel*, p. 30.

28. This section is based on Sami Khalil Mar'i and Nabih Daher, *Facts and Trends in the Development of Arab Education in Israel* (Haifa: The University of Haifa, Institute for Research and Development of Arab Education, 1976) (Hebrew). The book is a demographic analysis of Arab student population and teachers on all levels of the educational hierarchy, which uses a comparative approach of Jewish education in Israel and data based on the *Statistical Abstracts* published yearly by Israel's Central Bureau of Statistics (1949–1975).

29. Abdullah Abdul-Daim, *Education in the Arab World* (Beirut: Dar El'Ilm Lilmalayeen, 1974), pp. 28–30 (Arabic).

30. Salim Nashef, *Education on the West Bank* (Tul-Karm: College of Agriculture, 1973).

31. Emanuel Kupileivitch, "Education in the Arab Sector: Facts and Problems," *Education in Israel* (Ministry of Education and Culture, 1973), p. 331 (Hebrew).

32. *Ibid.*, p. 329.

33. Israel Bureau of Statistics *Statistical Yearbook*, 1974, Table 6/22, p. 613 (Hebrew).

34. *Ibid.*

35. Israel Ministry of Education and Culture Division of Curricula, "The Regional Pedagogical Center in Service of Teachers" (Jerusalem, May 1975) (pamphlet).

Chapter 2—School and Society in Arab Villages in Israel

1. David Reisman et al., *The Lonely Crowd* (New Haven: Yale University Press, 1950).

2. Carl Frankenstein, *Psychodynamics of Externalization—Life from Without* (Baltimore: Williams and Wilkins, 1968).

3. Henry Rosenfeld, *They Were Peasants* (Kibbutz HaMequchad, 1964) (Hebrew).

4. Abner Cohen, *Arab Border-Villages in Israel* (Manchester: Manchester University Press, 1965).

5. Rosenfeld, *They Were Peasants*, pp. 74–93.

6. Y. Ben Porat, *Arab Manpower in Israel* (Jerusalem: Morris Falk Institute of Economic Research in Israel, 1966).

7. A general discussion of the cultural factors involved in the tension existing in the Arab village can be found in Henry Rosenfeld, *They Were Peasants* (Kibbutz HaMe'ouchad, 1964) (Hebrew).

8. Rustom Bastuni, "Arab Society in Israel" *Hamizrach Ha Hadash* (*The New East*) 15(1 & 2)(1965) (Hebrew).

9. Carl Frankenstein, *Poverty, Disturbance and Primitivity* (Jerusalem: Mosad Szald, 1956) (Hebrew).

10. Dr. Yohanan Peres investigated the national identity of the young generation in Arab society and found that compartmentalization was expressed in the existence of "Arabness" along with and separate from "Israeliness," without these two components adapting to each other to emerge in a more integrative identity. See Yohanan Peres, *Aspects of Arab Education in Israel* (Research Report, Department of Sociology, Hebrew University, 1970), which presents evidence of a conflict between traditionalism and modernity expressing itself in contradictory behavior.

11. Jacob M. Landau, *Arabs in Israel, Political Studies* (Tel Aviv: Ma-archot, 1971) (Hebrew).

12. Abullatif Tibawi, *Arab Education in Mandatory Palestine* (London: Luzac, 1956).

13. From personal correspondence with Professor Abullatif Tibawi, London, a supervisor of Arab schools during the period of the British Mandate.

14. R. McGee, "Education and Social Change," *On Education—Sociological Perspective,* ed. D. A. Hausen and J. E. Gerstel (New York: John Wiley, 1967).

15. Clarence E. Beebey, *The Quality of Education in Developing Countries* (Cambridge: Harvard University Press, 1966).

16. Sami Khalil Mar'i, "The Education of Minorities in Israel," *Journal of Christian Education* 14(2)(1971):95–104.

17. During the last few years we have witnessed an attempt to face the problem. This is expressed primarily in the establishment of an Advisory Committee to the minister of education under the chairmanship of the deputy minister. The conclusions of this committee were published November 2, 1972, in a stenciled document: "Basic Trends in Arab Education." Another attempt to meet the problem was the discussions and activities of the Committee for Planning of Arab Education in the Eighties, and a third attempt followed the October 1973 War and the perplexing situations which teachers found themselves in with their

pupils. The Arab Department in the Ministry of Education attempts, with the cooperation of elements in the ministry and outside it, to meet the problem by initiating and activating educational experiments in the field. The focus of these experiments is the social-civic education of Arab pupils in Israel in the general context of the political situation in the Middle East.

18. Similar factors accelerated the processes of modernization in the American village. See Burton W. Kreitlow, *Community Backgrounds of Rural Education* (New York: Harper, 1954).

19. Frankenstein, *Psychodynamics of Externalization,* pp. 144–45.

20. H. D. Lasswell, "The Social Setting of Creativity," *Creativity and its Cultivation,* ed. H. H. Anderson (New York: Harper, 1959).

21. *Israeli Statistical Yearbook,* 1972.

22. In the Arab educational system, unlike the Jewish system, the distinction between the kindergarten teacher and the school teacher is not unequivocal. Most of the kindergarten teachers work also as school teachers and their official status is that of school teacher.

23. Many parents as well as teachers (especially veteran teachers from the time of the mandate) expressed bitterness and disappointment at the fact that there is play in the classroom. In former times school was more "serious," and playing went on only outside or in the street. Sometimes children were even forbidden to play in the street, especially in areas where teachers were in the afternoons.

24. Eli Saltz, *The Cognitive Basis of Human Learning* (Homewood, IH.: Dorsey, 1971).

25. Usually the male teachers ask the fathers to come to school on Parents' Day, and the female teachers ask the mothers. The general opinion of headmasters, teachers, and parents is that the mothers seem to respond to these invitations much more than fathers, perhaps because it has been the practice of the women in the village also to take upon themselves tasks outside the narrow framework of the home.

26. James S. Coleman, *Equality of Educational Opportunity* (Washington, D.C.: U.S. Office of Education, 1966).

27. Christopher Jencks, *Inequality: A Reassessment of the Effect of the Family and Schooling in America* (New York: Basic Books, 1972).

28. On tensions in the Arab village see Rosenfield, *They Were Peasants,* pp. 73–77.

29. One of the serious difficulties in the investigation of social status in the contemporary Arab village is the state of social-cultural transition. The ascriptive criterion is not valid because the society is no longer feudalistic, nor would the achievement criterion be reliable since the society is not yet modern. It seems that rural Arab society is at the height of the process of transition from an ascriptive society to an achievement-oriented society. There is overlapping, therefore, between clan and class, but obviously they are not identical any more.

30. For additional reading on the utilitarian and immediate approach to life see Paul Radin, *Primitive Man as Philosopher* (New York: Dover, 1957); and J. H. Copp, "Family Backgrounds of Rural Youth," *Rural Youth in Crisis* ed. L. G. Burchinal, (Washington, D.C.: U.S. Department of Health, Education and Welfare, 1965).

31. Frankenstein, *Poverty, Disturbance and Primitivity.*

32. Carl Frankenstein, *The Roots of the Ego* (Baltimore: Williams and Wilkins, 1966), p. 180.

33. Yohanan Peres, "Nationalist Education of Arab Youth," *Megamount* 16 (1)(1968) (Hebrew).

Chapter 3—Goals, Policies, and Administrative Status

1. Raymond Williams, *The Long Revolution* (New York: Columbia University Press, 1961).

2. Julia Evetts, *The Sociology of Educational Ideas* (London: Routledge and Kegan Paul, 1973), p. 127.

3. Aharon Kleinberger, *Society, Schools and Progress in Israel* (London: Pergamon, 1969), p. 123.

4. Emanuel Kupileivitch, "Education in the Arab Sectors: Facts and Problems" in Haim Ormian, ed., *Education in Israel* (Jerusalem: Ministry of Education and Culture, 1973), p. 326 (Hebrew).

5. *Law of State Education, 1953*, para. 34 (4), quoted in Joseph S. Bentwitch, "Arab Education in Israel," *New Outlook* 6(6)(July–Aug. 1963):19–23.

6. *Ibid.*

7. Kupileivitch, "Education in the Arab Sectors," *Education in Israel*, p. 325.

8. *Ibid.*

9. Bentwitch, "Arab Education in Israel," *New Outlook* 6(6)(July–Aug. 1963):20.

10. Israel, Ministry of Education and Culture, "Basic Goals in Arab Education: Conclusions of the Advising Committee Healed by the Deputy Minister, Mr. Aharon Yadlin, and Accepted by the Minister" (Jerusalem, February 11, 1972), p. 1 (mimeograph in Hebrew).

11. *Ibid.*

12. Israel, Ministry of Education, *Report of the Committee on Arab Education for the Eighties* (Jerusalem, 1975).

13. *Ibid.*, p. 13.

14. *Ibid.*, p. 14.

15. Bentwitch, "Arab Education in Israel," *New Outlook* 6(6)(July–Aug. 1963):22.

16. Rustom Bastouni, "Arab Society in Israel," *Hamizrah Hehadash* (*The New East*) 15(1 & 2)(1965):2 (Hebrew).

17. *State Controller*, Annual Report, No. 15 (1965), p. 106. Quoted in Sabri Jeries, *The Arabs in Israel* (Haifa: Al-Ittihad, 1966), p. 139, footnote 3 (Hebrew).

18. *Haaretz*, April 4, 1961 (independent Hebrew newspaper). Quoted in Jeries, *The Arabs in Israel*, p. 139.

19. *Yedi'out 'Aharonout* December 12, 1975 (Israeli Hebrew evening newspaper).

20. Diab El-'Obeid, Speech to the Knesset, November 11, 1972, p. 1–2 (mimeographed in Arabic). This speech can also be found in the Knesset Records of the same period.

21. Diab El-'Obeid, Speech to the Knesset, April 25, 1972 (Arabic).

22. Kupeleivitch,"Education in the Arab Sector," *Education in Israel*, p. 329.

23. *Al-Hamishmar*, July 6, 1976.

24. Mahmud Biadsi, "The Arab Local Authorities: Achievements and Problems," *New Outlook* 18(7)(1975).

25. Kupileivitch, "Education in the Arab Sector," *Education in Israel*, p. 330.

26. Kleinberger, *Society, Schools and Progress in Israel*, p. 317.

27. Israel, Central Bureau of Statistics, *Bulletin of Educational Statistics*, No. 19, June 1969, p. 15 (Hebrew).

28. Kleinberger, *Society, Schools and Progress in Israel*.

29. Khalil Nakhleh, "Nationalist Consciousness and University Education in Israel" (1976) pp. 16–17.

30. The current mayor of Nazareth (1978), Tawfik Zayyad, is a member of the Communist party. Without the tremendous support of the "academics," he could not have been elected. His deputy is a representative of the academics.

31. Nabih El-Kasem, *The Reality of the Druzes in Israel* (Jerusalem: Dar-El-Aitam, 1976), pp. 184, 236 (Arabic).

32. Kleinberger, *Society, Schools and Progress in Israel*, pp. 129–30.

33. *Ibid.*, p. 125.

Chapter 4—Curricula

1. Israel, Ministry of Education and Culture, *Proposals for Curricula in Secondary Schools* (Jerusalem: Department of Secondary Education, 1957) (Hebrew); idem, *Curriculum for Arab Secondary Schools* (Jerusalem: Department of Education for Arabs, 1968) (Arabic).

2. Yohanan Peres, A. Ehrlich, and Nira Yuval-Davis, "National Education for Arab Youth in Israel," *Race* 12(1)(July 1970):151.

3. Mahmood Me'ari, *A Comparative Survey of School Curricula in the Arab Sector in Israel*, A Supplementary Report to the Final Report of the Committee for the Planning of Arab Education for the 1980s (Jerusalem, January 1975), p. 34 (Hebrew).

4. See note 1, above. The goals quoted here are based upon the translation of the official goals by Peres et al., "National Education for Arab Youth in Israel," *Race* 12(1)(July 1970):153–154.

5. *Ibid.*, p. 48.

6. Joseph S. Bentwich, "Arab Education in Israel," *New Outlook* 6(6)(July, August 1963):19–23.

7. *Ibid.*

8. Peres et al., "National Education for Arab Youth in Israel" *Race* 12(1) (July 1970):161.

Chapter 5—The Segregation-Integration Issue

1. A discussion of the gaps in education, housing, and economic status, between Western and Oriental Jews in Israel is presented in Chapter 7, "Problems of

Equality," in Aharon Kleinberger, *Society, Schools, and Progress in Israel* (London: Pergamon, 1969).

2. Moshe Smilansky, "Coping of the Educational System with the Problems of the Disadvantaged," in H. Ormians, ed., *Education in Israel* (Jerusalem: Ministry of Education and Culture, 1973) (Hebrew).

3. Kleinberger, *Society, Schools, and Progress in Israel.*

4. *Ibid.*

5. Yehuda Amir, "Contact Hypothesis in Ethnic Relations," *Psychological Bulletin* 71(5):319–42.

6. L. Freedman, *Public Housing: The Politics of Poverty* (New York: Holt, Rinehart and Winston, 1969).

7. For the Chinese case see D. Y. Yuan, "Voluntary Segregation: A Study of New York Chinatown," *Phylon* 24(3):255–66; for the American Indian case see A. Lesser, "The Right Not to Assimilate: The Case of the American Indian," in M. H. Fied, ed., *Readings in Anthropology, Vol. 11: Cultural Anthropology,* T. Y. Cornwell, (New York, 1968), pp. 583–93.

8. Kleinberger, *Society, Schools, and Progress in Israel.*

9. Amir, "Contact Hypothesis in Ethnic Relations," *Psychological Bulletin* 71(5):319–42.

10. Carl Frankenstein, *The Liberation of Thinking from its Bonds* (Jerusalem: The School of Education, Hebrew University, 1973) (Hebrew).

11. Erick Cohen, *Integration vs. Separation in the Planning of a Mixed Jewish Arab City in Israel* (Jerusalem: The Hebrew University, The Levi Eshkol Institute for Economic, Social, and Political Research, 1973), p. 18.

12. *Ibid.*

13. *Ibid.,* p. 7.

14. *Ibid.,* p. 9.

15. *Ibid.,* p. 12.

16. Abraham Benjamin, *Experiment in Co-existence: Ma'alot-Tarshiha* (Jerusalem: The American Jewish Committee—Israel Office, 1975).

17. *Ibid.,* p. 9.

18. *Ibid.,* p. 17.

19. Cohen, *Integration vs. Separation,* p. 17.

20. John Hofman, "Readiness for Social Relations Between Arabs and Jews in Israel," *Journal of Conflict Resolution* 16, (2)(1972):247.

21. Benjamin, *Experiment in Co-existence,* p. 7.

22. Hofman, "Readiness for Social Relations," *Journal of Conflict Resolution* 16(2)(1972):244.

23. *Ibid.,* p. 247.

24. *Ibid.*

25. Yohanan Peres, "Arab-Jewish Relations," in John Hofman, ed., *Proceedings of the Convention on the State of Research on Human Relations Between Arabs and Jews* (Haifa: University of Haifa, 1971), p. 10 (Hebrew).

26. *Ibid.,* p. 13.

27. John Hofman, "Readiness for Social Relations Between Arabs and Jews in Israel, 1975" (Haifa: University of Haifa, Institute for Research and Development of Arab Education, 1976) (Hebrew) (research report).

28. Dan Shivtan, "Arab-Jewish Relationships," in Hofman, *Proceedings,* p. 38.

Chapter 6—Higher Education

1. John Hanson, *Imagination and Hallucination in African Education* (East Lansing: Institute for International Studies in Education, Michigan State University, 1965).

2. UNESCO, *Annual Yearbook*, 1968–1969, Table 12.2.

3. L. G. Gowan, *Education and Nation-Building in Africa* (New York: Praeger, 1965), p. 140.

4. Hanson, *Imagination and Hallucination*.

5. Abdullah Abdulda'im, *Education in the Arab World* (Beirut: Dar-El-Ilm Lilmalayeen, 1974) (Arabic).

6. Carl Cross, "The Agony of Japanese Higher Education" (Michigan State University, 1970) (mimeograph).

7. Research devoted to the issue is abundant: Mary Ann Bowman, "An Economist's Approach to Higher Education," *International Review of Education* 16(3)(1970); M. Peston, "Toward an Economic Theory of Higher Education," *Higher Education Review* 10(1968); G. Psacharopolos, *Results of Education: International Comparison* (London: Elseview, 1973).

8. Harold Howe, "The Value of College: A Non-Economist's View," *Educational Record* 57(1) (Spring 1976).

9. Sami Khalil Mar'i, "A Study of Higher Education in Three Split Villages Between Israel and the West Bank," *Hamizrah Hahadash* (The New East) 26(1 & 2)(1976) (Hebrew).

10. Israel Bureau of Statistics, Jerusalem, 1972, 1973, 1974.

11. Salim Nashef, "Education on the West-Bank" (College of Agriculture, Tul-Karm, 1972) (mimeograph).

12. Sami Khalil Mar'i and Nabih Daher, *Facts and Trends in Arab Education in Israel (1947–1976)* (Haifa: University of Haifa, Institute for Research and Development of Arab Education, 1976).

13. Yohanan Peres, A. Ehrlich, and Nira Yuval-Davis, "National Education for Arab Youth in Israel: A Comparison of Curricula," *Race* 12(1) (July 1970).

14. Abraham Benjamin and Rachel Peleg, "Vocational Aspirations of Arab High School Seniors and Their Social Implication" (Haifa: University of Haifa, Institute for Research and Development of Arab Education, 1976).

15. Ben Meir, *Crisis in Israeli Society* (Jerusalem: Karta, 1973) (Hebrew).

16. Sami Khalil Mar'i, "Scholastic Achievement of Arab High School Pupils in Israel" (Haifa: University of Haifa, Institute for Research and Development of Arab Education, Haifa, 1977) (research report).

17. Mary Ann Bowman, "An Economist's Approach to Higher Education," *International Review of Education* 16(3)(1970).

18. Harold Howe, "The Value of College: A Non-Economist's View," *Educational Record* 57(1)(Spring 1976):9.

19. Jacob M. Landau, *The Arabs in Israel: Political Studies* (Tel Aviv: Ma'arachout, Israel's Defense Army, 1971) (Hebrew).

20. *Ibid.*, p. 66.

21. Khalil Nakhleh, "Cultural Determinants of Palestinian Collective Identity: The Case of the Arabs in Israel," *New Outlook* 18(7)(1975):38.

22. Eli Reches, "Changes in the Attitudes of Arab Intellectuals in Israel Since 1967" (Lecture given at the Shiloah Institute, Tel Aviv University, March,

1976). The lecture is summarized and translated into Arabic by A. El-Sa'di and published in the Arabic journal *Al-Intilak* (Jerusalem: Arab Department of the Labor Party, July 1976), p. 11.

23. *Ibid.*

24. *Ibid.*, p. 10.

25. *Ibid.*, pp. 10–11.

26. Khalil Nakhleh, "Nationalist Consciousness and University Education in Israel" (Haifa: University of Haifa, Institute for Research and Development of Arab Education, 1976), p. 101 (research report).

27. Sa'id Zeedani, "Blood is the Ranson of the Land," *Pesek Zman* (May 5, 1976) (Hebrew).

28. Yuval Peleg, "Fifth Column—Not in Israel," *Pesek Zman* (May 5, 1976), p. 5 (Hebrew).

Chapter 7—Student Variables

1. Sami Khalil Mar'i, "Scholastic Achievement of Arab Secondary School Students in Israel and on the West-Bank" (Haifa: The University of Haifa, Institute. for Research and Development of Arab Education, 1976).

2. *Ibid.*

3. John Hofman, "Readiness for Social Relations Between Arabs and Jews in Israel," *Journal of Conflict Resolution* 15(2)(1972).

4. Mar'i, "Scholastic Achievement of Arab Secondary School Students in Israel and on the West Bank."

5. Benjamin S. Bloom, et al., *Taxonomy of Educational Objectives: The Cognitive Domain* (New York: Longmans, 1956).

6. Elhanan Meir, Saul Solberg, A. Barach, "A Cross-Cultural Comparison of the Structure of Vocational Interests," *Journal of Cross-Cultural Psychology* (4)(1973).

7. Abraham Benjamin and Rachel Peleg, "Vocational Aspirations of Arab High School Seniors and their Social Implications" (Haifa: University of Haifa, Institute for Research and Development of Arab Education, 1976) (Hebrew).

8. Abraham Benjamin and Rachel Peleg, *The Arab Student and the University* (Tel Aviv: Am-Oved Publishers, 1976) (Hebrew).

9. Hofman, "Readiness for Social Relations Between Arabs and Jews in Israel," *Journal of Conflict Resolution* 15(2)(1972).

10. John Hofman, "Readiness for Social Relations Between Arabs and Jews in Israel" (Haifa: University of Haifa, Institute for Research and Development of Arab Education, 1976) (Hebrew).

11. *Ibid.*, Table 1.

12. Benjamin and Peleg, *The Arab Student and the University.*

13. Benjamin and Peleg, "Vocational Aspirations of Arab High School Seniors and their Social Implications."

14. *Ibid.*, p. 10.

15. *Ibid.*, p. 36.

16. *Ibid.*, p. 6. For recent empirical studies on the attitudes of Jews toward

Arabs see Abraham Benjamin, "Sensitivity Workshop for Arab and Jewish Students" (Jerusalem: American Jewish Committee, 1970 (Hebrew); Kalman
Benyamini, "The Image of the Israeli, the American, the German, and the Arab
in the Eyes of Israeli Youth," *Megamout* 16(4)(1969) (Hebrew); Z. Austervil
and Z. Grinbuem, "The Attitude of Israeli Jews Towards Arabs: A Comparison of
Three Measures," *Megamout* 18(3)(1972).

17. H. Lindgren and F. Lindgren, "Creativity, Brainstorming and Orneriness:
A Cross-Cultural Study," *The Journal of Social Psychology* 67(1965):23–30.

18. Sami Khalil Mar'i, "The Creativity of American and Arab Rural Youth:
A Cross-Cultural Study," *Studies in Education* 1(1)(1972) (Hebrew).

19. Sami Khalil Mar'i, "Creative and Critical Thinking Abilities of Arab
Youth In Israel and on the West-Bank" (Haifa: University of Haifa, Institute for
Research and Development of Arab Education, 1977).

20. Paul Torrance, *Thinking Creatively with Words* (Minneapolis: Personnel
Press, 1966); Paul Torrance, *Thinking Creatively with Pictures* (Minneapolis: Personnel Press, 1966).

21. R. Ennis, "A Concept of Critical Thinking," *Harvard Educational Review*
32(1)(Winter 1962):8–111.

22. Bloom et al., *Taxonomy of Educational Objectives.*

23. J. W. Getzels and P. W. Jackson, *Creativity and Intelligence* (New York:
Wiley, 1962).

24. Paul Mussen, "Early Socialization: Learning and Identification," in G.
Mandler et al., eds., *New Directions in Psychology III* (New York: Holt, Rinehart,
1967).

25. Sami Khalil Mar'i, "Towards a Cross-Cultural Theory of Creativity,"
Journal of Creative Behavior 10(2) (Second Quarter, 1976).

26. Joel Shanan, "The Tendency for Active Coping: A Basis for Mental
Health," *Megamout* 15 (1967) (Hebrew).

27. Joel Shanan and H. Sharon, "Personality and Cognitive Functioning of
Israeli Males During Middle Years," *Human Development* 8 (1965).

28. Joel Shanan and S. Nisan, "Sentence Completion, A Tool for Personality
Assessment," *Megamout* 77(3)(1961).

29. Joel Shanan, "Educational, Social, and Psychological Adjustment of
Immigrants in their First Year" (Jerusalem: Hebrew University, 1973) (report).

30. T. Naftali, "Patterns of Coping in Adolescents" (Master's thesis, The
Hebrew University, Jerusalem, 1973).

31. Sami Khalil Mar'i and Mohammad Manna', "Active Coping Behavior of
Arab Youth in Israel and on the West Bank," *'Eyyunim Bechinnuch* (*Studies in
Education*) (11)(1976) (Hebrew).

Chapter 8—The Changing Socioeconomic and Political Conditions

1. Arieh Luva Eliav, *Israel's Ladder* (Tel-Aviv: Zemura, Bitan, Modern Publishers, 1976) (Hebrew).

2. Sami Khalil Mar'i and A. Benjamin, "The Attitudes of Arab Society To-

wards Vocational Education," (Haifa: University of Haifa, Institute for Research and Development of Arab Education, 1976). The author assumes full responsibility for the data and interpretations presented herein.

3. Abraham Benjamin and Rachel Peleg, "Vocational Aspirations of Arab High School Seniors and Their Social Implications" (Haifa: University of Haifa, Institute for Research and Development of Arab Education, 1976) (Hebrew).

4. Yousef Waschitz, "Commuters and Entrepreneurs," *New Outlook* 18(7) (Oct.–Nov. 1975).

5. John Hanson, *Imagination & Hallucination in African Education* (East Lansing: Michigan State University, Institute for International Studies in Education, 1965).

6. P. J. Foster, "The Vocational School Fallacy in Development Planning" (Chicago: University of Chicago, Conference on Education and Economic Development, 1963).

7. Dan Shivtan, "Arab-Jewish Relations in Israel," in John Hofman, ed., *Proceedings of the Convention on the State of Research on Arab-Jewish Relations* (Haifa: University of Haifa, 1971), p. 38 (Hebrew).

8. Aharon Kleinberger, *Society, Schools & Progress in Israel* (Oxford: Pergamon Press, Ltd., 1969), p. 320.

9. Waschitz, "Commuters and Entrepreneurs," *New Outlook* 18(7)(Oct–Nov. 1975):47–48.

10. John Hofman, "Readiness for Social Relations Between Arabs and Jews in Israel," *Journal of Conflict Resolution* 16(2)(1972).

11. Arieh Luva Eliav, *Land of the Deer* (Tel Aviv: Am Oved Publishers, 1972).

12. Arieh Luva Eliav, *Israel's Ladder* (Tel Aviv: Zemorah, Bitan, Modern Publishers, 1976) (Hebrew).

Chapter 9—Education at the Crossroads of Cultures

1. Dean McCannel, *The Tourist* (New York: Shocken, 1976).

2. Norris B. Johnson, "On the Relationship of Anthropology to Multi-cultural Teaching and Learning," *Journal of Teacher Education* 28(3)(May–June 1977): 10–15.

3. *Ibid.*

4. Arturo Pacheco, "Cultural Pluralism: A Philosophical Analysis," *Journal of Teacher Education* 28(3)(May–June 1977).

5. Ward Goodenough, "Multiculturalism as the Normal Human Experience," *Anthropology and Education Quarterly* 7(4)(1976):4–6.

6. Pacheco, "Cultural Pluralism: A Philosophical Analysis," *Journal of Teacher Education* 28(3)(May–June 1977):17.

7. William E. Connolly, ed., *The Bias of Pluralism* (New York: Lieber-Atherton, 1973).

8. Johnson, "On the Relationship of Anthropology to Multi-cultural Teaching and Learning," *Journal of Teacher Education* 28(3)(May–June 1977).

9. *Ibid.*, p. 11.

Appendix B—The Study of Minority Education

1. K. L. Pike, *Language in Relation to a Unified Theory of the Structure of Human Behavior* (The Hague: Mouton, 1966).

2. J. W. Berry and P. R. Dasen, "Introduction: History and Method in the Cross-Cultural Study of Cognition," in J. W. Berry and P. R. Dasen, eds., *Culture and Cognition: Readings in Cross-Cultural Psychology* (London: Methuen, 1974).

Index

Aba-Hushi, 100–101
Abdel-Nasser, Gamal, 125
Abduldaim, Abdullah, 107
Academics (Arab): as political power, 64, 198n30; surplus of, 168
Acre, 12, 95–99
Administration: of Arab affairs, 55–58; of Arab education, 55–60; 65–69
Arab Departments: separate, 55–56; rationale for, 66; critique of, 66–67
Arab Education Department: creation of in 1948, 19; Director of, 19, 23, 58; closing of suggested, 58; politicization of, 64; Arabization of suggested, 65; blocks innovations, 66; and vocational programs, 148–49
Arabists, 55, 57–58
Ashkenazim: and rejection of Arabs, 103; higher education among, 109; scholastic achievement of, 132; cultural dominance of, 167; and the occupational structure, 171; culture of favored, 178
Aspirations, vocational, of Arab students, 136–38
Assimilation, and secularism, 55
Autonomy in education: lack of under Turkish rule, 5; under British mandate, 17; under Israeli authority, 19; demands for, 27; as an alternative in education, 67–69

Bagrout (matriculation exam): and curriculum, 86; and intellectual abilities, 112–13; and university admission, 113; chances of passing, 124–25; national test, 132; gaps in between Arabs and Jews, 133; analyzed, 134; biases of, 135
Baka-al-Gharbieh, 60
Balfour, Arthur J.: Declaration of, 16; visiting Palestine, 17
Barach, A., 136
Bar-Ilan University, 124
Benjamin, Abraham, 99–101, 112, 136–38, 152–54, 158–61
Ben Meir, 112
Bentwitch, Joseph E., 51–52, 54, 86
Berry, J. W., 191
Biadsi, Mahmud, 60
Bible, and curriculum, 85
Bowman, Mary-Ann, 119
British evacuation of Palestine, 2

Carmiel, 6
Christian Schools: in Great Syria and Palestine, 10–11; status and significance of, 10, 13, 17; under Israeli rule, 61–64; autonomy of, 61–63; and Moslem students, 61–62
Clan (*see also* hamula): weakening of, 32; and modernization, 32; and

205

feudalism, 32; and political parties, 33; and teachers, 33, 37; and military administration, 33
Classrooms: crowded, 24; need for, 24; shortage in, 59
Cohen, Erik, 95–97
Coleman, James, 43
Committee on Arab Education: formation of, 53; reaction of to Yadlin Document, 53; suggestion of, 53–54; and vocational education, 150
Communist Party (see also Rakah): popularity of, 13; and academics, 198n30
Compulsory education: Law of, 18; enforcement of, 19–20
Confiscation (of land): and security, 6; and Judaization, 6; and Carmiel, 6–7, 26; and Upper-Nazareth, 6–7, 26; students against, 124, 127; debated, 183–88
Coping ability: of Arab youth, 142–44; and modernization, 142–43; and minority status, 142–43
Corporal punishment: use of, 31; students' refusal of, 176
Curricula: attitudes of parents toward, 46–47; and national identity, 48; and religious education, 48; state specified, 70; of history, 71–77; in language and literature, 77–85; compared in religious studies, 85–87; national relevance of, 112; and cultural estrangement, 113; lack of relevance in, 133; change of, 135; participation of Arabs in, 180

Dasen, P. R., 191
Discrimination: in marketing and pricing, 7; in jobs, 7, 137; against Arabs, 51; in government grants, 60; in job opportunities, 134; in education, 137; promoted against Arabs, 138
Druze: integration of, 66–67; and blurring of national identity, 67

Efrat, Aharon, 59
Egypt, 1, 107–108
El-Ard, 4

Elementary education: under Turkish rule in Palestine, 9–11; private Christian, 10; private Moslem, 10–11; under British mandate, 13–15; number of students in, 19–20; sex differences in, 20; and female teachers, 40; goals for, 50–51; and higher education, 111–13
Eliav, Luva Arieh, 145, 170
El-Kasem, Nabih, 67
El-'Obeid, Diab, 58, 64
Employment, of youth, 21
Ennis, R., 139
Equality: of educational opportunity within Arab society, 43–45; and class-clan membership, 44; Arab youth deprived of, 51; in job opportunities, 167–72
Extended family: and economic transformations, 8; breakdown of, 29

Female education: in Palestine under Turkish rule, 13; under British rule, 14–17; in Israel, 20; and female teachers, 41–42
Female teachers: influence of, 39–42; and female education, 41; and status of women, 42
Feudalism: and land ownership, 5; disappeared, 32; and status, 163–64; effects of abolishment, 166
Finance of Arab education, 58–60
Frankenstein, Carl, 39, 46, 94–95
Future perceptions of Arab students, 136–38

Gaza Strip, xi, 1, 121, 126
Geraisy, Sami, 4, 7
Getzels, J. W., 141
Giv'at Haviva, 168
Goals: of Jewish education, 50; of Arab education, 50–55; of teaching history, 71–73; of teaching language and literature, 77–79

Haifa, 66, 96, 100–102
Hamula (see also Clan) and socioeconomic status, 156–57, 164
Harbi (school), 9

Hebrew University of Jerusalem, 16, 57, 87, 95, 123, 129
Higher education: gaps between Arabs and Jews in, 106; among Palestinians, 106–27; and nation building, 107, 120; and economic return, 111–12, 115–19; and elementary education, 111–13; and secondary education, 112–13; and military administration, 115; and security, 115; and socioeconomic mobility, 119; and political socialization, 129–30; and aspiration of Arabs, 137; and contribution to status, 156–57
Histadruth, 55, 169
Hofman, John, 102–103, 138, 170
Howe, Harold, 108

Individualization: in rural Arab communities, 29–30; and modernization, 30
Integration: threats of, 6; administrative, 66; as discriminatory, 93; voluntary, 93; between Arabs and Jews, 95–99; in Acre, 95–97; in Ma'alot-Trarshiha, 99–100; experiment of in Haifa, 100–102; possibility of, 104–105; and democracy, 130; between Jewish subgroups, 132; blocked by social reality, 138
Intellectual abilities: of Arab youth, 138–41; and sex differences, 139–40
Intellectual functioning: and matriculation exams, 135; and course content, 135
Iran, 107–108
Istanbul, 10

Jackson, P. W., 141
Jaffa, 22
Jam'iyyat El Makased El-Kheiriyyah, 11
Jenks, Christopher, 43
Jeries, Sabri, 4
Jerusalem, 12, 17, 22
Job opportunities: availability of, 6; low status in, 7; closed for Arab workers, 8; of Arab University students, 115–18; limited, 116–17; discrimination in, 134; equality in, 167–72
Johnson, Noris Brok, 179
Jordan, 1, 13, 22, 109, 113, 120, 131, 134

Kibbutz: education in, 5; and autonomy of education, 67–68
Kleinberger, Aharon, 16, 60, 63, 91, 169
Knesset, 50, 58–59, 170
Koran, in curricula, 85–86
Kupileivitch, Emanuel, 23–24, 50–52, 60
Kuwait, 107–108, 118

Landau, Jacob, M., 2, 124
Land Day, 127–28, 183–88
Law of State Education, 50
Lebanon, 108, 110
Lindgren, F., 139
Lindgren, H., 139
Lubrani, Uri, 56

Ma'alot, 99–101
Male education: in Palestine under Turkish rule, 13; during British mandate, 14–17; in Israel, 20
Manna', Mohammad, 142
Mapam, 3, 60
McConnel, Dean, 176
Me'ari, Mahmood, 74, 76, 80–81
Meir, Elhanan, 136
Military administration: meaning of, 2; rationale for, 2; and teachers, 19, 38; and political leadership, 25; and clan structure, 33; as mediator, 55–56; and higher education, 115
Minority education, study of, 189–92
Modernization: and cultural contradictions, xi; processes of, 5, 26; and individualization, 30; and teachers, 38; and working class, 39; and coping ability, 142–43; and new opportunities, 143; indications of, 163–64; and secondary education, 174; and university students, 175;

and elementary and secondary students, 176
Monoculturalism: in Jewish education, 177–79; dangers of, 178
Mosque, and religious education, 9–10
Multiculturalism: defined, 177; in Arab and Jewish schools, 177–79
Mussen, Paul, 141

Nahariyah, 96
Nakhleh, Khalil, 64, 126
National identity: and school curricula, 47–48; and religious education, 48; the blurring of, 53; distortion of among the Druze group, 67; emphasized in Jewish schools, 76; in Arab schools, 77; denial of in the curriculum, 86; blurred by curriculum, 73, 87; denied in the school, 87–89
Nationalism (Arab), and education, 11, 13, 18
Nazareth, 5, 65, 99

October War, 126
Oriental Jews (see also Sephardim): and Zionism, 80; and slums, 91; and integration, 94–95; and rejection of Arabs, 103; and scholastic achievement, 132

Pakistan, 107
Parents: and teachers, 30, 34; personality of, 32; and female education, 40–42; attitudes of toward religious education, 47–48; attitudes of toward vocational education, 146–67; toward secondary education, 151–52; toward work, 153–54
Peled, Matty, 53
Peleg, Rachel, 112, 136–38
Peleg, Yoval, 186
Peres, Yohanan, 72–73, 84, 87, 103
Physical conditions of Arab schools, 59–60
Pluralism: and education, 179–80; democratic, 179; criticized, 179–80

Rakah (see also Communist Party), 185, 188
Ram-Allah, 17, 22
Reches, Eli, 115, 126
Relations, Arab-Jewish: political, xiii; in Palestine, 1; in Haifa, 100–101; study of, 102–104; and job discrimination, 169; and definition of the state, 181
Religious education: status of, 9, 13, 26; and national identity, 48; attitudes of parents toward, 47–48; and the curriculum, 85–87
Religious Party (Jewish): and religious state education, 5, 64, 68; goals of, 68
Rushdi school, 8

Saudi Arabia, 118
Scholastic achievement: of Arab students, 131–36; of Sephardic Jews, 132; of Ashkenazi students, 132
Secondary schools: under Turkish rule, 9; during British mandate, 15; and mobility of graduates, 15; student distribution in, 21–22; and higher education, 111–13; role of during British mandate, 146; parents' attitudes toward, 151–52, 162; and modernization, 164
Secularism: in education, 11; of Arab education and culture, 54–55; imposed upon Arab education, 68
Security: and military administration, 2; and university admission, 23–24; needs of, 90; and job inequality, 168–71
Segregation: general, 6; between Jews, 91; discriminatory trend of, 93; voluntary, 93; in service of integration, 94; of Arabs in Israel, 95; in Acre, 95–99; dominance of, 104–105; idealized, 105
Seker (achievement test): purposes of, 132; abolished, 132
Sephardim (see also Oriental Jews): and scholastic achievement, 132; and cultural domination, 167, 178; distribution in labor force, 171
Shahani school, 9
Shivtan, Dan, 104, 169
Six-Day War, 123

Smilansky, Moshe, 91
Solberg, Saul, 136
Syria, 8–13, 16

Tarshiha, 99–101
Tawjeehi (Jordanian matriculation),
    113, 134–35
Teachers (Arab): lack of autonomy,
    15–17; strike and demonstration,
    17; unqualified, 18, 23; and military
    administration, 19, 38; shortage of,
    23, 59; activism of, 27; and parents,
    31–32, 34–35; and clan structure,
    33–34, 37; status of, 33; as change
    agents, 36–37; dual allegiance of,
    137–38; as government agents, 37–
    38; and modernization, 38; female,
    39–42; salaries of, 59; alienation of,
    65; and national conflicts, 176
Technion, 124
Tel Aviv, 148
Thinking abilities (*see also* Intel-
    lectual abilities): of Arab youth,
    138–41; and sex differences, 139–40
Tolidano, Shmuel, 56
Torrance, Paul, 139
Totah, Khalil, 17
Turkey: rule over Palestine, 8–13;
    education under, 9–13

Um-al Fahm, 60
UNESCO, 107
University of Haifa, 23, 99, 101–102,
    124, 150
University of Tel Aviv, 104, 124, 169
University students (Arab): numbers
    and distribution, 23; problems of,
    23–24; reaction to activism of, 56;
    ratios of, 106–14; job opportunities
    of, 115–17; attitudes of, 121–24;
    struggle of, 123–29; activism of,
    123–29; and high school pupils,
    124–25; and land confiscation, 124,

127; and improvement of curricula,
    124; against guard-duty, 128–29;
    political socialization of, 129–30;
    lack of mobility of, 136; and status
    aspirations, 137; and modernization,
    175
Upper-Nazareth, 6–7

Vocational-technical education: pro-
    grams of, 21–22; in Arab and
    Jewish schools, 21–22; distribution
    of students in, 59; and developing
    societies, 106–107; inequality in,
    145; issue of, 146–50; parental atti-
    tudes toward, 146–67; fallacy of,
    168

Wali(s), and education, 9, 11
Waschitz, Yosef, 169–70
Weizmann, Chaim, 192
West Bank, xi, 1, 27, 106, 109–17,
    119, 121, 126, 131, 134, 139–40,
    142–43
Women: status of, 42; liberation of, 53
Workers: and modernization, 39, 175;
    as agents of change, 141; in Tel
    Aviv, 148; in Jewish urban centers,
    174

Yadlin, Aharon, 52, 59
Yadlin Document: quoted, 52; reac-
    tion to, 53; and blurring of na-
    tional identity, 53

Zeedani, Sa'id, 128, 183
Zionism: pre-state movements of, 3;
    and textbooks, 18; identification
    with values of, 76; and Oriental
    Jews, 90

aRaB eOucation in isRael

was composed in ten-point Linotype Times Roman and leaded two points,
with display type handset in Libra, and printed on 55-pound Glatco offset
by Joe Mann Associates, Inc.;
Smyth-sewn and bound over boards in Columbia Bayside Vellum
by Maple-Vail Book Manufacturing Group;
and published by

SYRACUSE UNIVERSITY PRESS
SYRACUSE, NEW YORK 13210

Contemporary Issues in the Middle East Series

THE MIDDLE EAST IN WORLD POLITICS
A Study in Contemporary International Relations
TAREQ Y. ISMAEL

"This book should become a basic reader because of its balance and general treatment of the subject matter. Academic libraries on all levels as well as public libraries with a potential reading audience would do well to obtain a copy."—*Choice*

Cloth ISBN 0-8156-0101-8 $12.00
Paper ISBN 0-8156-0102-6 $ 5.00

THE ARAB-ISRAELI DILEMMA   Second Edition
FRED J. KHOURI

Comments on the 1968 edition: "A well-researched history of the Arab-Israeli problem written with insight and ob-jectivity."—Drew Middleton, *Saturday Review*

"An excellent book, well documented and very balanced in approach."—*Choice*

Paper ISBN 0-8156-2178-7 $5.95

THE ARAB LEFT
TAREQ Y. ISMAEL

"Overall, a well-organized and lucid guide through the tangled labyrinth of Arab New Left thinking and practice that should be useful to everyone interested in understanding the forces at work in this troubled area."—*Book Forum*

"Original Arabic sources are utilized. Recommended to gradu-ate and undergraduate libraries. Useful in courses on Middle East politics, social movements, and non-Western political thought."—*Choice*

Cloth ISBN 0-8156-0124-7 $15.00
Paper ISBN 0-8156-0125-5 $ 5.95

SYRACUSE UNIVERSITY PRESS   •   SYRACUSE, NEW YORK   13210

ISBN 0-8156-01